MW00898227

CHRISTIAN
CoreStrength

by Andrew W.G. Matthews

A one-year discipleship guide for Christian doctrine and living

About The Author

REV. ANDREW W.G. MATTHEWS is a graduate of Texas A&M University with a B.A. in Economics, Reformed Theological Seminary with a Masters of Divinity, and PhD studies in the area of biblical wisdom literature. He is currently an ordained minister in the Presbyterian Church in America (PCA). Rev. Matthews has been a pastor in Presbyterian, Baptist, and non-denominational churches throughout the United States, Australia and Great Britain. He has also written a short booklet to help new believers called CHRISTIAN JUMPSTART.

To order more copies of CHRISTIAN CORESTRENGTH or to obtain other resources produced by the author please email,

andrewwg.matthews@gmail.com

Miriam Webster

1828

© Andrew W.G. Matthews

ISBN 978-1484033289

Scripture quotations are from The Holy Bible,
English Standard Version® (ESV®), copyright © 2001 by Crossway, a publishing ministry of Good News Publishers.
Used by permission. All rights reserved.

Cover by: William Ntim Aburam

Printed in the Untied States of America

Table of Contents

TABLE OF CONTENTS (CONT'D)

SECTION D: CHURCH LIFE (CONT'D)

SECTION E: THINKING DEEPER   91

INTRODUCTION

The great commission of Jesus in Matthew 28:18-20 calls the church to make disciples of all nations. This is the mandate of the church, but the church has not been very effective in its implementation. The churches' Christian education programs haphazardly and unsystematically attempt to develop believers in the Lord. A twenty-five minute sermon once a week and an occasional Sunday school class is not enough exposure to teach the immense terrain of Bible content and Christian doctrine.

A pastor of a church needs to have a plan by which to build his congregation in the faith. The apostle Paul referred to himself as *"a skilled master builder"* (1 Corinthians 3:10). He built a foundation of faith and he wanted to make sure that he built it with the right materials, and that what he built would stand in the day of judgment. In our day, believers are too often raised up without a foundation or in a disorderly manner. The dry wall is put in before the roof is installed! This lack of skilled building creates shaky or shallow believers. CHRISTIAN CORESTRENGTH has been written to provide a plan of learning that progresses in an orderly fashion, and also covers every major doctrine and practice of Christianity.

Another failure found in the church's discipleship is the lack of effective reproduction and multiplication of disciple-makers. The church needs to be making disciples who can then turn around and make other disciples. Paul instructed Timothy in 2 Timothy 2:2, *"and what you have heard from me in the presence of many witnesses entrust to faithful men who will be able to reach others also."* This is a four-link discipleship chain: Paul, Timothy, faithful men, and others. The gospel of Christ must be passed on from generation to generation. This is not only to be a task for the pastors and elders of the church. All believers need to be passing the baton of faith in Christ to their families, to the lost, and to fellow believers within the church.

The reality is that the average Christian does not know where to start with discipleship. I have been to discipleship conferences where the biblical case for discipleship was laid and an exhortation to disciple was given, however no practical plan or resources were provided. How many people left the conference feeling burdened to disciple but ill-equipped and unable to proceed? Church leaders do not serve the church well when they give a mandate to disciple, yet put nothing practical in the hands of the people to help them implement the task.

Imagine this hypothetical situation. You have a new neighbor from a distant land who greets you at your front door and informs you that he read a gospel tract, which instructed him how to place his faith in Jesus for eternal life. He had repeated the prayer and was told that he should now go to church. Having seen the "Honk if you love Jesus!" bumper-sticker on the back of your minivan he comes to you for assistance with his new-found faith. What do you do? Here is someone just begging to be discipled. You have a blank canvas to work with. What will you teach him first? What book of the Bible do you read first? Genesis or the Gospel of John? Perhaps books of the Bible are not the way to go. Should you do doctrines first, but which doctrines? Jesus Christ, sin, or faith?

The purpose of CHRISTIAN CORESTRENGTH is to put a tool into your hands so that you have the means (and no excuses) to take someone under your care and teach them the faith. CHRISTIAN CORESTRENGTH follows a plan to teach the Christian faith in such a manner that key doctrines are taught and important Bible passages are studied so as to lay a solid foundation of faith, and then build up believers to bring them to maturity. The first section, *Core Beliefs*, lays the foundation of essential truths which all believers need to know if they would confess Christ. The writer of the book of Hebrews, states that there are *"basic principles"* that need to be learned before we move on to more *"solid food"* (Hebrews 5:12). Once you lay the foundation of core beliefs you can go on to study the doctrines of salvation in the second section, *Such a Great Salvation*. Your understanding of salvation must proceed from the theoretical to the practical so in the third section, *A Closer Walk with God*, you will look at many Christian practices which will aid you to *"work out your salvation"* (Philippians 2:12). Since the Christian life is to be lived within the community of the church you will also study a number of key facets of *Church Life* in the fourth section. Lastly, you will examine some deeper theological and worldview issues in the fifth section, *Thinking Deeper*. As pilgrims living in a fallen world you need to understand these issues to aid you in your interactions and involvement within the cultures you live.

CHRISTIAN CORESTRENGTH can be used in a number of contexts. Since each lesson is only two pages long it is succinct enough to study in an hour, which is sufficient time for the Sunday School hour of most churches or over lunch with friends. Large or small groups can study the material, or it can be used in one-on-one discipleship. Though it sounds like an oxymoron, you could even "disciple yourself" if you do the book on your own. I would highly recommend this course for all officers and lay leaders in the church. If you are considering entering the ministry, or going to seminary, this course will expose you to most of the topics and terminology that you will face throughout your studies.

You will get the most out of the study if you read over the *Scripture Pre-Reading*, the lesson, and do ahead of time the exercises and *Hitting Home* questions. The preparation for each lesson may take approximately thirty minutes. To go through a lesson with another person should take between forty and ninety minutes depending on how much talking you engage in. What is important is that you cover the material and not get lost down "rabbit trails."

Initially you may study CHRISTIAN CORESTRENGTH for your own edification, but at some point you need to be thinking and praying about whom the Lord is leading you to disciple. I define *discipleship* as *personally engaging others with the Word of God.* Many people consider the prospect of discipling someone else intimidating because they do not feel mature enough themselves to be a leader. In some cases this fear is warranted. That is why you should study CHRISTIAN CORESTRENGTH yourself. Once you have obtained sound teaching, and greater maturity through the Lord, you should prayerfully consider whom the Lord is leading you to teach. Discipleship is a form of kingdom advancement and spiritual warfare, so do not be discouraged if you discover that many obstacles are thrown at you once you have committed to it. In some cases you will engage in evangelism to start someone along the path of Christ. In other cases God will use you to strengthen the faith of an existing child of God. In whatever manner God uses you, evangelism and discipleship can be the the most exhilarating and significant works of the Christian life. My prayer for you is the same as that of the apostle Paul who said, *"and I pray that the sharing of your faith may become effective for the full knowledge of every good thing that is in us for the sake of Christ."* (Philemon 7)

Andrew W.G. Matthews

SECTION A:

CORE BELIEFS

"According to the grace of God given to me, like a skilled master builder I laid a foundation, and someone else is building upon it. Let each one take care how he builds upon it. For no one can lay a foundation other than that which is laid, which is Jesus Christ." (1 Corinthians 3:10-11)

In order to build a house one has to first lay a foundation. In the Christian faith certain truths need to be laid down which are foundational and essential to all that we believe. The truths found in the *Core Beliefs* section are the essential Christian doctrines which define the very essence of being a Christian. If we are unclear about any of these truths we will struggle mightily in our faith. The starting point in this book, found in *Lesson 1*, is the "The Gospel." The gospel is the key to the kingdom, and without a correct understanding of how we can receive God's grace through Jesus Christ there is no point in proceeding through this book. The remainder of this section, *Core Beliefs*, covers many essentials of the faith which are a part of the gospel itself: doctrines concerning God and Christ, the state of man, salvation through faith, and the importance of the Word of God.

The writer to the Hebrews stated that his readers began with *"the basic principles of the oracles of God."* (Hebrews 5:12) He included among the basic principles the doctrine of Christ, repentance and faith, the resurrection, and eternal judgment (Hebrews 6:1-2). The core beliefs of the Christian faith are likened to the *"milk"* which babies must feed on until they can eat *"solid food"* (Hebrews 5:12). The core beliefs are basic and they are necessary, and the Christian never really leaves the core beliefs when moving on to advanced doctrines, but grows in a more profound understanding of the various dimensions of the basic principles. For this reason it is essential that we lay a solid foundation of sound doctrine in the core beliefs of our faith.

LESSON 1: THE GOSPEL

KEY DOCTRINE: The gospel is the message of God's saving grace for all who trust in God's Son, Jesus Christ.

MEMORY VERSE: *"For I am not ashamed of the gospel, for it is the power of God for salvation to everyone who believes, to the Jew first and also to the Greek."* (Romans 1:16)

SCRIPTURE PRE-READING: Genesis 1:1-3, 26-31; 3:1-19; John 3:16-21; 14:1-17; Romans 1:16-17; 3:21-26; 5:1-11

The gospel is the starting and finishing point of the Christian faith. The gospel contains the truth that God exists and that He is gracious to sinful people. He has shown His great love toward us by sending His own Son Jesus Christ to earth to die for our sins. When we recognize our guilt before God, repent of our unbelief, and place our faith in Christ's death for us, God forgives us through Jesus and grants us an eternal relationship with Him.

THE EXISTENCE OF GOD

The starting point of the Christian faith is to believe and trust in God. The first verse in the Bible says, *"In the beginning God created the heavens and the earth."* (Genesis 1:1) It simply declares that God exists and that He created all things. The first step of faith is our recognizing the reality of God's existence. Hebrews 11:6 says that *"without faith it is impossible to please God, for whoever would draw near to God must believe that he exists and he rewards those who seek him."* He is the eternal God—all-knowing, all-powerful, ever-present, and full of goodness, love, truth, and righteousness. He longs to bless those who want to be in a relationship of trust with Him.

THE PROBLEM OF MAN

The problem with man is that we are no longer in a loving and obedient relationship with God. To understand our problem, we must start in the beginning when mankind was created. Genesis 1:26 states, *"Then God said, `Let us make man in our image, after our likeness.'"* The next verse in Genesis 1:27 explains that both men and women alike were created in God's image and likeness. This means that our nature is based upon the character of God. Our ability to think, feel, love, achieve, learn, and make decisions is derived from God's nature. God did not create us so that we could go off and do our own thing. There was an initial perfect relationship between the first man and woman with God, and it was only in this position of trust and obedience that the first humans were able to live content and happy.

Due to the cunning deception of the devil Adam and Eve disobeyed God and became sinners. Since that first act of disobedience, all descendants of Adam and Eve have been born with a human nature that is opposed to wanting to obey and love God. Being a sinner is essentially a state of resistance or hostility to God's rule over our life. The book of Romans states that all people recognize that God exists but they fight against knowing and following God. Romans 1:19-21 says:

> *"For what can be known about God is plain to them, because God has shown it to them. For his invisible attributes, namely, his eternal power and divine nature, have been clearly perceived, ever since the creation of the world, in the things that have been made. So they are without excuse. For although they knew God, they did not honor him as God or give thanks to him, but they became futile in their thinking, and their foolish hearts were darkened."*

People who claim to be "a-theists" (*no-God*) are actually "anti-theists" (*against-God*) in their hearts.

As an exercise read Romans 3:23 and answer the following questions.

- How many have sinned?_____ Are there any exceptions?_____

- What does it mean to "fall short of the glory of God?"

Section A: Core Beliefs

A Leopard Can't Change its Spots

Sometimes we recognize that we are making wrong decisions and do one of two things: (1) we might simply try to be a better person and endeavor to "do the right thing" toward our fellow man, or (2) we become diligently involved in religious activities.

Either approach is flawed in that both are attempts at trying to improve or change our nature in order to be accepted by God. It assumes that we have the ability to make ourselves better and that we have the power in and of ourselves to be good. However, the Bible describes our sinful nature as being a kind of death. Ephesians 2:1 says, *"And you were dead in the trespasses and sins in which you once walked, following the course of this world, following the prince of the power of the air, the spirit that is now at work in the sons of disobedience."* The dead cannot make themselves alive nor can they keep God's commandments. This verse goes on to say that we were by nature objects of His wrath. Therefore, due to our sin, all mankind deserves to be judged by God eternally.

God Makes the Move

God makes the first move since we cannot help ourselves. Ever since Adam and Eve's first disobedience God has initiated relationships with us that are based upon grace—*not* our performance. He knows our sin but enters into a relationship with us by providing a means of forgiveness for us. The way in which we can now enter into a relationship with God is by the forgiveness given to us through Jesus Christ, the Son of God. Probably the most well-known verse in the Bible, John 3:16, teaches this, *"For God so loved the world, that he gave his only Son, that whoever believes in him should not perish but have eternal life."*

God sent His Son Jesus into the world to take on the nature of a man while at the same time keeping his eternal, divine nature. Jesus' purpose for coming was to show the world the very nature of His Father in heaven and to perform a great act of salvation for the forgiveness of sin. When Jesus was sent to the cross by the Jews and the Romans at the end of His ministry, He became the means of salvation for believers. Since we, as sinners, deserve to die for our sins, God's perfect justice requires a punishment. When Jesus died on the cross He bore our sins and took God's wrath upon Himself. When Jesus was raised on the third day God was demonstrating that His wrath had been satisfied and death had been defeated.

So What Now?

Since Jesus died do all people now go to heaven? No, His death is only effective for those of us who believe in Him. If we recognize our fallen, sinful state before God and our desperate need for the forgiveness that Jesus purchased on the cross, then we must respond in faith. We need to trust in the love God has for us in Jesus and confess sins we have committed, including our sin of not worshipping God. If we look to Christ and hope in His grace, He will forgive us, *"For, 'everyone who calls on the name of the Lord will be saved.'"* (Romans 10:13)

The gospel is called *"the power of God for salvation"* (Romans 1:16) because from the beginning of our faith until we go to heaven God will keep us in our salvation. God forgives us, declares us to be righteous, and begins a transforming process to make us righteous. Throughout our whole life we will continue to trust in the gospel to receive forgiveness and cleansing from our sin. That first seed of faith that trusted in God for salvation will be the same faith that moves us to trust in His mercy for every need in our life, *"as it is written, 'The righteous shall live by faith.'"* (Romans 1:17)

Hitting Home

1. Have you come to a place where you see yourself as a sinner needing forgiveness?

2. Have you tried in the past to "get right with God" by reforming yourself or becoming more religious?

3. If you were to die tomorrow, do you know that you would go to heaven? What are you basing that upon?

4. Write out a testimony of how you have come to a saving faith in Christ. (Use a separate sheet of paper.) Take time to share this testimony with someone else!

LESSON 2: GOD

KEY DOCTRINE: God exists, and we were created to worship and glorify Him forever.
MEMORY VERSE: *"Holy, holy, holy, is the Lord God Almighty, who was and is and is to come!"* (Revelation 4:8b)
SCRIPTURE PRE-READING: John 1:1-5; Exodus 33:18-20; 34:4-7; Psalm 139:1-18; Hebrews 11:1-3

Foremost in the Christian faith is that we are to know and worship God. God is a being who has existed for all eternity, even before He created the heavens and the earth. There is only one God, and He exists in three persons: the Father, the Son, and the Holy Spirit. God has no limits, and He is perfect in all of His attributes. God's chief purpose is to glorify Himself by revealing His nature and works to all.

THE GREAT "I AM"

Our first step in faith is our recognition of the existence of God. Hebrews 11:6 states that if we *"would draw near to God* [we] *must believe that he exists and that he rewards those who seek him."* Faith embraces that God *is*. The Bible teaches the eternal existence of God in a number of ways. In Exodus 3 at the burning bush, God tells Moses that His name means *"I AM WHO I AM."* His name, and thus His nature, denotes *being*. In Revelation 1:8 God describes Himself as *"the Alpha and the Omega...who is and who was and who is to come, the Almighty."* He existed before the creation of the world. He exists now, and He will exist forever. God is the first cause, and all things that exist owe their existence to Him.

ONE AND THREE

There is only one true God. Polytheism teaches that there are many gods, but the Bible recognizes the LORD God as the *only* real God. In Isaiah 44:6 God proclaims, *"Thus says the LORD, the King of Israel and his Redeemer, the LORD of hosts: 'I am the first and I am the last; besides me there is no god.'"* The most important verse for an Israelite is Deuteronomy 6:4 which says, *"Hear, O Israel: The LORD our God, the LORD is one."* The LORD is the one true God, and no other god is to be served.

God exists in three persons: the Father, the Son, and the Holy Spirit. All three persons are recognized as being equal in power and glory and having all of the attributes of God. How the Trinity works is a mystery that our finite minds cannot fully comprehend, however Scripture reveals that God exists in three persons. In Matthew 3:16-17 at Jesus' baptism, all three persons of the Trinity were present: Jesus, the Holy Spirit who descended like a dove, and God the Father who spoke and declared Jesus to be His beloved Son. [LESSON 7: THE TRINITY will examine these doctrines more closely.]

GOD CREATED EVERYTHING

The first verse of the Bible says, *"In the beginning, God created the heavens and the earth."* Since God created all things He is owed all worship and reverence. In Psalm 148:3-10 all the heavens sing His praises because of His power to create. The living creatures in heaven cast down their crowns and proclaim, *"Worthy are you, our Lord and God, to receive glory and honor and power, for you created all things, and by your will they existed and were created."* (Revelation 4:11) God created all things by simply speaking them into existence. In Genesis 1 God said, *"Let there be..."* and it came to be. All three members of the Trinity were involved in the creation, for the Bible states that *"the Spirit of God was hovering over the face of the waters"* (Genesis 1:2), and *"All things were made through him* [Jesus]*"* (John 1:3). God's creative power becomes a great source of hope for His people, *"My help comes from the LORD, who made heaven and earth."* (Psalm 121:2)

GOD IS SPIRIT

Jesus told the Samaritan woman in John 4:24 that *"God is Spirit, and those who worship him must worship in spirit and truth."* For God to be a spirit means that He has a being and personhood. In other words, God is not a mere force, power, or idea, but rather He is a person with emotions, an intellect, and a will. Another characteristic of being a spirit is that God exists apart from the creation He made. Although He fills all creation, He is not a part of it. He does not have a material body nor can He be seen by the human eye. God is *"...immortal, invisible, the only God."* (1 Timothy 1:17) For this reason, God forbids the use of images or carvings in His worship. Nothing in creation can depict what God is like. We can only know and rightly worship God through His Spirit and the Word of God.

GOD WITHOUT LIMITS

There are a number of attributes, or characteristics, that God possesses which are unique to Him. These attributes describe His greatness and power, and show that He has no limits. To demonstrate this concept, theologians often add the prefix *"omni"* to many of these attributes. God is...

- **Omnipotent (*All-Powerful*):** *"I know that you can do all things, and that no purpose of yours can be thwarted."* (Job 42:2)
- **Omniscient (*All-Knowing*):** *"I declared them to you from of old, before they came to pass I announced them to you."* (Isaiah 48:5)
- **Omnipresent (*Present Everywhere*):** *"Where shall I go from your Spirit? Or where shall I flee from your presence? If I ascend to heaven, you are there! If I make my bed in Sheol, you are there!"* (Psalm 139:7-8)

WHAT IS GOD LIKE?

We understand and also possess many of God's attributes and characteristics because He made us in His image. The following characteristics describe the character and nature of God. As we get to know God we learn and come to love that He is unchanging in all the perfections of His character. God is...

- **Holy:** God is perfect in righteousness and separate from all sin. *"Holy, holy, holy is the LORD of hosts; the whole earth is full of his glory!"* (Isaiah 6:3)
- **Sovereign:** God is in control of all things. *"For the LORD, the Most High, is to be feared, a great king over all the earth...God reigns over the nations; God sits on his holy throne."* (Psalm 47:2, 8)
- **Good:** God blesses His creation with His kindness. *"They shall pour forth the fame of your abundant goodness and shall sing aloud of your righteousness...The Lord is good to all, and his mercy is over all that he has made."* (Psalm 145:7, 9)
- **Just:** God punishes sin and rewards righteousness. *"And I heard the altar saying, 'Yes, Lord God the Almighty, true and just are your judgments!'"* (Revelation 16:7)
- **Loving:** God is gracious and affectionate to His people. *"The LORD passed before him and proclaimed, 'The LORD, the LORD, a God merciful and gracious, slow to anger, and abounding in steadfast love and faithfulness, keeping steadfast love for thousands, forgiving iniquity and transgression and sin'"* (Exodus 34:6-7)
- **Wise:** God understands all things and achieves His purposes. *"The LORD by wisdom founded the earth; by understanding he established the heavens"* (Proverbs 3:19)

TO GOD BE THE GLORY

God has one goal—to glorify Himself. He does this through creation, salvation, and judgment. This purpose—to be recognized, feared, loved, and praised—is not egotistical but rather the appropriate acknowledgment of His worth. God is good and deserving of all worship. In respect to mankind, God will either receive glory through His judgment on condemned sinners or through the praise He receives from redeemed saints. In the end all people will bow down to the Lord and know that He alone is God. *"Who will not fear, O Lord, and glorify your name? For you alone are holy. All nations will come and worship you, for your righteous acts have been revealed."* (Revelation 15:4)

HITTING HOME

1. Do you accept the existence of God as truth, or are you looking for some kind of argument or proof?

2. What is your conception of God? Does it line up with what God says about Himself in the Bible?

3. Do you recognize that God wants to be in a relationship with you?

4. How has your understanding of God changed throughout your study of this lesson?

LESSON 3: SIN

KEY DOCTRINE: Mankind has fallen from the original perfect likeness of God and now requires salvation from sin.
MEMORY VERSE: *"for all have sinned and fall short of the glory of God"* (Romans 3:23)
SCRIPTURE PRE-READING: Genesis 2:15-24; 4:6-11; Exodus 20:1-17; Psalm 51:3-5; Mark 7:20-23; Romans 7:7-25; 3:9-18

We do not know ourselves until we know God. We tend to think that we are pretty good at heart until we measure ourselves against the perfect standard of God. Mankind does not realize that if they are not living for the glory of God and obeying God's commandments, then they are living in sin. Sin affects all of us, and we cannot by our own efforts rid ourselves of sin. It is only through the grace of Jesus that we can be set free from the bondage of sin.

THE NATURE OF MAN

How would you describe the nature of mankind? (Circle one)

a. Essentially good, but having the ability to do bad.
b. Essentially bad, but having the ability to do good.
c. Neither good nor bad, simply a biological creature.
d. Essentially bad and needful of God's grace to do good.

In our society, most of us tend to choose option "a" since we have a positive view of ourselves. We recognize that "nobody's perfect" and that we all make mistakes. Then there are those of us who have some religious background and, recognizing man's sinfulness, choose option "b," but still believe that with diligent effort and religious instruction we can right ourselves. Those of us who choose option "c" reject the question of good and bad and simply understand man as a product of evolution. However, of the four options, "d" is the best description of the nature of mankind.

IT BEGINS IN THE BEGINNING

To understand ourselves, we must go to the very beginning of our origin. The old saying, "to err is human" was not the case in the beginning.

"Then God said, 'Let us make man in our image, after our likeness. And let them have dominion over the fish of the sea and over the birds of the heavens and over the livestock and over all the earth and over every creeping thing that creeps on the earth.' So God created man in his own image, in the image of God he created him; male and female he created them." (Genesis 1:26-27)

In the very beginning, mankind (the first man and the first woman) was created in the perfection of God's *image* and *likeness*. To bear God's image means recognizing that our essential character and personality is modeled after God. As God thinks, feels, and relates, we also think, feel, and relate. Concerning the moral nature of Adam and Eve, they were made perfect just as God is perfect. So it was that in the beginning, Adam and Eve were glorious just as God is glorious.

THE FALL OF MANKIND

God gave mankind one rule to obey in Genesis 2:17, *"but of the tree of the knowledge of good and evil you shall not eat, for in the day that you eat of it you shall surely die."* In chapter three of Genesis, the serpent deceives Eve and she, and then Adam, eats of that forbidden tree. It was in this disobedience of Adam that sin entered into human nature and the world. Since that time, every descendant of Adam—all mankind—has failed to worship God and keep His commandments.

A Failure of Worship

"Hear, O Israel: The LORD our God, the LORD is one. You shall love the LORD your God with all your heart and with all your soul and with all your might." (Deuteronomy 6:4-5) This important verse became the basis of what Jesus considered the greatest commandment. The first of the Ten Commandments states that we are to have *"no other gods before me."* (Deuteronomy 5:7) Because of our sin nature, we do not worship God perfectly. In fact, as sinners we are unable to worship God

CORESTRENGTH † CORESTRENGTH † CORESTRENGTH † CORESTRENGTH † CORESTRENGTH

perfectly with our entire being. Who amongst us dare claim to worship God with everything that we have?

A Failure of Obedience

The Westminster Shorter Confession Question and Answer 14 states that sin is "any want of conformity unto, or transgression of, the law of God." In other words, when we fail to keep God's moral commandments, we have sinned. His laws address how we are to worship God and how we are to treat others. Everyone of us at some point has sinned against another.

HATE EVIL!

The discussion of sin should not be merely academic, rather it is a topic that daily impacts all of us personally and destructively. We must not gloss over our sin or the sin around us as something to be trifled with. God hates sin, and we must also learn to hate sin. *"O you who love the LORD, hate evil!"* (Psalm 97:10) The following four categories of sin comprise some of the main types of desires, passions, and lusts that fuel our sinful thinking and then give birth to wrongdoing:

- **Sins of Pride:** The desire to have ourselves glorified is our way of replacing God in our life. This manifests itself in pride, arrogance, vanity, haughtiness, envy, jealousy, and boastfulness.
- **Sins of Sensuality:** The desire to satisfy physical pleasures makes a god out of our body. This includes indulging in glutinous eating, drunkenness, drug addiction, and all sexual perversions such as promiscuity, adultery, homosexuality, pornography, rape, and incest.
- **Sins of Violence:** Sin manifests itself in our hatred and violence against our neighbor—lying, deceit, malice, anger, slander, hatred, murder, cruelty, abuse, rape, and torture.
- **Sins of Greed:** Our covetousness has no bounds, leading us to steal, cheat, horde, refuse to show mercy and charity, and disregard the well-being of our neighbor in our pursuit of personal gain.

FREQUENTLY ASKED QUESTIONS

The following list of questions comprises some of the objections that we have when we consider the nature of mankind:

- *If I have a sinful nature, why do I know right from wrong?* (Romans 2:14-15; Matthew 23:1-3)
  <u>Answer</u>: Since we are made in God's image, we still have sensitivity to right and wrong in our consciences.
- *Why, then, is the world full of "nice" or "good" people?* (Romans 2:14-15; 13:1-4)
  <u>Answer</u>: The fall of man does not mean that everyone acts like a monster. We still have a conscience and make attempts to do what is right, though none of our acts are pure before God. There are also many laws in society which prevent us from acting in a worse manner. God in His grace often restrains us from greater sin and changes us for the better.
- *What is God's response to sin?* (Genesis 2-4; Romans 3:19; John 3:16)
  <u>Answer</u>: God promised Adam that he would die if he disobeyed. That promise of death was fulfilled in Adam and each of us since. God will judge sin in this world and in eternity.

HITTING HOME

1. To what extent do you think man is sinful or inherently good in nature?

2. Do you consider that you deserve to be judged by God because of your sin and punished eternally in hell? How well do you know yourself?

3. Have you ever tried and failed to reform yourself through your own strength?

4. When we come to the end of our own strength, we throw ourselves upon the grace of God. Have you reached that point in your life?

Section A: Core Beliefs   7

LESSON 4: GRACE

KEY DOCTRINE: A holy God enters into a relationship with sinful people only by His grace that He lavishes on them.

MEMORY VERSE: *"For by grace you have been saved through faith. And this is not your own doing; it is the gift of God"* (Ephesians 2:8)

SCRIPTURE PRE-READING: Exodus 33:12-34:9; Luke 15:1-32; John 1:14-18; Jonah 4; Ephesians 2:1-10

Since the original fall of Adam and Eve, God enters into relationships with sinners due to His grace. We are unable to become good enough to merit God's favor, so He shows compassion upon us. God's grace is the most glorious aspect of His character and it is the basis of our faith. Through the coming of His son Jesus, God fully revealed the riches of His grace.

WHAT IS GRACE?

Grace is known for being a beautiful and positive word in the English language. Perhaps the most well-known hymn in America is "Amazing Grace." But what is grace? It has often been called "unmerited favor" or likened to "mercy." A simple definition of grace is "love for sinners," because grace is the undeserved love that God lavishes on sinful people who only deserve punishment. Since God is holy and we are sinful, He should punish us but He chooses to love us instead. This bestowal of God's grace upon us speaks volumes about the nature of God and not of anything pertaining to us.

SHOW ME THY GLORY!

In Exodus 33:12-34:9, Moses asks for God to reveal His glory to him. This is a bold and profound request, as Moses shows his desire to know the full revelation of God's essential nature and character. Read the above passage and answer the following questions.

- In verse 33:19, what does God promise He will reveal?

- In verses 34:6-7, list all the words that describe the grace of God.

- In verse 34:7, how does God treat the guilty?

When God revealed His glory, He highlighted within His character His graciousness toward sinners. God did not simply use one word to describe His goodness, but rather He used five words to describe grace. He is not stingy with His grace; He is abounding in it and shows it to thousands of generations. If this is what God describes as His glory, then we should be greatly encouraged at the prospect of being in a relationship with Him.

A RÉSUMÉ OF GRACE

The Bible is an historical account of God showing His graciousness to a select group of people from Adam onwards. God was not just befriending those who were "perfect;" the Bible is not bashful about broadcasting the flaws of its main characters. When we look at the broad sweep of biblical history, we see that God has consistently shown grace to fallen individuals and nations:

- Adam and Eve sinned and suffered the consequences, but did not die immediately. (Genesis 3)
- Noah and his family survived the flood. (Genesis 6-9)
- An idol-worshipper, Abraham, was chosen to be the "father of the nation of Israel." (Genesis 12:1-3; Joshua 24:2)
- Jacob the deceiver was chosen and blessed. (Genesis 25-50)
- Moses the murderer was still used by God. (Exodus 2-4)
- The people of Israel were redeemed from Egypt and taken to the Promised Land. (Exodus-Joshua)

- David was helped in the wilderness and forgiven after committing adultery and murder. (1 Samuel)
- The evil city of Nineveh repented after Jonah's preaching. (Jonah)

GRACE AND TRUTH THROUGH JESUS CHRIST

Jesus came with the purpose of revealing the glorious nature of His Father. We cannot see God, but when we look at Jesus we can see what God is like. *"No one has ever seen God; the only God, who is at the Father's side, he has made him known."* (John 1:18) The apostle John stated that Jesus revealed His glory as He dwelt among us (John 1:14), and that glory consists of the abundance of *"grace and truth."* (John 1:14, 17) This glorious *"grace and truth"* of Jesus is the same glory of the *"steadfast love and faithfulness"* that God revealed on Mt. Sinai to Moses (Exodus 34:6). In essence, just as God showed His glory to Israel, He now shows His glory to us through his Son.

When we look at the ministry of Jesus, we see that He revealed the glorious character of God's grace through all that He did. The people of Israel should have recognized that God's grace had visited them in the person and work of Jesus, because so much of His ministry exhibited God's grace:

- Because of God's love, Jesus was sent for us. (John 3:16)
- Jesus' healing of the multitudes revealed His power and compassion. (Mark 1:32-34)
- Jesus' teaching on love and forgiveness displayed God's grace. (Matthew 5-6)
- Jesus showed that He is a friend of sinners. (Matthew 9:10-13)
- Jesus died on the cross for sinners. (Romans 5:6-11)

AMAZED BY GRACE

The apostles of Jesus wrote and preached about God's amazing grace. Their letters explain the good news of how God reconciled us to Himself through Jesus' death and resurrection. The forgiveness of God given through faith in Christ was the foundation and goal of all of their teaching.

- In Ephesians 2:5-8, what is the reason that God saves people?

- In Ephesians 3:14-19, what does Paul pray that the Ephesian Christians will know?

BUT NOT CHEAP GRACE

In the second part of the description of God's name in Exodus 34:6-8, God says that He *"will by no means clear the guilty."* Sin will be judged, and the guilty will be punished for their crimes. Yes, God is overflowing with grace, yet at the same time He remains just. The genius of the gospel is that God is able to show both grace and justice at the cross so that He never compromises His holy character (Romans 3:21-26). We either bear the punishment for our own sin or Christ does. Such grace should inspire awe since it came at the great cost of God's only Son. Psalm 130:4 says, *"But with you there is forgiveness, that you may be feared."*

HITTING HOME

1. To what degree do you recognize that grace is at the core of God's character? Or, is your primary conception of God an angry judge?

2. Is your relationship with God based upon your works or upon your faith in His grace?

3. Did God choose to love "holy people" in the Bible, or did His love *make* them holy?

4. Which aspects of Jesus' ministry most impress you about the grace of God?

5. If God has been gracious to you, how should that change your relationship with others?

LESSON 5: JESUS CHRIST

KEY DOCTRINE: Jesus Christ is the Son of God who grants forgiveness and eternal life to all who place their faith in Him.
MEMORY VERSE: *"And the Word became flesh and dwelt among us, and we have seen his glory, glory as of the only Son from the Father, full of grace and truth."* (John 1:14)
SCRIPTURE PRE-READING: Matthew 8:1-9:8; Mark 15:21-39; Luke 1:26-38; 24:1-9; John 1:1-14; Colossians 1:15-20

The central person of the Christian faith is Jesus Christ. He was the promised Messiah of the Old Testament who came to save His people from their sin. Before He came to earth, the Son of God existed for all eternity with His Father as the second person of the Trinity of God. Jesus of Nazareth was both fully God *and* fully man. His ministry on the earth demonstrated that He was God's Son, and by His death on the cross, He made atonement for the sins of God's people.

THE PROMISED MESSIAH

The need for a Savior started in the beginning right after the fall. In Genesis 3:15 God announced for the first time of a Savior who would defeat the devil, *"he shall bruise your head, and you shall bruise his heel."* Throughout the Old Testament Israel waited for her promised Messiah. During the darkest days of Israel's failings God's prophets spoke of a coming time of grace and victory when salvation would come through the Christ. But what would He be like? From the Old Testament we can learn what kind of Savior God would send:

* He would defeat Satan, but would be wounded in the process. (Genesis 3:15)
* He would be a prophet who speaks God's words. (Deuteronomy 18:15)
* He would be a conquering king. (Psalm 2)
* He would be a suffering servant. (Isaiah 53)

JESUS IS FULLY GOD

The Son of God has always existed in eternity with the Father. The Son became incarnate in the world when He was born of Mary. These four passages speak about the eternal, divine nature of Jesus—that the Son of God is equal with the Father in nature and glory: Hebrews 1:2-3; John 1:1-2, 14; Philippians 2:6-7; and Colossians 1:15-16.

When the angel Gabriel announced to the virgin Mary that she was going to conceive a child, he told her that the Holy Spirit's power would overshadow her. This child would be *"holy—the Son of God"* (Luke 1:35), not just any human child but the fully divine Son of God. The Gospels clearly demonstrate the divine nature of Jesus Christ through a multitude of ways:

* The Father identified Him as His Son. (Matthew 3:17; 17:5)
* Jesus performed miracles. (Mark 1:29-34)
* Jesus forgave sin. (Matthew 9:6)
* Jesus had command over nature. (Matthew 8:27)
* Jesus had power over demons. (Matthew 8:29-32)
* Jesus received worship. (John 9:38)
* Jesus demonstrated omniscience. (John 1:48; 4:17-19)
* Jesus testified of His own divinity. (John 8:58)
* The divine titles given Him. (John 20:28)

JESUS IS FULLY MAN

Jesus was born of a human mother Mary, and it was from her that He received His human nature. The book of Hebrews states, *"Since therefore the children share in flesh and blood, he himself likewise partook of the same things...Therefore he had to be made like his brothers in every respect"* (Hebrews 2:14, 17). Jesus had flesh and blood just like us. The Gospels present the humanity of Jesus in that Jesus was born, matured, and lived in a normal, human manner. Like us, Jesus felt hunger, thirst, and weariness, as well as exhibited normal human emotions like grief, joy, and anger. Also like us, Jesus was tempted, however unlike us and due to His divine nature He never gave in to temptation.

Having a fully human nature grants Jesus the ability to be the perfect intercessor and advocate on our behalf. He knows our weaknesses and is able to give us grace to fit our needs. *"For we do not have a high priest who is unable to sympathize with our weaknesses, but one who in every respect has been tempted as we are, yet without sin. Let us then with confidence draw near to the throne of grace, that we may receive mercy and find grace to help in time of need."* (Hebrews 4:15-16) In this respect Jesus's humanity is necessary for atonement. If Jesus was not fully human, He could not take our place and receive the punishment required for our sins.

JESUS' THREE-YEAR MINISTRY

After Jesus was baptized by John the Baptist, His ministry was officially inaugurated. From that point on, Jesus assumed the role of the Christ culminating with the end goal of His crucifixion and resurrection. He did not, however, go straight to the cross as soon as He was baptized. Instead, Jesus spent three years teaching throughout the land of Israel and beyond. The purpose of Jesus' ministry as recorded in the four Gospels was:

- **To reveal the Father's nature through perfect obedience**
  "Whoever has seen me has seen the Father...Believe me that I am in the Father and the Father is in me, or else believe on account of the works themselves." (John 14:9, 11)
- **To speak God's Word and make disciples**
  "And when Jesus finished these sayings, the crowds were astonished at his teaching, for he was teaching them as one who had authority, and not as their scribes." (Matthew 7:28-29)
- **To demonstrate His divine nature, thereby evoking faith**
  "Now Jesus did many other signs in the presence of the disciples, which are not written in this book; but these are written so that you may believe that Jesus is the Christ, the Son of God, and that by believing you may have life in his name." (John 20:30-31)

JESUS' DEATH AND RESURRECTION

After Peter confessed Jesus as the Christ and the Son of God, Jesus informed the disciples that He would suffer and die in Jerusalem at the hands of the religious leaders and the Romans, but would rise again on the third day. Jesus made this same prediction of His death and resurrection two more times in the Gospel accounts. His death and resurrection was always the end goal of His ministry. In Luke 13:31-35 Jesus openly challenged Herod by declaring His plan to continue performing miracles until He came to Jerusalem where He knew that He would die. Why such a focus on His death? Because only through His death could atonement be made for sin. On the cross Jesus bore the sins of His people and, thus, endured our just punishment from God. Jesus' cry of *"It is finished"* (John 19:30) meant that His death fully satisfied God's justice by paying the price required for us to receive God's acceptance.

The predictions of Jesus' death are always coupled with His resurrection because only at His resurrection would the true victory over death and sin be manifested. At the resurrection, we see that Jesus is no longer under God's judgment and that the power of death has been defeated. The resurrection shows to the world that Jesus was fully obedient to His Father and that His perfect sacrifice was accepted by Him. After the resurrection, God gave Jesus all authority under heaven and earth, and Jesus now reigns as Lord over all of creation and His people.

HITTING HOME

1. How does Christ's humanity encourage you as you walk by faith?

2. Jesus asked Peter, *"who do you say that I am?"* (Matthew 16:15) How would you answer?

3. Have you come to the place in your life where you embrace the fact that Jesus had to die for you?

4. In what way are you taking part in Christ's ministry?

LESSON 6: SALVATION

KEY DOCTRINE: Anyone can be saved through faith in Jesus, the Son of God, who died for our sins.
MEMORY VERSE: *"For God so loved the world, that he gave his only Son, that whoever believes in him should not perish but have eternal life."* (John 3:16)
SCRIPTURE PRE-READING: Mark 10:46-52; John 3:1-21; Acts 16:25-34; Romans 4:1-8; Galatians 2:15-21; 1 Peter 1:3-9

As sinners, we cannot work our way into God's approval and forgiveness. We do not redeem ourselves. Salvation comes to sinners when we recognize our sin and embrace God's grace toward us through the death and resurrection of Jesus. Forgiveness and justification before God comes when we in faith trust in the mercy shown to us in Jesus Christ.

GETTING RIGHT WITH GOD THE WRONG WAY

By this point we have learned that there is a God and that we have sinned against Him. We also know that God responds to our sin with judgment and grace. We do not want judgment; so in an attempt to reform ourselves and please God, we try to obey all of His commandments and the moral rules that we know. This is a common error that many of us make. The Bible says that trying to earn acceptance with God by perfectly obeying His law is impossible. *"For by works of the law no human being will be justified in his sight, since through the law comes knowledge of sin."* (Romans 3:20)

Being accepted (justified) by God through law-keeping does not work for the following reasons:

* The Bible says we cannot be justified by our works. (Galatians 2:16)
* We cannot keep *all* of God's laws. (James 2:10-11)
* We cannot keep *any* of God's laws perfectly. (Matthew 5:27-28)
* Knowing God's laws only causes us to sin more. (Romans 7:8-9)
* Thinking we are keeping God's laws makes us arrogant. (Luke 18:9-14)
* Works-based righteousness is delusional (Mark 10:20-21) and hypocritical. (Matthew 23:27-28)

If we cannot be justified by God through keeping His commandments, then why did God give them to us? So that we would have knowledge of our own sin. *"Yet if it had not been for the law, I would not have known sin. For I would not have known what it is to covet if the law had not said, 'You shall not covet.'"* (Romans 7:7) A function of the law is to convict us of sin and expose our powerlessness so that we throw ourselves on the mercy of God.

SAVED BY FAITH

Once we realize that we cannot be righteous in our own strength, we need God's grace. The good news (the gospel) is that God's plan was to save us, not through our works of righteousness, but through faith in His grace given to us through His Son Jesus Christ:

* *"yet we know that a person is not justified by works of the law but through faith in Jesus Christ, so we also have believed in Christ Jesus, in order to be justified by faith in Christ and not by works of the law"* (Galatians 2:16)

* *"For God so loved the world, that he gave his only Son, that whoever believes in him should not perish but have eternal life."* (John 3:16)

We are saved when we submit to the person of Jesus Christ and the work that He did on the cross. First, we must recognize and accept Jesus Christ as God's Son who is the full revelation of God; Jesus demands our worship and obedience. Secondly, we believe that on the cross, Jesus took our sins upon Himself and died in our place. His death was the punishment by the Father for all of our sins. When we trust in Jesus, we are forgiven by God the Father and declared righteous before Him.

THE FULL GOSPEL

What happens when we trust in Jesus? We can now say that we are "saved," and this salvation is a multi-faceted blessing. The following is a list of many of the benefits of this great salvation:

- **Our sins are forgiven by God.** *"I am writing to you, little children, because your sins are forgiven for his name's sake."* (1 John 2:12)

God forgives us of all of our sins. We need not carry around the guilt and shame of our sins, and we no longer dread God's judgment. Psalm 103:12 says, *"as far as the east is from the west, so far does he remove our transgressions from us."*

- **We have the sure hope of heaven.** *"Truly, truly, I say to you, whoever hears my word and believes him who sent me has eternal life. He does not come into judgment, but has passed from death to life."* (John 5:24)

Since we are forgiven of our sins, we cannot be punished for them. We have already been given eternal life; therefore, as we approach our death, we can be bold in our hope of heaven.

- **We are considered righteous before God.** *"And to the one who does not work but believes in him who justifies the ungodly, his faith is counted as righteousness"* (Romans 4:5)

When we believe in Jesus, our faith is counted as righteousness before God. God imputes righteousness toward us. From this point on, God considers us to be a "saint." Though we still sin, God does not consider us to be a "sinner."

- **We are at peace with God.** *"Therefore, since we have been justified by faith, we have peace with God through our Lord Jesus Christ."* (Romans 5:1)

We are no longer God's enemy. His anger is not burning against us; He is now reconciled and at peace with us. From now on, God is with us and for us.

- **We are called His children.** *"And because you are sons, God has sent the Spirit of his Son into our hearts, crying, 'Abba! Father!'"* (Galatians 4:6)

After being reconciled with God and called righteous, God adopts us into His spiritual family. God is our eternal Father, and Christ is our big brother and head. Now as His children, God loves us, is committed to our well-being, and hears our prayers.

- **We are given a new spiritual nature.** *"Therefore, if anyone is in Christ, he is a new creation. The old has passed away; behold, the new has come."* (2 Corinthians 5:17)

At salvation we experience a new spiritual birth whereby the Holy Spirit creates in us a new heart. This new spiritual nature enables us to keep God's commandments and do good works.

- **God's love is with us forever.** *"For I am sure that neither death nor life, nor angels nor rulers, nor things present nor things to come, nor powers, nor height nor depth, nor anything else in creation, will be able to separate us from the love of God in Christ Jesus our Lord."* (Romans 8:38-39)

In Christ nothing can sever us from the love of God. So we will always sing, *"Give thanks to the LORD, for he is good, for His steadfast love endures forever."* (Psalm 136:1)

HITTING HOME

1. How have you tried, or how are you trying, to work your way into God's grace? Have you started going back to church and changing your ways?

2. When we realize that we cannot be righteous in our own strength, we look in faith to Christ's mercy toward us. Have you gotten to that broken point in your life where only by trusting in His grace can you be forgiven?

3. Are you able to define a specific point in time when you believed in Christ or was it a process of trusting in Christ? (Go back and read your written testimony from lesson one.)

4. From the list of the benefits of salvation (see **THE FULL GOSPEL**), which of these stand out as having special significance to you?

LESSON 7: THE TRINITY

KEY DOCTRINE: God is comprised of three persons who are all equal in substance, having the same attributes, power, and glory: the Father, the Son, and the Holy Spirit.

MEMORY VERSE: *"Go therefore and make disciples of all nations, baptizing them in the name of the Father and of the Son and of the Holy Spirit"* (Matthew 28:19)

SCRIPTURE PRE-READING: Judges 13; Psalm 110; Matthew 2:13-17; Hebrews 1:1-14

Since the foundation of the Christian church, theologians have come to understand that God exists in three persons: the Father, the Son, and the Holy Spirit. The existence of three persons in the Godhead is hinted at in the Old Testament but is fully revealed in the New Testament. God the Father, Jesus the Son, and the Holy Spirit fully share all of the attributes and nature of God but assume different roles in the working out of God's redemptive plan.

WHAT'S IN A WORD?

The term *"Trinity"* is not used in the Bible. There are some religions that refuse to believe in the Trinity, such as Judaism, Islam, the Unitarians, and the Jehovah Witnesses. What do we mean by the term *Trinity*? Christianity is monotheistic in that we affirm that there is only one true God. Yet we say that in God there are three persons: Father, Son, and Holy Spirit. These all have the same nature or substance. Equally, they share the divine attributes of omnipotence, omniscience, holiness, eternality, etc. Though the term *Trinity* is not used in the Bible, the concept or understanding behind the word is demonstrated so that it is an appropriate term to use to describe God.

OLD TESTAMENT HINTS

Is the concept of the Trinity taught throughout the whole Bible—Old and New Testaments? The main emphasis of the Old Testament is that God is the only true God, thereby refuting polytheism. However, the doctrine of there being multiple persons in God is hinted at, or given glimpses of, in a number of ways:

- God's use of the first person plural. *"Let **us** make man in **our** image."* (Genesis 1:26) See also: Genesis 11:7; Isaiah 6:8.
- Two references to God in one verse, yet two different persons. *"The Lord* [the Father] *says to my Lord* [the Son]*: 'Sit at my right hand, until I make your enemies your footstool.'"* (Psalm 110:1) In Matthew 22:41-45 Jesus testified that Psalm 110:1 referred to His Father's promise to Him.
- An Angel of the Lord appears in many passages where He is distinct from the LORD, yet is recognized as God. In Judges 13, all three persons of the Trinity are referred to, *"the LORD* [the Father]*," "the angel of the LORD* [the Son]*,"* and *"the Spirit of the LORD* [the Holy Spirit]*."*
- The Holy Spirit in the Old Testament is referred to as *"the Spirit of God"* (Genesis 1:2) or *"the Spirit of the LORD."* (Ezekiel 11:5)
- The LORD sends a Savior who is also considered to be God. Read Zechariah 2:10-11 and notice that the LORD sends the LORD.

NEW TESTAMENT PROOFS

In the New Testament the doctrine of the Trinity is not specifically defined but is clearly demonstrated in the deeds of God. All three members of the Trinity are present.

God the Father
- At Jesus' baptism and transfiguration, the Father calls Jesus His Son. (Matthew 3:16-17; 17:5)
- Jesus refers to and prays to His Father. (John 14:7-11; 17:1-5)
- The epistles refer to: *"God our Father and the Lord Jesus Christ."* (Ephesians 1:2)
- When *"God"* is used, it generally refers to God the Father. (Hebrews 1:1-2)

God the Son

The following passages are some of the most important texts which demonstrate Jesus' divine nature: John 1:1-3,14; Philippians 2:6-7; Colossians 1:15-19; and Hebrews 1:2-3. In John 1:1-3 Jesus is *"the Word, the Word was with God, and the Word was God...all things were made through him."* These important passages make reference to Jesus having equal substance, likeness, and equality with God and that through Him all things were created.

God the Spirit

The Holy Spirit tends to get short shrift in the church (except for Pentecostals) because we can falsely think that He is just a force or power and not a person. In the New Testament Jesus is the focus; the Spirit's role is to point people to Jesus and dwell within them after salvation. The following passages demonstrate that the Holy Spirit is fully God:

- These passages list all three members of the Godhead with equal standing: Matthew 28:16; 1 Corinthians 12:4-6; and 2 Corinthians 13:14. *"The grace of the Lord Jesus Christ and the love of God and the fellowship of the Holy Spirit be with you all."* (2 Corinthians 13:14)

- The Spirit is a person and not just a force. He speaks: *"the Holy Spirit said"* (Acts 13:2); He grieves: *"And do not grieve the Holy Spirit of God"* (Ephesians 4:30); He teaches and comforts: *"the Helper, the Holy Spirit, whom the Father will send in my name, he will teach you all things and bring to your remembrance all that I have said to you."* (John 14:26)

- In Acts 5:3-4, lying to the Spirit of God is lying to God.

- The Spirit exhibits omnipresence and is equated to God in Psalm 139:7-10.

- The Holy Spirit accomplishes God's work of salvation upon man, *"he saved us...by the washing of regeneration and renewal of the Holy Spirit"* (Titus 3:5).

- The Holy Spirit keeps us in our salvation, we *"were sealed with the promised Holy Spirit, who is the guarantee of our inheritance until we acquire possession of it"* (Ephesians 1:13).

THREE IN ONE

God the Father, Son, and Holy Spirit all share the same divine attributes, but are three persons. Since they all share the same attributes, they cannot exist independently of each other. They have a perfect unity and oneness. How does that work? We must admit that we cannot fully comprehend the Trinity. In our humility we must accept that some truths are mysterious and wonderful. We should not get frustrated if we cannot fully wrap our head around this. Many people in history have fallen into error when trying to understand the Trinity. The three persons are not three separate Gods, and there is not one God who assumes three different personas. Finally, we should not consider God the Father as the true God with Jesus and the Spirit being merely sub-gods.

The differences between the three members of the Godhead appear in the roles they assume. The Father ordains, creates, and rules over all things. In His plan of redemption, the Father chooses Christ to be the Savior of those whom He has elected. The Son comes to earth to be the atoning sacrifice for salvation and is crowned the Lord over all things. The Holy Spirit applies Christ's work on the cross unto people to save them and maintains their faith throughout their lives.

HITTING HOME

1. Which "version" of God do you prefer, the God of the Old Testament or the Christ of the New Testament? Jesus said that if we have seen Him, then we have seen the Father (John 14:9). How does this affect your understanding of Jesus' ministry?

2. What do you not yet understand about the relationship of the three members of the Trinity?

3. What significant role does the Holy Spirit play in the plan of salvation?

4. How does your understanding of the Trinity affect your prayer life?

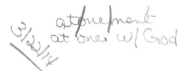

atonement
at 'ones' w/ God
3/22/14

LESSON 8: THE CROSS

KEY DOCTRINE: On the cross Jesus effectively provided atonement for God's children by incurring the wrath of God for their sins.

MEMORY VERSE: *"but we preach Christ crucified, a stumbling block to Jews and folly to Gentiles, but to those who are called, both Jews and Greeks, Christ the power of God and the wisdom of God."* (1 Corinthians 1:23-24)

SCRIPTURE PRE-READING: Matthew 26:36-68; 27:11-61; 28:1-10; Romans 3:21-26; 5:6-21; Hebrews 9:11-28

The most important event in the New Testament is the death and resurrection of Jesus. No other event in the four Gospels receives as much coverage as the last hours of Jesus' earthly life. It is only through the death and resurrection of Jesus that salvation comes to man. His teachings and example alone are not enough to provide forgiveness and spiritual change within a person. His death and resurrection is the key to the miracle of forgiveness, new life, a relationship with the Father, and deliverance from sin and death. For this reason, "Christ crucified" became the central focus of the gospel message.

IS W.W.J.D. ENOUGH?

Many of us tend to approach Christianity by looking at Jesus as a great moral teacher. He sets the perfect example by which to live, and His teachings should be the foundation of a good Christian life. The acronym W.W.J.D. (What Would Jesus Do?) became the mantra for living the Christian life in the 90's; however, such a view of Christ is not sufficient for salvation.

An approach to Christianity which solely looks to Jesus as a teacher misses the essential element of His death on the cross. It is this last part of His ministry that is the key to Jesus' plan of salvation. The theological significance of the cross must be explained; otherwise, it will be misunderstood as *"a stumbling block"* or *"foolishness"* (1 Corinthians 1:22) to the world. It is only through Jesus' sacrifice on the cross that forgiveness and salvation come to mankind.

THAT BLOODY OLD TESTAMENT RELIGION

Critics of Christianity are often offended by all the bloodshed associated with salvation. In the Old Testament the Jewish priests offered animal sacrifices to God on behalf of the people. These bloody sacrifices were said to atone for the peoples' guilt of sin. Leviticus 16:20-22 describes how the priest would lay his hands upon a goat while confessing the sins of Israel, and then let it loose into the wilderness. At the same time the priest would kill another goat and sprinkle its blood within the temple. These acts provided atonement for the people before the LORD. Atonement is the means by which God, who has suffered an offense by the unrighteous acts of mankind, is reconciled with man. The just punishment for sin is a sentence of death. In the Old Testament the death of animals was the temporary means by which the sins of humans could be atoned; the animal died instead of the human.

CHRIST IN OUR PLACE

In the New Testament the book of Hebrews explains that, *"it is impossible for the blood of bulls and goats to take away sins."* (Hebrews 10:4) Animal sacrifices merely pointed to the effectual sacrifice of Christ. Jesus became the perfect priest who offered Himself as a spotless lamb to atone for our sins once and for all. Christ knew that His ultimate purpose in His ministry was to die on behalf of His people. At Calvary, Jesus did not simply lose a religious power struggle, rather He intentionally laid His life down to be the perfect sacrifice, perfectly obeying the will of the Father.

At the cross both God's mercy and His justice are displayed. He makes Jesus *"to be sin"* (2 Corinthians 5:21) for us in order to bear the punishment of God's wrath, and thereby satisfy God's justice. Once God's justice and wrath have been appeased, or propitiated, God is able to enter into a reconciled relationship with us. As Romans 3:26 states God accomplishes the goal of being both *"just and the justifier"* of His people. God shows grace toward a people whom He loves while still maintaining His holy justice. God's forgiven people must always recognize that their salvation was bought at the great cost of God's beloved Son.

The following key passages highlight the redemptive nature of Christ's death:
- *"But he was wounded for our transgressions; he was crushed for our iniquities; upon him was the chastisement that brought us peace, and with his stripes we are healed."* (Isaiah 53:5)
- *"The next day he saw Jesus coming toward him, and said, 'Behold, the Lamb of God, who takes away the sin of the world!'"* (John 1:29)
- *"Christ redeemed us from the curse of the law by becoming a curse for us--for it is written, 'Cursed is everyone who is hanged on a tree.'"* (Galatians 3:13)

FOR WHOM DID CHRIST DIE?

If we understand that the purpose of Christ's death on the cross was to atone for sin, then we can correctly answer the question, "for whom did Christ die?" (Circle one)

 a. Christ died for the sins of all people, and all people must therefore be saved.
 b. Christ potentially died for all people, contingent on them believing in Him. *work?*
 c. Christ died only for those people whom He foresaw would believe in Him.
 d. Christ died for specific people, whom God brings to faith.

Of these four explanations, only answer "d" accurately represents the biblical presentation of the work of the cross. If we understand that Jesus' death actually pays for people's sins, then it holds that those people for whom He died cannot be punished eternally. Jesus' death was effective for all those for whom He died. If we do not hold this position, we do not think that Jesus' death achieved anything ultimately, but that our salvation rests upon the faith and work of sinners to bring it about.

This understanding of the cross fits within the wider understanding of how God, from the beginning, chose specific people to be recipients of His mercy and come to salvation. Jesus refers to these people as the ones whom the Father had given Him, *"I am not praying for the world but for those whom you have given me, for they are yours"* (John 17:9). Those for whom Christ died are called to faith and repentance. *"And those whom he predestined he also called, and those whom he called he also justified, and those whom he justified he also glorified."* (Romans 8:30) Therefore the cross becomes the power and wisdom of God, not only to bring us to Christ, but also to preserve us for our heavenly inheritance. *"My Father, who has given them to me, is greater than all, and no one is able to snatch them out of the Father's hand."* (John 10:29)

BOASTING IN THE CROSS

The more we understand the value and effectiveness of Christ's work on the cross, the greater we will love Him for it. The brighter the spotlight shines on Jesus, the less we will seek to boast in *our* faith and *our* repentance. We will instead look to **His** sacrifice and **His** grace. What amazing grace awaits those who draw near to Him, for He is *"able to save to the uttermost."* (Hebrews 7:25) We can have peace knowing that all of our present and future sins have been paid in full, which should grant us greater assurance and the desire to boast in the cross. As the apostle Paul aptly proclaimed, *"But far be it from me to boast except in the cross of our Lord Jesus, Christ"* (Galatians 6:14).

HITTING HOME

1. Do you believe that Jesus died for *you* because of your personal sin? What does Jesus' death and resurrection mean to you?

2. What do you think about God's requirement that His wrath can only be satisfied with a death?

3. Picture all of your sins being placed on Jesus' shoulders and Him taking your punishment. How thankful are you for the cross?

4. How confident are you that Christ's one sacrifice will save you and keep you to the end? Is your assurance of salvation based upon God's grace at the cross, or in your own resolve?

5. Do you think that you can now share clearly the message of the cross with another person?

LESSON 9: THE BIBLE

KEY DOCTRINE: The Bible is the infallible (unfailing) and inerrant (without error) Word of God that contains all that believers need for faith and godly living.

MEMORY VERSE: *"All Scripture is breathed out by God and profitable for teaching, for reproof, for correction, and for training in righteousness, that the man of God may be competent, equipped for every good work."* (2 Timothy 3:16-17)

SCRIPTURE PRE-READING: Deuteronomy 8:1-6; Psalm 19:7-11; 2 Timothy 3:12-17; Hebrews 1:1-2; 4:12-13; 2 Peter 1:20-21, 3:14-18; Revelation 22:18-21

Any person who believes in Jesus has come to faith from hearing a message from the Bible. The Bible is the Christian's source of revelation about God, so its truthfulness is essential to our faith. The Scriptures themselves maintain that the Holy Spirit inspired and used men to write these sixty-six books of the Bible to present a trustworthy revelation for us. It is through the Scriptures of the Old and New Testaments that we come to faith in Christ, obtain a knowledge of God, and grow in godly character by the Holy Spirit.

HAS GOD SPOKEN?

The crucial issue that confronts believers is accepting the Bible as God's Word. God has not hidden Himself from us but has revealed Himself so that we can believe in Him. If God did not speak to us, we would have no hope of knowing Him. *"So faith comes from hearing, and hearing through the word of Christ."* (Romans 10:17) God's word must come to us so that we can believe in Him. Faith is not what we imagine about God; our faith is a response to God's word revealing His nature. Thus, faith is not "blind" nor ignorant of fact and truth. We trust in a God who can speak and reveal Himself to us, so that we know in whom we believe.

The devil was the first to question whether God really speaks to people. He asked Eve, *"Did God actually say, 'You shall not eat of any tree in the garden?'"* (Genesis 3:1) The question *"Did God actually say"* is what many people who resist the faith express in their criticism of the Bible. They reject the idea that God has spoken to people throughout history and had these revelations written down in the pages of the Bible. We, however, must come to the Bible with the belief that it is the Word of God, *"living and active, sharper than any two-edged sword, piercing to the division of soul and of spirit, of joints and of marrow, and discerning the thoughts and intentions of the heart."* (Hebrews 4:12) We also must recognize that our very lives are dependent upon *"every word that comes from the mouth of the God."* (Matthew 4:4)

THUS SAITH THE LORD

The Bible claims that God has spoken through men throughout the ages. God has used men as messengers of His Word to speak to the people. *"Long ago, at many times and in many ways, God spoke to our fathers by the prophets, but in these last days he has spoken to us by his Son"* (Hebrews 1:1-2). Often an Old Testament prophetic book will start with, *"The word of the LORD that came to..."* (see Hosea, Joel, Micah, Zephaniah). Many Bible narratives give an account of what God specifically said to the people of that day. When Moses met God at the burning bush in Exodus 4:12, God said, *"Now therefore go, and I will be your mouth and teach you what you shall speak."* When the prophet proclaimed his oracle he would say, *"Thus says the LORD."* As such, his message was not his own opinion, but rather a message from God.

In the New Testament, the apostle John met Jesus on the island of Patmos, and the book of Revelation came from those visions he had. The apostle Paul in Galatians 1:12 said that Jesus Himself taught him, *"For I did not receive it from any man, nor was I taught it, but I received it through a revelation of Jesus Christ."* The letters of the apostles were thus considered Scripture due to the recognition that God was the source and authority behind all that they wrote. The apostles also knew that they had been given an apostolic commission from Jesus to be the authoritative teachers of the early church.

SCRIPTURE CANNOT BE BROKEN

We believe that the Bible is God's Word because the Bible itself says that it is. Our doctrine of Scripture is derived from Bible passages which speak on the nature of God's Word. Jesus' view of the Old Testament was that it is infallible Scripture that cannot be broken (John 10:35). He stated that *"not an iota, not a dot"* (Matthew 5:18) of the Law and the Prophets could pass away, but all must be fulfilled. The Revelation of Jesus Christ states that nothing should be added or subtracted from the words of the prophecy. Since the Scriptures are *"breathed out by God"* (2 Timothy 3:16), they are God's authoritative Word. The Bible is the final word on all matters to which it speaks; therefore, the believer must submit himself to the Word instead of *"doing whatever is right in his own eyes."* (Deuteronomy 12:8)

BREATHED BY GOD, PENNED BY MAN

The Bible is considered God's Word because it maintains that the writers of the Bible were directly influenced by God in their writing—it is not just a man's personal opinion. The Holy Spirit influenced the writers in such a way that every word was exactly what God wanted them to write. *"knowing this first of all, that no prophecy of Scripture comes from someone's own interpretation. For no prophecy was ever produced by the will of man, but men spoke from God as they were carried along by the Holy Spirit."* (2 Peter 1:21-22) Likewise in 2 Timothy 3:16, *"All Scripture is breathed out by God."* These verses teach that the Bible is created by the power of the Holy Spirit. This inspiration extends to every word that was written by the author in its original language, not just the gist of what they were saying.

The Bible does not apologize for using humans in its transcription. God did not skip the human writer and simply drop a golden book from heaven for someone to find. He used people of varied background and education to write within their own circumstances. The Holy Spirit used the personalities of each writer to produce a unique work. As such, the Gospel of John's style of writing is different from Luke, and the epistles of Paul are different from Peter's. This may disturb people because they fear that any human involvement detracts from the credibility of the writing. "To ere is human," right? Not when the Holy Spirit is carrying them along (2 Peter 1:22).

BIBLE FACTS

- Only the 66 books of the Old and New Testaments are Scripture. (Revelation 22:18-19)
- The main theme of the Bible is that God is glorifying Himself through His grace and power in redemption and judgment.
- The Bible is alive in that the Holy Spirit uses it to convict, illuminate, and transform the reader. The Scriptures are not just a source of instruction in conduct for believers but also a means of comfort and encouragement in the faith.
- The first "autographs" (the original document written by the human author) were inspired; later copies (modern translations) can have errors, but the Holy Spirit has overseen the transmission of the Scriptures faithfully throughout history.
- Scripture interprets Scripture. Since the Bible is not self-contradictory, biblical passages help interpret other passages.
- Contemporary language translations are interpretations of the original languages.

HITTING HOME

1. When you read the Bible, what effect should it have upon you? (Hebrews 4:12)

2. What should be the desire of your heart in respect to knowing God's word? (Psalm 1:2; 1 Peter 2:2)

3. How regularly do you read the Bible and hear teaching from it? Do you think that amount is sufficient?

4. How high is the respect that you have for the authority and effectiveness of the Word of God to transform your life?

LESSON 10: ETERNITY

KEY DOCTRINE: After death, the souls of people will either go to be with the Lord Jesus in heaven or go to a place of eternal judgment (hell).

MEMORY VERSE: *"For we must all appear before the judgment seat of Christ, so that each one may receive what is due for what he has done in the body, whether good or evil."* (2 Corinthians 5:10)

SCRIPTURE PRE-READING: Ecclesiastes 12; Matthew 13:24-30, 36-43; Luke 16:19-31; 2 Corinthians 5:1-10; Revelation 20:10-21:1-8

Death is an inevitable reality that we all will face, yet it is a sober truth that most people choose to ignore. The Bible teaches that all of us will die and then face a judgment from God, who will separate the righteous from the wicked. It is only if we have trusted in Jesus in this life that we can be confident that we will spend eternity in heaven with God.

THE BIG QUESTION

What happens to us when we die? This is not a question we like to deal with. It is also a matter which we tend to procrastinate in dealing with, just like we put off doing our annual taxes until the deadline. Yet, like taxes, death is inevitable and we must consider what happens to us after death. Which statement below best describes your present understanding of what happens after death?

a. The righteous people go to heaven; the wicked people go to hell.
b. We all go to some better place.
c. Nothing happens. We simply do not exist anymore.
d. We start over again in another life.

Since we cannot find the answer through the scientific method of observation, we must approach the question from a position of faith. What does the Bible say happens to people after they die?

BODY AND SOUL

First of all, the Bible affirms that we are made up of both a body and a soul, *"then the Lord God formed the man of dust from the ground and breathed into his nostrils the breath of life, and the man became a living creature."* (Genesis 2:7) Our body is a perishable *"tent"* (2 Corinthians 5:2), and our soul, or spirit, is our essential character, which comprises our thinking, emotions, values, and our ultimate being. When we die our bodies perish and return to the ground, "dust to dust, ashes to ashes." However, our soul having been given by God and made in His image exists forever, *"and the dust returns to the earth as it was, and the spirit returns to God who gave it."* (Ecclesiastes 12:7)

Given the reality of an eternal soul, the view that we are simply material creatures and at death we stop existing is not consistent with the Bible. Thus, we can rule out option "c" listed above. There is also no evidence in Scripture of a doctrine of reincarnation where we come back to life in another body (option "d"). That leaves dealing with some form of eternal life in heaven or hell.

HEAVEN OR HELL

Is there such a thing as a last judgment where God will separate the righteous from the wicked? Jesus clearly taught that we will be judged according to our deeds and go to heaven or hell. *"Behold, I am coming soon, bringing my recompense with me, to repay everyone for what he has done."* (Revelation 22:12) Read the *Parable of the Weeds* in Matthew 13:24-30 and 36-43 and answer the following questions.

• What are the two final destinations of the grain and the weeds? (v. 30, 42-43)

• To whom does each belong? (v. 37-39)

• What is the character of the weeds and the grain? (v. 41-42)

The teachings of Jesus are consistent with the glimpse of the future that we see in the book of Revelation. There is both a lake of fire into which the devil, his demons, and the wicked are cast, and a place of life and bliss where the faithful will live in glory (Revelation 20:10-15; 21:1-5; 22:14-15). There is a separating of the righteous and the wicked, and Jesus makes His judgment based upon what we have done while we are alive. Romans 2:6-8 states, *"He will render to each one according to his works: to those who by patience in well-doing seek for glory and honor and immortality, he will give eternal life; but for those who are self-seeking and do not obey the truth, but obey unrighteousness, there will be wrath and fury."*

Considering the four answers to "**THE BIG QUESTION**" above, most of us recognize that answer "a" is probably the right answer, but in practice choose answer "b" as applying to ourselves and all of our friends and family. Hell is not a pleasant option, so we tend to think that only the really wicked people go there (Hitler and Osama bin Laden). Even if we affirm that the righteous go to heaven and the wicked are sent to hell, how should we define "the righteous" and "the wicked?" The offensive message of the Bible is that we all start in "the wicked" category until we cross over to "the righteous" side when we believe in Jesus.

ETERNITY STARTS NOW

Although we start off on a path to destruction, we can be assured that our final destination will be heaven when we place our trust in Jesus. After we have placed our faith in Jesus, God makes a change in our character so that we now begin to live and do deeds worthy of those being prepared for heaven. We can have a confidence that we will go to be with God and experience joy because we know that our sins have been forgiven in Christ. Once we have been declared righteous by God, we are no longer subject to the condemnation of hell. *"There is therefore now no condemnation for those who are in Christ Jesus."* (Romans 8:1)

Some might think it is presumptuous (or self-righteous) to be confident that we are going to heaven some day. However, our confidence is not founded upon our good deeds, but solely on what Christ did in dying for us. We recognize that our good deeds are done by Christ living through us but they are never the ultimate ground of our assurance of heaven.

IF I DIE TODAY?

Most of the Bible references about heaven and hell talk about the end of time when the great judgment happens. Before that time, when people die and are buried their souls will experience either joy or agony. If we are saved, when we die our soul will immediately go to be with the Lord Jesus in heaven:

- *"For to me to live is Christ, and to die is gain...My desire is to depart and be with Christ, for that is far better."* (Philippians 1:21, 23)

- *"So we are of good courage. We know that while we are at home in the body we are away from the Lord, for we walk by faith, not by sight. Yes, we are of good courage, and we would rather be away from the body and at home with the Lord."* (2 Corinthians 5:6-8)

As a Christian we can live without the fear of death because Christ conquered the power of death. It is far better to be with the Lord than to live in this fallen world. Death for us will be an entrance into the joyous welcome and presence of the Father and the Son. As King David penned, *"You make known to me the path of life; in your presence there is fullness of joy; at your right hand are pleasures forevermore."* (Psalm 16:11)

HITTING HOME

1. If you were to die today, where would your soul go? Why do you believe that?

2. What do you think about the concept of an eternal judgment? Is it too harsh? If you think so, how is it just that the wicked in this life face no consequences for their actions?

3. Have you come to a place in your Christian walk where the idea of dying and going to be with the Lord is an attractive prospect?

SECTION B:

SUCH A GREAT SALVATION

"Therefore we must pay much closer attention to what we have heard, lest we drift away from it. For since the message declared by angels proved to be reliable, and every transgression or disobedience received a just retribution, how shall we escape if we neglect such a great salvation?" (Hebrews 2:1-3)

Salvation is not a small thing. Our salvation is called *"such a great salvation"* in this verse from Hebrews. We might be tempted to think that "being saved" refers only to the forgiveness of our sins or our justification. Perhaps we see it as the assurance of going to heaven some day. However, the good news of the gospel should not be limited to only one facet of the gospel's *"great salvation"* promise. The salvation we experience in Christ has past, present and future aspects. We were saved in the past (justification); we are being saved in the present (sanctification); and we will be saved in the future (glorification).

Understanding the doctrines of salvation helps in our salvation. Obviously, knowing the gospel is necessary to enter the kingdom of God, but life in the kingdom will make more sense and be more victorious, when we comprehend the process of salvation itself. Understanding our salvation not only benefits us, but also magnifies the grace of God. From start to finish God is in the "driver's seat" of our salvation. God chooses us in Christ before all eternity, and calls us by His Spirit to believe in Jesus. His power gives us life, and by His grace we are preserved for our inheritance in heaven. What assurance we obtain, and what glory God receives when we know that God is mighty to save.

LESSON 11: ELECTION

KEY DOCTRINE: Before the creation of the world God chose in Christ those whom He will save eternally.
MEMORY VERSE: *"even as he chose us in him before the foundation of the world, that we should be holy and blameless before him. In love he predestined us for adoption as sons through Jesus Christ, according to the purpose of his will."* (Ephesians 1:4-5)
SCRIPTURE PRE-READING: Deuteronomy 7:6-11; John 10:22-30; 17:1-2, 9-22; Romans 8:28-30; 9:6-29; Ephesians 1:1-14

If we are a Christian it is because God chose us before the creation of the world to be saved in Jesus. He chose to love us and be gracious to us by including us in His redemptive plan. Jesus died for our sin on the cross and then God opened our hearts by the Spirit to trust in Jesus. Once we know that God is behind our salvation from the beginning to the end we should give Him all the praise and glory for His amazing grace. God chose us not because of our worth but solely because of His grace.

CHOSEN BY GOD

If we have become a Christian we must not be tempted to pat ourselves on the back for how wise we are for choosing Jesus. It was all God's doing, we are just the fortunate recipients of His grace. The people He saves are deliberate, planned, and chosen and that plan began before we were born, in fact, before the world was created. The Bible uses a number of different words to communicate the truth that God chose us to be saved in Jesus: we are *the elect*; we were *predestined* for salvation; God *foreknew* us; *grace was given* to us before time began. The following verses are a few of the primary passages which clearly teach this doctrine:

* *"For **those whom he foreknew he also predestined** to be conformed to the image of his Son, in order that he might be the firstborn among many brothers."* (Romans 8:29)
* *"Blessed be the God and Father of our Lord Jesus Christ, who has blessed us in Christ with every spiritual blessing in the heavenly places, even as **he chose us in him before the foundation of the world**, that we should be holy and blameless before him. **In love he predestined us** for adoption as sons through Jesus Christ, according to the purpose of his will, to the praise of his glorious grace, with which he has blessed us in the Beloved."* (Ephesians 1:3-6)
* *"For we know, brothers **loved by God**, that **he has chosen you**"* (1 Thessalonians 1:4)
* *"But we ought always to give thanks to God for you, brothers **beloved by the Lord**, because **God chose you** as the firstfruits to be saved, through sanctification by the Spirit and belief in the truth."* (2 Thessalonians 2:13)
* *"God, who saved us and called us to a holy calling, not because of our works but because of his own purpose and **grace, which he gave us in Christ Jesus before the ages began**"* (2 Timothy 1:9)
* *"To those **who are elect** exiles of the dispersion in Pontus, Galatia, Cappadocia, Asia, and Bithynia, **according to the foreknowledge of God the Father**"* (1 Peter 1:1-2)

JESUS TAUGHT ELECTION

The above verses all come from the writings of the apostles but election is not simply an apostolic teaching. Jesus Himself taught that God chooses to save whom He will. He did not use the terms *predestination* or *election*, but Jesus often made references to people whom God *gave* to Him. When Jesus gives credit to God for people coming to faith in Him, He is acknowledging the doctrine of election. Read through the following texts and identify what Jesus says about election:

* Jesus states that God hides truth from some and reveals it to others. (Matthew 11:25-26)
* Though many were invited only the *"chosen"* will go to the feast. (Matthew 22:1-14)
* Jesus states that everyone who comes to Him does so because of God's action--giving, drawing, teaching, and granting. (John 6:36-40, 44-45, 62-65)
* The *"sheep"* of Jesus are the ones given to Him by God and will listen to His word. The Pharisees could not obey Jesus because they were not His sheep. (John 10:25-30)
* The Son gives eternal life to all whom God has given Him. (John 17:1-2)

WHY DOES GOD LOVE?

The issue of fairness (everyone treated the same) is often raised in objection to the doctrine of election. It may seem arbitrary and cruel, but this is not the case. God is both just and loving in the act of election. If we demand fairness (justice) then we should insist upon judgment for all or heaven for all. None of us are entitled to be shown God's love and mercy; it is His gift to give. God does make a general appeal to all people to trust in Christ. Unfortunately, due to the hardness of our hearts we cannot come to Christ without God enabling us.

Election is always equated with love in the Bible. If we do not like the doctrine of election, it means that we do not want God's love placed upon us for all of eternity. When God elected us, He chose to love us. *"Yet I have loved Jacob."* (Malachi 1:2) The fact that God chooses to love some speaks to His grace. *"But God, being rich in mercy, **because** of the great love with which he loved us"* (Ephesians 2:4). Why does He choose to love us? The answer is simple and circular--**because**. *"I will be gracious to whom I will be gracious, and will show mercy on whom I will show mercy."* (Exodus 33:19) God loves us simply because of His love; it is all by grace. As an interpretation exercise read Ephesians 1:1-14 and answer the following questions.

- What does it mean that we are *"blessed in Christ with every spiritual blessing in the heavenly places"*? (v. 3)

- When were we chosen in Christ? (v. 4)

- What are the two purposes of God's election of us? (v. 4-6, 12)

- By what means did we come to believe in Christ? (v. 13)

GOD'S ODD CHOICE

Why does God choose some and not others? This is a mystery to us and is part of God's secret counsels (Deuteronomy 29:29). However, we can know that it has nothing to do with how good we are. God is not like a team captain who is picking all the good players first. In fact, the opposite is more likely true. *"It was not because you were more"* (Deuteronomy 7:7) He chooses the least! *"But God chose what is foolish in the world to shame the wise; God chose what is weak in the world to shame the strong; God chose what is low and despised in the world, even things that are not, to bring to nothing things that are, so that no human being might boast in the presence of God."* (1 Corinthians 1:27-29) The fact that we are saved is no credit to our righteousness or strong spiritual inclinations. We need to fall on our face and in humble gratitude and thank Him for His mercy to wretches like us.

AN UNSHAKEABLE CONFIDENCE

When God predestines us to be saved we are chosen *"in Christ."* (Ephesians 1:3-4) That is, God has purposed that Jesus will die for our sins, the Spirit will convert us and keep us, and then we will ultimately be brought to perfection, like Jesus, in heaven some day. His grace given to us in Christ starts and finishes the work of salvation. The ultimate assurance we have that we will make it to heaven some day is based upon our knowledge that, *"I have loved you with an everlasting love; therefore I have continued my faithfulness to you."* (Jeremiah 31:3)

HITTING HOME

1. Can you recognize and acknowledge that the Bible teaches the doctrine of election even if you have a hard time submitting to it? If you have objections to these teachings are they philosophically or biblically based?

2. Explain the doctrine of election without using the terms, election and predestination.

3. In what way does this doctrine humble you? Have you been giving yourself more credit than you deserve for your salvation?

4. Explain how these truths can be a great source of comfort and assurance to you.

LESSON 12: CALLING

KEY DOCTRINE: God calls His elect through the Holy Spirit-empowered Word of God.
MEMORY VERSE: *"What man of you, having a hundred sheep, if he has lost one of them, does not leave the ninety-nine in the open country, and go after the one that is lost, until he finds it?"* (Luke 15:4)
SCRIPTURE PRE-READING: Isaiah 41:8-10; Luke 14:12-24; 15:1-10; Act 2:39; 1 Corinthians 1:26-31; 1 Thessalonians 1:2-7

Those people whom God has chosen in eternity to save He will call to faith in Christ. God does this by blessing the reading or preaching of the Bible, specifically the message of the gospel. Without the Holy Spirit's working on us we would continue to resist the truth and stay in our state of unbelief. Through the Holy Spirit we are given *"ears to hear"* (Mark 4:9) in order that we may respond with faith in Christ.

STILL HAVEN'T FOUND WHAT I'M LOOKING FOR

Many of us make a mistake when we say that we "found God." The church makes the same error when it refers to people as "seekers." On a practical level there is a sort of searching or seeking that takes place by us as we come to God, but the reality is that God is the true seeker who finds His lost people. Before we are saved we search for happiness and satisfaction in the world from people, possessions, and accomplishments. In the process of searching we may become dissatisfied and look for a spiritual solution. However, often we want a spirituality that still affirms our right to be independent from God, and affirms everything that we hope about ourselves. The true God and Lord Jesus Christ is not what the sinful heart really wants. We resist the knowledge of God before we are saved, because we fear our sin being exposed by God's truth:

- *"For everyone who does wicked things hates the light and does not come to the light, lest his works should be exposed."* (John 3:20)

- *"For the wrath of God is revealed from heaven against all ungodliness and unrighteousness of men, who by their unrighteousness suppress the truth."* (Romans 1:18)

In Luke 14:12-24, Jesus told a parable about a man who invited many people to his great banquet. All the invitees had excuses why they could not come, so he sent his servant out far and wide to bring in the non-desirables of society and to compel them to come in. This parable teaches that we have great resistance to the knowledge of God and entering His kingdom. The apostle Paul, in 1 Corinthians 1:18-2:16, described how the gospel message is foolishness to people of this age. *"The natural person does not accept the things of the Spirit of God, for they are folly to him, and he is not able to understand them because they are spiritually discerned."* (1 Corinthians 2:14)

GOD ON THE HUNT

When we find God, we discover that God found us. God always takes the initiative to search and seek after us. Jesus described God, using three parables in Luke 15, as one who searches for lost people and rejoices in finding them. The very mission of Christ was to come into the world to save sinners (John 3:17). He is like a farmer who wants to bring in a harvest of people (John 4:35-36), a fisherman who is catching men and woman (Luke 5:10), or a shepherd who is looking for lost sheep (John 10:16).

It is actually more theologically specific to say that the Holy Spirit seeks out God's elect for salvation. Jesus' role in redemption was accomplished by living perfectly and dying on the cross for our sins. The Holy Spirit's role is to bring in those for whom Christ died. Jesus said He would send the Holy Spirit into the world to convict the world of its sins. *"But if I go, I will send him [the Holy Spirit] to you. And when he comes, he will convict the world concerning sin and righteousness and judgment"* (John 16:7-8).

Jesus described the Holy Spirit as being like an invisible wind that blows; we cannot see the wind but we can see the effects. Likewise, we cannot see the Holy Spirit but we can see the effects of Him working on people and bringing them to salvation. That is why Jesus told Nicodemus that he had to be *"born again."* (John 3:1-8) Only the Holy Spirit can create life within us and cause us to enter the kingdom of God.

HEARING THE CALL

The Scriptures demonstrate in a number of ways that it is the Holy Spirit who brings us into faith. The power of the Holy Spirit accompanies the preaching of the gospel of Christ to bring about the conversion of a person:

- God teaches people and draws them to salvation in Christ. (John 6:44-45)
- God opens hearts to hear the Word of God. (Acts 16:14)
- The Holy Spirit powerfully convicts people to respond to the gospel. (1 Thessalonians 1:5-6)
- Light (God's truth) is shone into hearts, bringing belief in the gospel. (2 Corinthians 4:1-6)

The Holy Spirit needs to powerfully call us to salvation because if it were left up to us alone we would not choose Christ. Jesus recognized this truth when He thanked His heavenly Father for His role in bringing people to faith. Read Matthew 11:25-30 and answer the following questions.

- Whom does Jesus invite to come to Him? (v. 28-30)

- Who will not come to faith and why? (v. 25-27)

- Who comes to Jesus and what is the cause? (v. 25-27)

- Is the general call of "*all*" (v. 28) to come to Jesus a contradiction of the specific call of God on some? (v. 25)

SPREAD THE WORD

As part of God's world-wide plan to save His people He sends out messengers to spread the gospel message. The gospel should be preached far and wide, for as many people as possible need to hear how Jesus can deliver them from their sin. We do not know who will eventually believe, so we attempt to reach every ear with the message. We are like a sower who throws the seed of the Word broadly, trusting that God will cause it to take root and grow (Matthew 13:1-9). There should be urgency to spreading the Word because nobody will believe upon Jesus unless they have heard about Him, and who will hear unless we tell them (Romans 10:14-15)? The plan of God to call people to Himself necessitates that believers go forth and spread the Word of the gospel.

This participation in the calling of God for His elect is not a passive activity. We participate in spreading the gospel knowing we will face resistance and setbacks, but we go forth with confidence that the Chief Shepherd has said, *"I have other sheep that are not of this fold. I must bring them also, and they will listen to my voice."* (John 10:16) The saving work of the Holy Spirit overcomes initial resistance, excuses, and attempts at hiding from God. His sheep will hear the voice of Jesus*, "so there will be one flock, one shepherd."* (John 10:16)

God is the one who saves people. We cannot force a conversion through persuasion and apologetics. This truth should relieve any pressure we might put on ourselves to say and do just the right thing in order to "close the deal," so to speak. We share our faith, love people, and live lives of righteousness, trusting that God will use us to find His lost sheep. Let us humbly seek first the kingdom of God, and when a person comes to faith we can rejoice with Jesus who says, *"Rejoice with me, for I have found my sheep that was lost."* (Luke 15:6)

HITTING HOME

1. Did you ever in your life resist the Bible, the gospel or Christians you knew?

2. Do you have a testimony of how God drew you to Himself? What people and experiences did He use to wake you up and get your attention?

3. How do you feel knowing that God searched and sought you out to bring you into His family?

4. In what ways are you participating in seeing someone else come to faith? Can you discern God using you and working on the other person?

LESSON 13: REGENERATION

KEY DOCTRINE: Regeneration is the act of the Holy Spirit whereby He creates new life within the heart of a spiritually dead person.

MEMORY VERSE: *"he saved us, not because of works done by us in righteousness, but according to his own mercy, by the washing of regeneration and renewal of the Holy Spirit"* (Titus 3:5)

SCRIPTURE PRE-READING: Ezekiel 36:26-27; 37:1-14; John 3:1-8; Ephesians 2:1-10; Titus 3:3-7

How does a person get saved from being lost and blind, to being found and gaining sight? It is truly a miracle, as only God can bring a person out of their state of spiritual death. Regeneration describes the work of God when He, through the Holy Spirit, creates new life within a sinner, causing that sinner to hear and respond in repentance and faith to the gospel of Jesus Christ.

DEAD MEN WALKING

Most people who are alive do not know that they are actually dead--not in the physical sense, but in the spiritual sense. Mankind is spiritually dead in that we are unable to make completely pure moral decisions that pass the test of God's righteousness. Our natures are predisposed against God's holiness and are not seeking to be in a relationship with Him. In Ephesians 2:1-3 Paul describes our state of fallen humanity:

"And you were dead in the trespasses and sins in which you once walked, following the course of this world, following the prince of the power of the air, the spirit that is now at work in the sons of disobedience—among whom we all once lived in the passions of our flesh, carrying out the desires of the body and the mind, and were by nature children of wrath, like the rest of mankind."

When Jesus saw the religious leaders of His day He said to them, *"Woe to you, scribes and Pharisees, hypocrites! For you are like whitewashed tombs, which outwardly appear beautiful, but within are full of dead people's bones and all uncleanness."* (Matthew 23:27) He recognized that for all the outward show of goodness, these men were still spiritually dead and unrighteous in the sight of God. The Pharisees were not a special class of villains; they were respected in society and were probably sincere in their attempts to please God. They are no different from people today who go through the outward practices of religion yet their hearts are still dead.

Being spiritually dead causes not only the inability to do righteous acts before God but also hinders the ability to hear and respond to God's truth. We will not understand the Word of God unless the Holy Spirit reveals it to us. *"The natural person does not accept the things of the Spirit of God, for they are folly to him, and he is not able to understand them because they are spiritually discerned."* (1 Corinthians 2:14) Dead men cannot hear the truth.

BORN AGAIN

Many people do in fact respond to Jesus and believe in Him. How does this happen if we are spiritually dead? God has to create spiritual life in us which then enables us to respond. Read the account of Jesus' conversation with Nicodemus in John 3:1-21 and answer the following questions.

- What must happen to a person in order for them to enter God's kingdom? (v. 3)

- Which comes first; entering the kingdom or being born again? (v. 5)

- Can you see the work of the Spirit causing life in a person? (v. 8)

- How does the darkness respond to the light? (v. 19-20)

- How then do people in darkness come into the light? (v. 21)

The term *born again* refers to the act of *regeneration* as used in Titus 3:5, the *"washing of regeneration."* Another way the Bible refers to *regeneration* is being *made alive*; God has *"made us alive together with Christ."* (Ephesians 2:5) Eternal life began for us when Jesus gave us of His own spiritual and imperishable nature.

NEW CREATIONS

Just as God created the world by the power of His spoken word in Genesis chapter one, God is creating new life in people through Jesus. We do not assist or help in being born again, it is all of God. *"Therefore, if anyone is in Christ, he is a new creation."* (2 Corinthians 5:17) God, who created all things good, now creates a new person who is capable of doing good. *"For we are his workmanship, created in Christ Jesus for good works, which God prepared beforehand, that we should walk in them."* (Ephesians 2:10) As a new creation we are to walk in righteousness doing those deeds which God has prepared beforehand for us to do. These deeds will then glorify His goodness.

The Old Testament book of Ezekiel uses two images which convey how God creates new life in us. In describing the rebellious nation of Israel, the LORD said of them that they had a *"heart of stone"* (Ezekiel 36:26). The Lord prophesied that He would take out their hard hearts and put His Spirit in them and give them a *"new heart"* which would be a *"heart of flesh"* (Ezekiel 36:36-37). When His Spirit came upon Israel it would be like a wind that blew upon *"dry bones,"* which would become *"an exceedingly great army."* (Ezekiel 37:10) This prophesy was originally fulfilled when the nation of Israel returned from exile in Babylon, but it also points to the greater work of the Holy Spirit in our day, creating new hearts and new life in regenerate believers.

COME TO JESUS

The normal means by which the Holy Spirit creates life in people is through the preaching of the Word of God. The apostle Paul said that he was not ashamed of the gospel, *"for it is the power of God for salvation to everyone who believes"* (Romans 1:16). The power of the Holy Spirit accompanies the message of Jesus to bring about salvation. Read the following passages and answer the accompanying questions.

- How did the Holy Spirit use the Word of God? (1 Thessalonians 1:4-5)

- What was the means by which these believers were born again? (1 Peter 1:23)

- What happened to Lydia to cause her to believe? (Acts 16:14)

Does the doctrine of regeneration take away our responsibility to respond to the gospel? Can we sit back and be passive, waiting for God to move? Regeneration does not negate the commandment that we *must* repent and believe in Jesus in order to be saved, it simply enables it. Read the following passages and notice the requirements that are placed upon those who are hearing the gospel.

- Peter commands the people to repent. (Acts 2:37-38)

- Paul instructs the Philippian jailer to believe. (Acts 16:31)

There are two commands given: *repent* and *believe*. The combination of these two actions comprises the act of Christian conversion. We must repent of our former unrighteous life of sin, both our particular sins and our sin of not worshipping God. We also must believe in Jesus, recognizing that He is the Son of God who has taken the punishment for our sin. When a person comes to Christ in this manner the promise of Jesus in Matthew 11:28 is fulfilled, *"Come to me, all who labor and are heavy laden, and I will give you rest."*

HITTING HOME

1. Do you remember a time in your life when you heard truth but never understood or responded to it?

2. Can you recall a time before your conversion when you tried to outwardly look religious but inwardly were unrighteous and full of sin? Was there ever a time in your life when you felt powerless to change yourself or stop sinning?

3. How did you come to faith? Do you remember the sermon, testimony, or Bible passages that was used to bring about your conversion?

4. What was the first evidence in your life that Jesus had made you alive?

LESSON 14: JUSTIFICATION

KEY DOCTRINE: Justification is the act by which God forgives a person's sins and accepts them as righteous in His sight.
MEMORY VERSE: *"Therefore, since we have been justified by faith, we have peace with God through our Lord Jesus Christ."* (Romans 5:1)
SCRIPTURE PRE-READING: Genesis 15:1-6; Psalm 32:1-5; Mark 2:1-12; Romans 3:21-26; 5:1-11; Galatians 4:1-7; Hebrews 12:5-11

Perhaps the most pivotal question in religion is how a sinful person can be accepted by a holy God. Many of us seek to solve this problem by trying to make ourselves righteous and earn His approval. The law declares that all have sinned before a holy God and deserve His wrath. The gospel promises that we will be accepted by God when we place our trust in Jesus' atoning death. Once justified, God adopts us as His own children who have the Spirit of His Son.

WHAT IS YOUR ETERNAL DESTINATION?

If you were to die right now, where would you go? How we answer this question reveals much about our understanding of the Christian faith. We might admit that we do not know were we would go. Perhaps we assume we are going to heaven because we are good at heart. Maybe we point to our church membership or to the fact that we believe that God exists as our hope for heaven. It is true that the wicked go to hell and the righteous go to heaven. So the million dollar question then is how do we become righteous before God?

WEIGHED, MEASURED, AND FOUND WANTING

Once we recognize that the righteous go to heaven and the wicked go to hell we have a motivation to stop sinning and keep God's commandments. Our hope is that if we do enough good deeds the scales of justice will eventually tip in our favor. We go to church, give some money, and try to break our bad habits. Of course, none of this actually affects any real change in our essential character. When we start trying to get rid of our sin, we end up sinning more, and eventually we come to the place where we can identify with the apostle Paul who said, *"For I know that nothing good dwells in me, that is, in my flesh. For I have the desire to do what is right, but not the ability to carry it out. For I do not do the good I want, but the evil I do not want is what I keep on doing."* (Romans 7:18-19)

Attempts at achieving a state of righteousness by trying to keep God's commandments will always fall short. The very attempt at trying to fix ourselves only proves that we are sinners to begin with. We are like a child who knocks over Mother's vase and, while attempting to secretly fix it, we are discovered with the glue and broken pieces in our hands. *"For if I rebuild what I tore down, I prove myself to be a transgressor."* (Galatians 2:18) The Bible states clearly that no one is able to be saved, or accepted by God, by trying to keep God's commandments, *"For by works of the law no human being will be justified in his sight, since through the law comes knowledge of sin."* (Romans 3:20)

JUSTIFIED BY FAITH

If we cannot change ourselves, how then can we become righteous? When we say that we "have been saved" we are actually referring to the state of justification. We are justified when God forgives our sins and declares us to be righteous in His sight. Standing before the holy Judge we are declared by God to be not guilty. But how do we get this verdict? Jesus explains how in Mark 2:1-12. The paralytic who was lowered through the roof was told by Jesus, *"And when Jesus saw their faith, he said to the paralytic, 'Son, your sins are forgiven.'"* (Mark 2:5) This enraged the Pharisees; how can a man forgive sins?! Jesus answered that He has the authority on earth to say, *"Your sins are forgiven."* (Mark 2:9) It is faith in Jesus that grants us acceptance and forgiveness, not our own works, *"yet we know that a person is not justified by works of the law but through faith in Jesus Christ, so we also have believed in Christ Jesus, in order to be justified by faith in Christ and not by works of the law, because by works of the law no one will be justified."* (Galatians 2:16)

At the moment we place our faith in Jesus, God imputes Christ's righteousness to our account, and we are declared righteous before God. *"And to the one who does not work but believes in him who justifies the ungodly, his faith is counted as righteousness"* (Romans 4:5). We trust in the perfect Son of

God who loved us and died on the cross for our sins. Our trust is in His righteousness and not our own. When we put our faith in Jesus, God, in His mercy and justice, forgives all our sins—past, present, and future. If we abandon the doctrine of justification by faith we lose the gospel and eventually fall into the danger of a works-based salvation and legalism.

Faith is the necessary means to bring about salvation because faith exalts God and diminishes self. Knowing in our hearts that our righteousness is not of our own doing keeps us humble. *"For by grace you have been saved through faith. And this is not your own doing; it is the gift of God, not a result of works, so that no one may boast."* (Ephesians 2:8-9) Our salvation is all by God's grace and not our works, therefore our only boast is in the Lord, *"so that, as it is written, 'Let the one who boasts, boast in the Lord.'"* (1 Corinthians 1:31) Read Romans 3:21-26 and answer the following questions.

- Through what means does one obtain *"the righteousness of God"*? (v. 21-22)

- What does it mean that Christ is a *"propitiation"*? (v. 25)

- Explain how God is both *"just and the justifier"*? (v. 26)

No Condemnation

The doctrine of justification should grant us assurance and peace in our faith. It is an unchangeable act of God--a person cannot become unjustified. When we are declared "not guilty" we cannot be condemned by God to hell. The Judge has already punished Christ for our sins, so God's justice forbids Him from punishing us once more. *"There is therefore now no condemnation for those who are in Christ Jesus."* (Romans 8:1) When we sin after we have been justified we should not be tempted to think that we might have lost our salvation. As our loving Father, God will discipline us, but He will not disown us. We are His justified children and therefore nothing *"will be able to separate us from the love of God in Christ Jesus our Lord."* (Romans 8:39) We can stand in His grace knowing that we are at peace with God. *"Therefore, since we have been justified by faith, we have peace with God through our Lord Jesus Christ."* (Romans 5:1)

The Adopted Children of God

After God forgives and accepts us into a reconciled relationship with Himself, He adopts us as His own children. God sent His Son into the world *"to redeem those who were under the law, so that we might receive adoption as sons."* (Galatians 4:5) God creates sons and daughters by granting us the Spirit of His Son to dwell in our hearts. *"And because you are sons, God has sent the Spirit of his Son into our hearts, crying, 'Abba! Father!'"* (Galatians 4:6) By virtue of creation all humans are children of God, however, only through the Spirit of Christ can we become the true spiritual children of God. The Holy Spirit bears witness to us that we are God's children (Romans 8:16), and then this Spirit causes our hearts to cry out to our heavenly Father, yearning to know and love Him.

We should never underestimate the wonderful blessing it is to be called a child of God. The Father loves His children and He will never take that love away (1 John 3:1-2). He has given us His Holy Spirit which is the guarantee and seal of our eternal inheritance and the power which maintains us in our salvation. Jesus is God's Son, and once we are adopted we become a child of God and heir with Jesus. A proof of our relationship with our Father is that God now disciplines us so that we share in His holiness, *"For the Lord disciplines the one he loves, and chastises every son whom he receives."* (Hebrews 12:6) Discipline is painful, but it produces the pleasing fruit of righteousness. We can rest assured that all of our heavenly Father's will for us is done through the eyes of love.

Hitting Home

1. Explain why justification comes through faith and not by words.

2. Do you ever struggle with feeling like you have lost your salvation? How do the doctrines of justification and adoption give you more assurance of your salvation?

3. Have you embraced Christ's forgiveness or are you still carrying around guilt for your past sins?

4. In what way have you experienced the Spirit of God causing you to call upon the Father?

LESSON 15: SANCTIFICATION

KEY DOCTRINE: Sanctification is the process by which the Holy Spirit transforms a Christian's character into the holy likeness of Jesus Christ.

MEMORY VERSE: *"Therefore, my beloved, as you have always obeyed, so now, not only as in my presence but much more in my absence, work out your own salvation with fear and trembling, for it is God who works in you, both to will and to work for his good pleasure."* (Philippians 2:12-13)

SCRIPTURE PRE-READING: Deuteronomy 4:1-8; Psalm 101; Mark 5:1-20; Romans 6:1-14; Colossians 3:5-11; 1 Peter 1:13-16

The sin of man grieves God. There will be no sinners in heaven, and God has no pleasure in the sinful actions of His children on this earth. God's plan is to change us by the Holy Spirit to be like Jesus. Sanctification is the transformation of God's people from our sinful selves into the holy character of God's Son. This transformation is not a passive process on our part, rather we are to be fully engaged as we endeavor to grow in obedience to God.

"BE HOLY AS I AM HOLY"

What happened throughout the Bible when men and women came face to face with God? Look at the following passages and describe the response of each of these men who encountered God.

- Exodus 3:1-6 _____
- Isaiah 6:1-7 _____
- Luke 5:1-11 _____

Each of these men recognized that they were in the presence of God, and the revealed holiness of God exposed their sin. They were unworthy to be in His presence and they feared the judgment of God. Their fear was legitimate, for God can justly condemn all sinners who stand before Him. It is only when God, in His graciousness, forgives us that we can then be at peace with Him.

In the Old Testament God called the people of Israel out of Egypt and gave to them His Ten Commandments and the whole Law. He wanted them to be distinct and separate from all the other nations in the world. They would be the only people who had a relationship with God and followed His holy laws (see Deuteronomy 4:4-8). In Leviticus 11:44 God commanded Israel, *"For I am the LORD your God. Consecrate yourselves therefore, and be holy, for I am holy."* The idea of holiness in the Old Testament was for the Israelites to be *separate* from the sinful practices and idolatry of other nations, and to have a *righteous* character like God.

The same concept is present in the New Testament when a person believes in Jesus. We have been separated from our former lifestyle, and declared to be holy. *"As obedient children, do not be conformed to the passions of your former ignorance, but as he who called you is holy, you also be holy in all your conduct"* (1 Peter 1:14-15). We are to now live in a way that is fitting for a person who is in a relationship with the holy God. The last two chapters of the Bible, Revelation 21-22, point to the ultimate purpose of God's redemptive plan, when God separates the righteous from the wicked and dwells with His people for all eternity. During our short time on this earth we are working toward this end goal of becoming a holy people ready to worship God in Spirit and truth.

THE NATURE OF SANCTIFICATION: DEATH AND LIFE

When we were converted we were declared righteous by God, so in His eyes we are holy. Why is it that we often do not feel or act in a holy way? This is because we still have a remaining sin nature which does not die easily. At the same time, God has given us a new nature by the Holy Spirit within us. The nature of sanctification is that the *old sinful life has to die* and the *new Spirit-created life has to grow.* Read Colossians 3:5-14 which shows this two-fold process working within us.

- What has to die or be *"put off"*? (v. 5-9)

- What has to grow or be *"put on"*? (v. 12-14)

- What is the goal of this process? (v. 10)

THE MEANS: THE HOLY SPIRIT AND OUR FAITH

On our own we cannot change ourselves, so it is essential that the Holy Spirit is the active agent behind our sanctification. *"His divine power has granted to us all things that pertain to life and godliness, through the knowledge of him who called us to his own glory and excellence"* (2 Peter 1:3). We will share in Christ's nature only by the Spirit of Christ bringing about this transformation, however we are not passive in this process. Sanctification necessitates the active involvement of a Christian's heart, mind and strength. We should not become lazy and assume that God will make us grow automatically. There is a dual working of us and the Holy Spirit in sanctification as we *"work out"* our salvation. Read Philippians 2:12-13 and complete the following exercises.

- List the words that refer to our responsibility in growing in salvation.

- Why should *"fear and trembling"* be associated with our sanctification?

- Explain what God's part is as seen in this passage.

Our role in working out our salvation is neither mysterious nor burdensome. We simply take advantage of the resources that God has equipped us with through His Word, the Spirit and the church. Here are a few practical disciplines that we can follow which will aid us in our spiritual growth.
- Read and study the Bible regularly to understand the whole counsel of God.
- Pray without ceasing! Through prayer we draw near to God and guard against temptation.
- Be aware of our own sins and temptations, being quick to confess and repent.
- Stay plugged into our church to hear the Word and partake of the Lord's Supper.
- Place ourselves in accountability with other Christians.

VICTORY IN JESUS

Lest we think that sanctification leads to legalism and works-based righteousness, the Bible teaches that our becoming like Jesus is a work of faith. We often make the mistake of trying to change our faults through self-examination, instead we should hold to the promise of 2 Corinthians 3:18, *"And we all, with unveiled face, beholding the glory of the Lord, are being transformed into the same image from one degree of glory to another. For this comes from the Lord who is the Spirit."* As we behold Jesus, we become like Him. Faith in Jesus is the effective means of our sanctification, for faith always looks away from ourselves and on to the grace we find in Jesus. We should rejoice in the gospel of salvation by faith, *"For in it* [the gospel] *the righteousness of God is revealed from faith for faith, as it is written, 'The righteous shall live by faith.'"* (Romans 1:17)

One aspect of trusting in Jesus is embracing the truth that Jesus will give us the victory in our sanctification. Though we have a remaining sin nature, the Bible teaches us that the power of the Lord Jesus in us is more powerful than our old nature (the flesh). *"We know that our old self was crucified with him in order that the body of sin might be brought to nothing, so that we would no longer be enslaved to sin."* (Romans 6:6) Our ultimate confidence in overcoming all the struggles of the Christian life is that our Lord, who *"in every respect has been tempted as we are, yet without sin"* (Hebrews 4:15) is able to grant us mercy and grace in our time of need (Hebrews 4:16).

HITTING HOME

1. Since becoming a Christian where have you seen victories over sin in your own life? Can you testify to how God gave you these victories?

2. What are some areas in your life and character that need to be changed in order for you to be more like Jesus?

3. Have you ever said, "That is just the way I am!" Can this statement be reconciled with the doctrine of sanctification, or not?

4. What actions can you take to *"work out your own salvation"* (Philippians 2:12) and *"put off"* (Colossians 3:9) the old sinful man?

LESSON 16: PERSEVERANCE

KEY DOCTRINE: Perseverance is the truth that all justified believers cannot fall out of grace, but will keep their faith through the power of God and be eternally saved.

MEMORY VERSE: *"And I am sure of this, that he who began a good work in you will bring it to completion at the day of Jesus Christ."* (Philippians 1:6)

PRE-READING: Isaiah 54:4-10; Luke 8:4-15; John 10:27-30; Romans 8:31-39; 1 Peter 1:3-9

The question of whether or not we can lose our salvation is important because during the trials of life we can easily feel that our faith will not last. This fear is compounded by the phenomenon of professing Christians who later deny their faith and leave the church or fall into great sin. The Bible addresses this matter by stating that true faith always lasts. The certainty of remaining in our state of salvation is rooted in three truths: the purpose of election, the finality of justification, and the power of the Holy Spirit.

FALLING AWAY

Is it possible to lose our salvation? What should we make of those people in the church who seem to lose their faith? Let us look at some possible explanations.

  a. They had real saving faith, and then they lost it and became unsaved.
  b. They were simply doing outward works and never had real faith.
  c. They had a superficial faith but not genuine saving faith.
  d. They have real faith but are going through a season of defeated living and doubt.

Of these four explanations only one of them is **not** possible: "a." Options "b," "c," and "d" can explain the phenomenon of professing Christians falling away. Options "b" and "c" both describe people who are religious and would call themselves Christians but do not actually have saving faith. Option "d" describes a true believer who for a time falls into sin.

Jesus teaches in the parable of the sower (Luke 8:4-15; see also: Matthew 13:1-23; Mark 4:1-20) how responses to the Word of God differ among people. There is a phenomenon where people who at a shallow level believe for a little while (the seed that fell on rocky soil), but eventually their faith dies. Trials or persecution reveal the false nature of their faith, and it falls away. Some people make a shallow, public profession of faith that has not reached the level of true justifying faith. The church is inhabited by many people who claim the name of Christ, and even subscribe to sound doctrine, but have never really trusted in the gospel of Jesus. The third commandment, *"You shall not take the name of the LORD your God in vain, for the LORD will not hold him guiltless who takes his name in vain."* (Exodus 20:7) would apply to these people. To *"take the name of the LORD your God in vain"* is not simply to curse with God's name, but is to outwardly claim to be a worshipper of the Lord yet not have true faith. Such a claim to a relationship with God does not bring about acceptance from the Lord--one still is guilty before God. This type of believer will one day say *"Lord, Lord,"* (Matthew 7:21) but He who searches the hearts of men will say, *"I never knew you; depart from me, you workers of lawlessness."* (Matthew 7:23)

The seed that lands amongst the thorns can describe the reality of true believers who live in defeat for a season due to sin in their lives (option "d" above). The temptations and cares of this life often choke out our ability to produce genuine fruit and live a victorious Christian life. Even though it may not look like we are "living the Christian life" we still have true faith in us. In this case the Lord, in His faithfulness, *will* discipline us and eventually bring us back to faith-filled living.

TRUE FAITH LASTS

The proof that we have true saving faith, not just a superficial profession, is that true faith will endure our whole life. Hebrews 3:14 says, *"For we have come to share in Christ, if indeed we hold our original confidence firm to the end."* The logic here is that a past conversion is shown to be genuine by one's continual perseverance in the faith. Likewise, Paul writes in Colossians 1:22-23 that God has purposed to *"present you holy and blameless and above reproach before him, if indeed you continue in the faith, stable and steadfast, not shifting from the hope of the gospel that you heard."* Throughout our life we must maintain the same trust in the gospel that we had when we first believed in Jesus. If our faith does not last, it never was.

There is an adage in the church, "once saved, always saved." This is a true statement, but it does not describe the active responsibility we have to persevere in our faith. We will be tested and tempted, and God requires us to continue trusting in Him. For the course of our whole life we must *"work out your own salvation with fear and trembling"* (Philippians 2:12). We need to be on guard against a complacency which thinks we can "kick back" and not work at our faith, since we are "safe." Likewise, if we think that our justification is now a license to "sin as much as we want" and still make it to heaven we should question our salvation. *"What then? Are we to sin because we are not under law but under grace? By no means! Do you not know that if you present yourselves to anyone as obedient slaves, you are slaves of the one whom you obey, either of sin, which leads to death, or of obedience, which leads to righteousness?"* (Romans 6:15-16) God's grace toward us should never serve as a license for sin.

ASSURANCE IN GOD'S SALVATION

The Scriptures teach that we can and should have assurance in our faith. When we understand the nature and power of God's saving purposes the assurance we gain can give joy and strength to our life. The following points explain why we can have confidence that we will complete our race of faith. These are focused on God's purposes and power and not on our own faithfulness and ability:

- **His Purpose:** Since God is the author of our salvation we can have confidence, knowing that we will make it to the end and experience our final victory. The theology behind this truth states that God predestined the whole process of our salvation, which culminates in the finished product--a person who is perfectly like Christ in heaven. Romans 8:29-30 teaches that there is an unbroken chain of salvation that finishes in glorification. Every person whom God predestines, He also calls, justifies, and glorifies. There are no missing steps. *"And I am sure of this, that he who began a good work in you will bring it to completion at the day of Jesus Christ."* (Philippians 1:6)

- **His Forgiveness**: When we were justified by God our sins were forgiven on account of Christ's death for us. If God declares us "not guilty," He cannot reverse that judgment at a later date, thus making Christ's death null and void. His sacrifice to forgive us is effective and *"finished"* (John 19:30).

- **His Power:** We have to believe to the end, but we continue to believe only by the power of the Holy Spirit in us. God gave us our first saving faith and He maintains that faith throughout the remaining trials of our life. First Peter 1:5 says that we, *"by God's power are being guarded through faith for a salvation ready to be revealed in the last time."* In this same way, Jesus spoke of His power to guard His sheep in John 10:28, *"I give them eternal life, and they will never perish, and no one will snatch them out of my hand."*

For these reasons we can have confidence and assurance in our faith. We will make it to heaven, not because of our diligent work and willpower, but because of God's purpose, power, and mercy. Our faith will be tested to see that it is genuine. The fires of life will refine it like pure gold. Nevertheless because God's plan for us to be with Him in heaven cannot be thwarted, we will appear before Christ and give Him all praise, glory and honor (1 Peter 1:7-8).

HITTING HOME

1. Do you know anyone you thought was a Christian who has left the faith? Explain.

2. How secure are you in your faith? What are you basing your assurance on—your works or God's grace?

3. Can you describe a time in your life when the cares and temptations of this world choked your faith and Christ-like living? What brought you back, or are you still struggling?

4. Do the teachings of perseverance encourage you in your faith or cause you to become complacent?

LESSON 17: GLORIFICATION

KEY DOCTRINE: Glorification is the perfected state of the believer when both body and soul will bear the glorified likeness of Jesus.

MEMORY VERSE: *"For those whom he foreknew he also predestined to be conformed to the image of his Son...And those whom he predestined he also called, and those whom he called he also justified, and those whom he justified he also glorified."* (Romans 8:29-30)

SCRIPTURE PRE-READING: Isaiah 65:17-24; Romans 8:18-30; 1 Corinthians 15:35-58; Revelation 17: 9-17; 21:1-8

There are three tenses to salvation: past, present, and future. We *have been* saved—justification; we *are being* saved—sanctification; and we *will be* saved—glorification. Our present process of sanctification never reaches perfection in this life. Our glorification will occur when we are done with our sinful wills and are given a new imperishable body like Christ. Though our souls will be glorified at our death, our bodies will not obtain glory until they rise at the second coming of Christ.

ONLY PERFECT IN THE END

There will come a time when we will reach perfection, when we will be like Christ. That time will only come when we see Christ at our death or at His return. In this life the process of sanctification is never complete. *Perfectionism* is a heresy which claims Christians can be sinless in this life. Though we can gain victory over sin, we never come to a point in our walk where we can say, "I have arrived." Look at how Paul describes his own progress in sanctification:

"Not that I have already obtained this or am already perfect, but I press on to make it my own, because Christ Jesus has made me his own. Brothers, I do not consider that I have made it my own. But one thing I do: forgetting what lies behind and straining forward to what lies ahead, I press on toward the goal for the prize of the upward call of God in Christ Jesus." (Philippians 3:12-14)

Paul recognized that he had not obtained perfection in Christ, but he strove to obtain all the blessedness of knowing Christ. Paul knew that Christ was continually calling him to greater holiness. If the apostle Paul never claimed to have reached perfection, how could we do so?

What about passages which refer to Christians not sinning (1 John 3:4-6, 9; 5:18)? For instance, 1 John 5:18 says, *"We know that everyone who has been born of God does not keep on sinning."* These verses teach that sanctification must occur in someone who is born of God, not that we will never sin after our conversion. A truly born-again believer cannot continue in a lifestyle of unrepentant sin. In the same epistle the apostle John states, *"If we say we have no sin, we deceive ourselves, and the truth is not in us."* (1 John 1:8) If we claim to have no sin, i.e. to be perfect, we are deceiving ourselves and we do not know Christ.

The realization that we never achieve perfection in this life is necessary in order to keep us humble instead of spiritually proud. The testimony from the saints throughout the ages is that the more they knew Christ the more they realized how sinful they were and how much further they had to grow. As the prophet Isaiah cried out after seeing the Lord, *"Woe is me! For I am lost; for I am a man of unclean lips, and I dwell in the midst of a people of unclean lips; for my eyes have seen the King, the LORD of hosts!"* (Isaiah 6:5) The more we see God's holiness the more we will see our own sin.

GOING TO CHRIST

We know that when we die our decaying bodies go into the ground. Our flesh returns to the dust, but our souls go on to heaven, where we have immediate fellowship with Christ. Paul said, *"For me to live is Christ, and to die is gain....My desire is to depart and be with Christ, for that is far better."* (Philippians 1:21, 23) As good as living a fruitful life was, Paul still considered death to be a "gain." Likewise, in 2 Corinthians 5:6, 8 Paul said, *"We know that while we are at home in the body we are away from the Lord...and we would rather be away from the body and at home with the Lord."* As believers we have the assurance that when we die we go to be with Christ. At the point of death our souls are perfected and all our sin is done away with. We will behold Jesus as He is and will be like Him in His glory. Our expectation of the incomparable glory and joy of heaven will guard our hearts as we consider the prospect of our own death. After death we shall hear Christ say to us, *"Enter into the joy of your master"* (Matthew 25:21) where *"at his right hand are pleasures forevermore."* (Psalm 16:11)   As an exercise read Revelation 7:9-17 and answer the following questions.

- Who and how many people are in heaven? (v. 9)

- What kind of praises to God do the people sing? (v. 10-12)

- Describe the character of the multitude? (v. 13)

- What blessings are they experiencing in heaven? (v. 15-17)

PERFECT BODY AND SOUL

When we die and our souls go to be with the Lord, we are not yet complete. Our bodies will still be decaying in the ground and separate from us. It is not until Christ returns in glory that our bodies are then transformed to be like Christ's body, and our souls are joined on to them. *"Behold! I tell you a mystery. We shall not all sleep, but we shall all be changed, in a moment, in the twinkling of an eye, at the last trumpet. For the trumpet will sound, and the dead will be raised imperishable, and we shall be changed."* (1 Corinthians 15:51-52) Our current bodies are all in the process of dying, but the bodies we shall receive will be immortal, undefiled and full of glory. *"It is sown in dishonor; it is raised in glory. It is sown in weakness; it is raised in power. It is sown a natural body; it is raised a spiritual body. If there is a natural body, there is also a spiritual body."* (1 Corinthians 15:43-44) For this reason Christians have historically honored the burial of the dead. The body is *sleeping*, waiting for the time when it will rise anew.

Christ is called *"the firstborn from the dead,"* (Colossians 1:18) because at His resurrection He rose with a glorified body which is the prototype of the resurrection bodies which we will possess in the last day. In the brief time Jesus was on the earth after He appeared to His disciples He possessed this new glorified body. Jesus could be touched and he could eat food, yet His body had special properties which enabled Him to appear and disappear at will. It is this type of immortal, spiritual body which we will all possess at Christ's return. Imagine what it will be like to have an imperishable body that never gets sick or grows old? As we get older this prospect of a body upgrade becomes a lot more appealing!

PARADISE RESTORED

At Christ's glorious return He will raise our dead bones and ashes and give them a glorified body, and our souls will be rejoined with them. We will meet Him in the air, and then we will reign with Christ in a new heaven and a new earth where sin, disease, and death will never exist (Revelation 21:1-6). Our new bodies and souls will be living on this new earth where perfection will remain forever. *"But according to his promise we are waiting for new heavens and a new earth in which righteousness dwells."* (2 Peter 3:13) In the beginning of creation we were never meant to die or live in a fallen world. Rather, we were meant to live in a perfect relationship with God in a perfect world. At the consummation of all things God will have achieved His purpose of restoring His world and living with His people, where we will experience all of His glory. *"Behold, the dwelling place of God is with man. He will dwell with them, and they will be his people, and God himself will be with them as their God. He will wipe away every tear from their eyes, and death shall be no more, neither shall there be mourning, nor crying, nor pain anymore, for the former things have passed away."* (Revelation 21:3-4)

HITTING HOME

1. As you have grown in your faith, how have you found new areas of sin that you were unaware of?

2. How does the reality that you will be given a glorified body change the way you think of, and relate to, your current mortal body?

3. In what ways do you long to be gone from this world and be together with Christ?

4. Knowing that there will be a new heaven and a new earth, how does it affect the way you are going to live in this world today?

SECTION C:

A CLOSER WALK WITH GOD

"Nevertheless, I am continually with you; you hold my right hand. You guide me with your counsel, and afterward you will receive me to glory...But for me it is good to be near God" (Psalm 73:23-24, 28)

Most of us who are reading this book are experiencing the present tense of salvation—we *are being* saved. As Christians we are in the process of obeying the apostle Paul's exhortation to *"work out your own salvation"* (Philippians 2:12). This section, and the whole of our Christian life for that matter, is the practical out-working of the doctrine of sanctification. It is one thing to intellectually grasp the doctrine of sanctification, but it is an entirely more difficult matter to put it into practice. We could say that this is where "the rubber meets the road" for our theology.

Theologians have noted that one can have knowledge about God without actually knowing God. In that case, all one's knowledge is in vain and not pleasing to God. The book of James rebukes dead orthodoxy saying, *"You believe that God is one; you do well. Even the demons believe--and shudder!"* (James 2: 19) Our faith must be lived out in our minds, emotions, and wills. Jesus said that anyone who obeyed God would discover whether His teachings were true or not. Our knowledge of God will become intimate and transformational as we seek to keep Christ's word. This section, A CLOSER WALK WITH GOD, highlights numerous practical aspects of living our Christian faith. We will study how to trust and obey, to fight the spiritual war, and to endure hardships. We will learn the necessity of holiness, of purity, of prayer, and of generosity, among other Christian virtues. As we walk with the Lord and *"grow in the grace and knowledge of our Lord and Savior Jesus Christ"* (2 Peter 3:18), we will experience God guiding us with His counsel and preserving us for His eternal kingdom in heaven.

LESSON 18: JESUS IS LORD

KEY DOCTRINE: Those who believe in Jesus must endeavor to obey His authoritative word.
MEMORY VERSE: *"If you love me, you will keep my commandments."* (John 14:15)
SCRIPTURE PRE-READING: Deuteronomy 6:1-25; Matthew 7:13-29; 17:1-13; John 14:15-24; James 2:14-26

We should never make the mistake of thinking that we can trust in Jesus for forgiveness but regard obedience to Jesus as merely optional. If we genuinely trust in Jesus' death for us then we embrace Him as our God whom we must worship and obey. Jesus, as God's final Word, calls upon us to show our faith and trust by obeying all that He has taught us. We obey and trust Jesus not only in His moral teachings but also in His promise of steadfast love toward us.

COVENANT KEEPING

In the Old Testament God entered into a covenant with the people of Israel. A covenant is a binding agreement between two parties with blessings, stipulations and punishments. When Israel entered into a covenant with the LORD after the exodus from Egypt, God made them pledge to worship Him alone and to obey all His commandments as presented at Mt. Sinai. In return God promised to provide for and protect Israel throughout their existence. If either party broke the covenant then there would be dire consequences.

Simply put, our covenant with God requires that we love Him with all of our heart, soul, and mind, and that we love our neighbors as ourselves (Matthew 22:37-39). This summarizes the whole law, and it is the greatest commandment for all believers. The principle of keeping covenant by remaining faithful in worshipping God and obeying His commandments is the same in the Old and New Testaments. If we have trusted in God's grace toward us through Christ's death on the cross then we will show our trust by our continual obedience to the teachings of Jesus. We are always required, as God's people, to demonstrate the genuineness of our faith by our worship of God and obedience to His moral commandments. *"If you love me, you will keep my commandments."* (John 14:15)

THE FINAL WORD

On the Mount of Transfiguration (Matthew 17:1-13) Jesus and three of His disciples were on a high mountain when Moses and Elijah appeared to them. Jesus' countenance shone like the sun and His clothing became white as light. The voice of God boomed from heaven saying, *"This is my beloved Son, with whom I am well pleased; listen to him."* (Matthew 17:5) In this one statement God affirms that Jesus is His *Royal Son* (Psalm 2:7), the *Suffering Servant* (Isaiah 42:1), and *the Prophet* of God (Deuteronomy 18:15), who surpasses even Moses and Elijah. When God commands us to *"listen to him"* (Matthew 17:5) He is asserting that Jesus is the final, authoritative revelation of the Father.

It is fitting that one of the names given to Jesus is *the Word* (John 1:1). Words communicate, and Jesus—*the Word*—is the final communication of the nature of God. When the Father purposed to reveal Himself to us He sent His own Son to manifest all that He is. *"No one has ever seen God; the only God [Jesus], who is at the Father's side, he has made him known."* (John 1:18) When Jesus preached on the Scriptures He could say, *"But I say to you,"* (Matthew 5:17, 22, 28, 32, etc.) implying that His interpretation and application of the Word was authoritative and accurate (Matthew 7:28-29). Jesus, *the Prophet* who is the Word of the LORD, had come to bring the final truth to God's people.

The Father has told us to listen to Jesus, and Jesus Himself says that we must obey His word if we love Him. At the conclusion of the Sermon on the Mount Jesus lays out a litmus test of who the true believers are, and what determines who will be welcomed into heaven. Read Matthew 7:15-27 and answer the following questions.

• How do we recognize the difference between "sheep" and "wolves"? (v. 15-20)

• In what will many false believers place their trust at the day of judgment? (v. 21-23)

• Why are these people rejected? (v. 23)

• What characterizes the person who knows Jesus? (v. 24-27)

Just as the Old Testament Law and covenant were binding upon the people of God, so too is obedience to the word of Christ in the New Testament. *"For since the message declared by angels proved to be reliable, and every transgression or disobedience received a just retribution, how shall we escape if we neglect such a great salvation?"* (Hebrews 2:2-3) We would be mistaken if we concluded that there are no ramifications of judgment for those who disobey the words of Christ since the gospel is a message about the love of God. The writer of the Hebrews states, *"How much worse punishment, do you think, will be deserved by the one who has spurned the Son of God, and has profaned the blood of the covenant by which he was sanctified, and has outraged the Spirit of grace? For we know him who said, 'Vengeance is mine; I will repay.' And again, 'The Lord will judge his people.'"* (Hebrews 10:29-30) The necessity of faithfulness to the Word of the Lord, and the consequences for disobedience, is the same yesterday, today, and forever.

TRUST IN THE LORD

Obeying our Lord is more than just keeping moral commandments; Jesus is not just a teacher of righteous living. Jesus is God, and the same covenantal promises that the LORD gave to Israel are fulfilled in our relationship with Christ. *"For all the promises of God find their Yes in him. That is why it is through him that we utter our Amen to God for his glory."* (2 Corinthians 1:20) We trust in Jesus as LORD who will show us His faithfulness in this life and throughout eternity.

The Gospel of John clearly identifies Jesus with the God of the Old Testament. Most of Jesus' teachings in John are not so much instructions about godly living but a progression of revelation of who He is. Jesus is the great I AM (Exodus 3:14; John 8:58), the bread of heaven (Deuteronomy 8:3; John 6:32-35), and the light of the world (Isaiah 42:6; John 8:12). As we understand who Jesus is and trust Him we gain eternal life and all the blessings of God's steadfast love for His children. When we confess *"Jesus is Lord"* (Romans 10:9) we are testifying that we obey Him and that we trust in His faithful care for us. The following list of promises contains some of the ways in which Jesus, as the Sovereign LORD, has promised to bless us:

- **Jesus gives us eternal life:** *"Whoever believes in the Son has eternal life; whoever does not obey the Son shall not see life, but the wrath of God remains on him."* (John 3:36)

- **Jesus has power over death:** *"Jesus said to her, 'I am the resurrection and the life. Whoever believes in me, though he die, yet shall he live, and everyone who lives and believes in me shall never die.'"* (John 11:25)

- **Jesus satisfies our hungry and thirsty souls:** *"Jesus said to her, 'Everyone who drinks of this water will be thirsty again, but whoever drinks of the water that I will give him will never be thirsty again. The water that I will give him will become in him a spring of water welling up eternal life.'"* (John 4:13-14)

- **Jesus defends us from the wicked:** *"The Lord will rescue me from every evil deed and bring me safely into his heavenly kingdom. To him be the glory forever and ever. Amen."* (2 Timothy 4:18)

- **Jesus meets our material needs:** *"And my God will supply every need of yours according to his riches in glory in Christ Jesus."* (Philippians 4:19)

HITTING HOME

1. In what areas of your life are you seeking the benefits of salvation without accepting Jesus' commandments to obey and worship Him?

2. Have you ever obeyed Jesus in such a way that it possibly jeopardized your career or subjected you to ridicule? Explain.

3. In what areas of your life have you become obedient to Jesus' word? Give an example.

4. Have you ever relied upon Jesus' word and promises and then seen Him show Himself faithful? Give an example.

LESSON 19: LIVING BY FAITH

KEY DOCTRINE: God is pleased with us when we trust in Him.
MEMORY VERSE: *"Now faith is the assurance of things hoped for, the conviction of things not seen. For by it the people of old received their commendation."* (Hebrews 11:1-2)
SCRIPTURE PRE-READING: Genesis 15:1-6; Numbers 13:25-14:25; Matthew 15:21-28; Hebrews 11:1-16; 1 Peter 1:3-9

Jesus asked a chilling question at the end of the parable of the persistent widow, *"Nevertheless, when the Son of Man comes, will he find faith on earth?"* (Luke 18:8) This rhetorical question reveals just how difficult it is to maintain faith in this world. When our faith is tested and refined we discover just how little faith we actually have. Our faith in God's mercy and power in this life pleases Him, and His plan throughout our life is to prove the genuineness of our faith and cause it to grow.

WHAT IS FAITH?

The only place in the Bible where faith is defined is in Hebrews 11:1, *"Now faith is the assurance of things hoped for, the conviction of things not seen."* In other words, faith is our sure hope in a promise or truth about God which He has revealed to us in His Word. Though we cannot see God, we know that He exists and that He will be true to what He has said about Himself.

This definition of faith applies to all areas where we are required to exercise our trust. In respect to justifying faith, our trust is that God has forgiven our sins due to the death, burial and resurrection of Jesus Christ. We simply trust in the promise of grace offered to us through Jesus, without looking at our works, morality or religiousness. The same Lord who declared to the paralytic man, *"Take heart, my son; your sins are forgiven"* (Matthew 9:2) also promises to forgive our sins when we believe in Him.

Saving faith is no different in nature than the faith we must exercise throughout our Christian walk. When the trials of life overwhelm us we are required to believe that the invisible God is in control and works all things according to His plan. *"And we know that for those who love God all things work together for good, for those who are called according to his purpose."* (Romans 8:28) In all these things we cannot foresee His deliverance, but we can cling to the promise that the unseen God will help us in our time of need, and that His love is working all things for our ultimate salvation.

The essential core of our faith is our hope and trust in God's merciful love toward us. A vital refrain that runs throughout the book of the Psalms is *"Give thanks to the LORD, for he is good, for his steadfast love endures forever."* (Psalm 136:1) In the midst of great afflictions the psalmist confessed, *"But I have trusted in your steadfast love; my heart shall rejoice in your salvation"* (Psalm 13:5). Though Satan and the world will throw fiery darts to destroy our faith, the steadfast love of the Lord is the rock upon which our hope can cling throughout our life.

GROWING FAITH

Though we would like to think that we are "faith-warriors" the humbling reality is that we actually have very little faith at all. Naturally we do not like having to rely upon God. We would prefer to manage things on our own—but, of course, with God's blessing on it! Faith is not something that we can self-generate. At our conversion we were given the smallest mustard seed of faith (Matthew 13:31-32), but it is enough to be saved! Our faith may start small, but the Holy Spirit, who originally gave us faith, will cause it to grow.

God causes our faith to grow by bringing trials into our life which test and stretch our faith. First Peter 1:6-7 says that, *"you have been grieved by various trials, so that the tested genuineness of your faith...may be found to result in praise and glory and honor at the revelation of Jesus Christ."* The painful trials of our life test whether our faith is genuine or not. Like gold that is refined by fire, our precious faith will be refined resulting in greater trust in and glory for God. We do not realize how little we trust God until we are forced to actually trust Him. The Christian life is like a gauntlet of trials and deliverances which God uses to build up our faith. This often repeated process, the **CYCLE OF FAITH**, involves a number of steps:

    Step 1: TRIAL--A grievous problem confronts us.
    Step 2: FAILURE--We attempt to solve the problem with our own resources but fail.
    Step 3: CONVICTION--The Holy Spirit convicts us of our need to trust in God.
    Step 4: PRAYER--We cry out for God's help and then wait upon His deliverance.

Step 5: DELIVERANCE--God delivers us in some glorious and often unexpected way.
Step 6: INCREASE--We glorify God more and our faith in His steadfast love grows.
Step 7: REPEAT--Repeat Step 1 but with greater faith than before!

FAITH IN ACTION

Genuine faith is always accompanied by works. In Hebrews 11:1-39 numerous examples are given of saints, who because of their faith acted. By faith Abel offered a sacrifice; by faith Noah built an ark; by faith Rahab hid the spies, and so forth. Their conviction of God's promises, presence, and power caused them to take risks and take stands. Living by faith should not produce passivity but fuel activity based upon the reality of the sovereignty and providence of God. We are able to act in faith because we trust in God's promise that He is with us.

One of the saints of the Old Testament who was commended for his faith was Caleb. Read the Numbers 13:25-14:25 account of Israel's refusal to enter the land, and answer the following questions.

* What were the reasons behind the negative report of the ten spies? (13:28-33)

* Describe the faith-filled arguments of Caleb. (13:30; 14:6-9)

* What conclusion did the people come to? (14:1-4, 10)

* What was God's judgment of the people and Caleb respectively? (14:11-12, 20-25)

Jesus taught His disciples that a person's faith could move a mountain, *"Truly, I say to you, if you have faith and do not doubt, you will not only do what has been done to the fig tree, but even if you say to this mountain, 'Be taken up and thrown into the sea,' it will happen. And whatever you ask in prayer, you will receive, if you have faith."* (Matthew 21:21-22) Though it seems incredible, this promise is still valid for the Christian. In many cases we manifest our faith by our trust in God to act as He pleases according to His inscrutable wisdom. However, in some cases God positions us so that we will invoke His mighty hand to answer our specific requests and accomplish the impossible--all for His glory. The Bible is replete with examples of His people praying with specificity and God answering them: Elijah's prayer concerning the rain (1 Kings 17:1; 18:41-46), Nehemiah's request for favor with the king (Nehemiah 1:11; 2:4-8), and Hezekiah's cry for deliverance from the Assyrian army (2 Kings 19:14-20, 35).

FAITH COMMENDED

When we lose hope and expect little from God, or rely upon our own strength, God is not pleased with us. Hebrews 11:6 says that *"without faith it is impossible to please him, for whoever would draw near to God must believe that he exists and that he rewards those who seek him."* Our faith and trust in God's love toward us is what gives Him pleasure. *"His delight is not in the strength of the horse, nor his pleasure in the legs of a man, but the Lord takes pleasure in those who fear him, in those who hope in his steadfast love."* (Psalm 147:10-11)

In the Gospels we sometimes see Jesus being surprised and pleased by the hope that men and women had in His power and mercy. Jesus marveled at the centurion's faith (Matthew 8:5-13), was impressed by the Syrophoenician woman's persistence (Mark 7:24-30), and was moved by the bleeding woman's hope (Mark 5:25-34). All of these and many others exhibited a confidence in the power and gracious character of Christ toward them. It is this hope that God wants to grow in us.

HITTING HOME

1. Discuss the three components of the definition of faith: assurance, promise, unseen? (Hebrews 11:1)

2. What current trial are you experiencing which is testing your faith? In what areas of your life are you discovering how little you trust God?

3. Have you experienced a testing of your faith where you truly doubted God's goodness and love toward you? Explain.

4. Describe a **CYCLE OF FAITH** experience in your own life, step by step? (See **GROWING FAITH**)

LESSON 20: FEAR GOD

KEY DOCTRINE: God requires a holy reverence and obedience from His children.
MEMORY VERSE: *"Serve the Lord with fear, and rejoice with trembling."* (Psalm 2:11)
SCRIPTURE PRE-READING: Psalm 2; Matthew 10:26-32; Hebrews 12:3-11, 18-29; Revelation 19:11-21

The Scriptures often describe a genuine believer as someone who fears the LORD. To fear God means to have a reverence and trust in Him which leads to obedience. We who fear the Lord will worship Him alone, obey His laws, tremble at His word, and hope in His mercy. In contrast with the wicked, *"there is no fear of God before his eyes."* (Psalm 36:1) Though God's grace has removed many fears from our life, we still have a reason to fear God's chastisements which sanctify our soul.

THE FEAR OF THE LORD

When the Bible refers to believers, it often describes them as those who *"fear the LORD."* For instance Psalm 34:11 exhorts, *"Come, O children, listen to me; I will teach you the fear of the LORD."* Also, Psalm 147:11 describes the person in whom God delights, *"but the LORD takes pleasure in those who fear him, in those who hope in his steadfast love."* In contrast, the wicked are described as those who have no fear of God. *"Transgression speaks to the wicked deep in his heart; there is no fear of God before his eyes."* (Psalm 36:1) At first, the idea of fearing God does not sound like a very positive thing-- we fear hurricanes, tax audits, and burglars. Is being afraid of God a good thing? Someone you fear is not exactly someone you want to draw near to—more like run away from. Thus we need to understand what is meant by the term *"fear the LORD."*

To *"fear the LORD"* is to recognize who God is in His holy and gracious character, and to respond to Him with reverence and hope. This fear will inspire us in obedience to His Word. Four primary characteristics are seen in a person who fears God:

- **To fear God is to worship Him.** *"It is the LORD your God you shall fear. Him you shall serve and by his name you shall swear. You shall not go after other gods, the gods of the peoples who are around you"* (Deuteronomy 6:13-14). Jesus quoted this verse back to the devil when He was tempted in the desert (Matthew 4:10). Instead of *"fear"* Jesus substituted the word *"worship"* thus communicating the essence of what it means to fear God--to worship Him.

- **To fear God is to be in awe of His power and judgment.** *"'You have not lied to men but to God.' When Ananias heard these words, he fell down and breathed his last. And great fear came upon all who heard of it."* (Act 5:4-5) When both Ananias and his wife Sapphira lied to the church, and thus to the Holy Spirit, concerning the donated proceeds of the sale of their land, the Lord judged them with a capital punishment. Great fear came upon the whole church, and they learned that Jesus is a holy God who is not to be trifled with.

- **To fear God is to be obedient to His commandments.** *"Therefore, my beloved, as you have always obeyed, so now, not only as in my presence but much more in my absence, work out your own salvation with fear and trembling"* (Philippians 2:12). An attitude of *"fear and trembling"* in our obedience before our holy God is necessary and is a great motivator for our sanctification.

- **To fear God is to hope in His love.** *"Behold, the eye of the LORD is on those who fear him, on those who hope in his steadfast love"* (Psalm 33:18). We who fear the Lord are, by definition, the only people who are genuinely hoping in His steadfast love.

If our faith lacks the above characteristics then we do not have saving faith. God spoke in Jeremiah's day against the rebelliousness of Israel saying, *"Know and see that it is evil and bitter for you to forsake the LORD your God; the fear of me is not in you, declares the Lord GOD of hosts."* (Jeremiah 2:19) If we do not fear God, it is because we do not actually believe that the Lord will hold us accountable for our actions, and this will lead us into greater sin. However, we must take heed of Jesus' warning, *"I am he who searches mind and heart, and I will give to each of you according to your works."* (Revelation 2:23)

NO FEAR!

The *fear of the LORD* is a right characteristic of our faith, but there are some types of fear that are not fitting for a child of God. In Zechariah's prophecy of the Messiah in Luke 1:74-75 he says, *"that we, being delivered from the hand of our enemies, might serve him without fear, in holiness and righteousness before him all of our days."* What kinds of blessings in the Christian life are included in the *"without fear"* reference by Zechariah? Read the following passages and identify what we are **not** to fear.

- 1 John 4:17-18: No fear of _____

- Romans 8:15: No fear of the _____

- Hebrews 2:14-15; 1 Corinthians 15:54-57: No fear of _____

- Psalm 27:1-2; 2 Timothy 1:7-8: No fear of our _____

- Isaiah 41:8-10: No fear of _____

- Luke 12:31-32: No fear of _____

A healthy fear of the Lord removes many of our unhealthy fears. As children of God we need not live under the fear of sickness, hardships, the devil, and death. Our hearts can be steadfast, trusting in the faithfulness of the Lord. *"The LORD is my light and my salvation; whom shall I fear? The LORD is the stronghold of my life; of whom shall I be afraid?"* (Psalm 27:1)

JUDGMENT BEGINS AT THE HOUSE OF GOD

Some say that it is right for non-believers to fear God, since they are still susceptible to eternal judgment, but Christians need not fear God. If we are justified before our heavenly Father should we then fear any of the judgments of God against us? It depends on what kind of judgments are in view. We need not fear the condemnation of hell, but we should fear the chastisement of His hand. This healthy fear of God's displeasure will help us in our obedience to God's Word. Our fear is rooted in an understanding that God is holy and He will discipline His church so that we share in His holiness. *"My son, do not regard lightly the discipline of the Lord, nor be weary when reproved by him. For the Lord disciplines the one he loves, and chastises every son whom he receives."* (Hebrews 12:5-6) Because of our heavenly Father's love for us He will discipline us painfully. *"For they* [human parents] *disciplined us for a short time as it seemed best to them, but he disciplines us for our good, that we may share his holiness."* (Hebrews 12:10)

This discipline is part of the judgment that God applies to His church in this world in order to prepare us for eternity. *"For it is time for judgment to begin at the household of God; and if it begins with us, what will be the outcome for those who do not obey the gospel of God?"* (1 Peter 4:17) God deals first with His church before He judges the world. This type of judgment on our sin, by the Holy Spirit, gives rise to our attitude of fear and trembling before God.

Living out our Christian life with fear before God is also necessary because not all people who profess Christ really belong to Him. Church members need to be reminded that people who fall away from the faith are subject to great judgments from the Lord. *"For if we go on sinning deliberately after receiving the knowledge of the truth, there no longer remains a sacrifice for sins, but a fearful expectation of judgment, and a fury of fire that will consume the adversaries."* (Hebrews 10:26-27) A healthy fear of the Lord guards us from the temptation of drifting away from our first profession of faith. *"Therefore let us be grateful for receiving a kingdom that cannot be shaken, and thus let us offer to God acceptable worship, with reverence and awe, for our God is a consuming fire."* (Hebrews 12:28-29)

HITTING HOME:

1. Have you ever thought the term *"fear of the LORD"* to be a peculiar one? Why?

2. In what ways does your faith possess a righteous fear of God?

3. Give an example of God's discipline and reproof in your life? Have you ever resisted a sin due to your fear of God's judgment?

4. If you had more fear of God how might your conduct in your family, church, and life change?

LESSON 21: THE INDWELLING SPIRIT

KEY DOCTRINE: The Holy Spirit within us enables us to believe and be obedient to God's will.
MEMORY VERSE: *"And I will ask the Father, and he will give you another Helper, to be with you forever, even the Spirit of truth, whom the world cannot receive, because it neither sees him nor knows him. You know him, for he dwells with you and will be in you."* (John 14:16-17)
SCRIPTURE PRE-READING: Joel 2:28-32; John 14:15-28; Acts 2:1-4; Romans 8:1-17; Galatians 5:16-26

The great expectation of the Old Testament prophets was that the Messiah would usher in the new covenant and the Spirit would be poured out upon all of God's people. The Holy Spirit given by Christ is the effective working of the power of Jesus within us that brings about our complete salvation. The Spirit of Christ makes us children of God, gives us a knowledge of God, equips us for service, and produces the fruits of true righteousness. As we set our minds on the things of the Spirit we will be filled by the Spirit.

A BLAST FROM THE PAST

One of the main differences between the Old and New Testaments is the extent to which the Spirit of God works in the lives of believers. During the Old Testament era the Holy Spirit often moved on men like Moses, Samson, Gideon, and Saul in powerful ways, but sometimes did not have an abiding presence throughout their lives. Though there were many Old Testament believers who had true faith and kept God's commandments, the collective nation of Israel was unable to keep God's covenant due to the weakness of their sin nature. The heart of the nation of Israel was likened to that of a lifeless stone which needed to be replaced by a *"heart of flesh."* (Ezekiel 36:26)

It was out of this failure that the prophets looked to the salvation of the Messiah and the blessings which would flow through the Spirit in a new covenant. Joel prophesied, *"And it shall come to pass afterward, that I will pour out my Spirit on all flesh"* (Joel 2:28) and also Jeremiah said, *"But this is the covenant that I will make with the house of Israel after those days, declares the LORD: I will put my law within them, and I will write it on their hearts."* (Jeremiah 31:33) Instead of the Spirit moving on a few leaders, in the new covenant the Spirit has been poured out on all of God's people so that, *"they shall all know me, from the least of them to the greatest, declares the LORD."* (Jeremiah 31:34) This was Moses' hope when he instructed his assistant Joshua, *"Are you jealous for my sake? Would that all the LORD's people were prophets, that the LORD would put his Spirit on them!"* (Numbers 11:29)

NOT I, BUT CHRIST WITHIN ME

Jesus instructed His disciples that it was better for Him to depart, for He would still continue to be with them through the Holy Spirit (John 16:7). It was in this sense that the apostle Paul considered that the life that he lived was actually Christ living through him by the Holy Spirit. *"I have been crucified with Christ. It is no longer I who live, but Christ who lives in me."* (Galatians 2:20) The gift of the Holy Spirit within a person is not some special privilege of a few super-spiritual folks, but it is the defining characteristic of a Christian. After the Holy Spirit was given to the church at the day of Pentecost Peter said to all present, *"Repent and be baptized every one of you in the name of Jesus Christ for the forgiveness of your sins, and you will receive the gift of the Holy Spirit. For the promise is for you and for your children and for all who are far off, everyone whom the Lord our God calls to himself."* (Acts 2:38-39) If you are not "Spirit-filled" you are not a Christian.

Only through the working of the Spirit within us will we be able to accomplish any good in our Christian lives. The apostle Paul considered that we are all merely *"jars of clay"* which house the precious treasure of Christ (2 Corinthians 4:7). Peter, who denied Jesus three times (Mark 14:66-72), was later emboldened by the power of the Holy Spirit and testified of Christ to the crowds and the Jewish high council (Acts 2:14-41; 4:1-12). It is the Spirit within us that gives us the boldness and ability to bear witness and equips us for obedience to Christ.

The Spirit of God produces worship; the only people who are truly worshipping God are those who have His Spirit. You are not a *spiritual* person unless you actually have the Holy Spirit. Jesus taught the Samaritan woman, *"But the hour is coming, and is now here, when the true worshipers will worship the Father in spirit and truth, for the Father is seeking such people to worship him. God is spirit, and those who worship him must worship in spirit and truth."* (John 4:23-24) The Spirit within us is described as being *jealous* (James 4:5), and He who searches hearts knows where our affections lie. He convicts us of our unbelief, reveals the idols in our heart, and fuels the passion to rejoice in God's glory.

To know God we must have His Spirit, and it is the Spirit within us that reveals truth about God. The Holy Spirit will be our teacher to guide us in our interpretation of the Scriptures, protect us from error, and reveal how the Word applies to our life. *"But the anointing that you received from him abides in you, and you have no need that anyone should teach you. But as his anointing teaches you about everything, and is true, and is no lie—just as it has taught you, abide in him."* (1 John 2:27) The Holy Spirit illuminates the meaning of the Scriptures and empowers the Word, so that it becomes *"living and active"* (Hebrews 4:12) and does a work of transformation within us.

THE FRUIT OF THE SPIRIT

Jesus said that you can know a tree by its fruit (Luke 6:43-45). Out of a person's heart will come forth either righteousness or wickedness. The Holy Spirit within our hearts should be emanating the good fruits of righteousness. Paul describes these righteous characteristics as the fruit of the Spirit: *"love, joy, peace, patience, kindness, goodness, faithfulness, gentleness, self-control"* (Galatians 5:22-23). When we are manifesting these traits it is the Spirit producing them in us.

In order to bring forth this type of righteous fruit Jesus must make us into a good tree (Matthew 12:33). Jesus has granted us His divine power through the Holy Spirit who enables us to escape the corruption of this age and walk in godliness (2 Peter 1:3-4). As Jesus declared, *"It is the Spirit who gives life; the flesh is no help at all."* (John 6:63) We need to recognize that the Spirit was given to us that we may walk in the holiness that only God can give. As an exercise to help us understand how the Spirit works in our lives read Romans 8:1-17 and answer the following questions.

- What defines the person who belongs to God? (v. 9, 14-16)

- How, and from what, are we set free? (v. 2-4)

- How does the Spirit work in relation to God's law? (v. 4)

- Describe the state of mind of a person living by the Spirit? (v. 6)

- If we are not living for the Spirit, what are we living for? (v. 5-8)

SETTING OUR MINDS

One of the great frustrations in our Christian life is how much we still sin after our conversion. We might wish that the Spirit within us would somehow automatically override our sin nature so that we could always live triumphantly, yet that is not the case. In both Romans 8:13 and Galatians 5:16-25 Paul describes an internal battle of the Spirit versus *the flesh*--our remaining sin nature. Though the Spirit is in us, we must still make a conscious decision *"to set the mind"* (Romans 8:6) on those desires and thoughts which we know are pleasing to the Spirit, and to resist those impulses of our sin nature. We set our mind on things that are pleasing to the Lord by reading the Bible daily and being vigilant in prayer, instead of focusing on the things of this fallen world. When our mind is focused on the things of the Spirit we experience what is called being *"filled with the Spirit"* (Ephesians 5:18). Instead of temptation, fear, and despair, the Spirit fills our hearts and minds with faith, hope, peace, courage and joy.

HITTING HOME

1. Have you ever recognized the Holy Spirit working and dwelling in you? Give an example.

2. Describe a time in your life when your sin nature fought against the Holy Spirit and the Spirit prevailed. How did the Spirit work in you to bring about the victory?

3. Can you see changes in your character which you can attribute to the fruit of the Spirit? Explain.

4. Write out some practical means by which you can set your mind on the things of the Spirit.

LESSON 22: THE CHRISTIAN'S WARFARE

KEY DOCTRINE: To persevere in their faith Christians must fight a spiritual war against their own sin, unbelievers, and demonic forces in this life.

MEMORY VERSE: *"I have fought the good fight, I have finished the race, I have kept the faith."* (2 Timothy 4:7)

SCRIPTURE PRE-READING: Job 1:6-2:10; Psalm 27:1-14; John 15:18-25; Ephesians 2:1-3; 6:10-20; 1 John 2:15-17

Christianity is not for wimps. Jesus taught that the path that leads to death is wide and easy, however the path that leads to life is narrow and hard (Matthew 7:13-14). When we align with Christ we declare war against our own sin nature, this fallen world, and demonic powers. Therefore we must prepare for this life-long battle, arming ourselves with our holy faith, the Word of God, and prayer.

THE AXIS OF EVIL

We will fight a spiritual war against three enemies which are defined in the Scriptures as *the flesh*, *the world*, and *the devil*. These three enemies all will seek to discourage our faith, lead us into temptation, and persecute us for our beliefs. Read Ephesians 2:1-3 and identify this triad of evil.

- The Flesh: _____

- The World: _____

- The Devil: _____

THE FLESH

We have learned in previous studies that we are all born with a sin nature, often called the *flesh*. Though in some contexts *flesh* simply refers to the body, in most cases *flesh* refers to the sins we commit, whether in body or in mind. As Ephesians 2:1-3 states, *"And you were dead in the trespasses and sins in which you once walked...among whom we all once lived in the passions of our flesh, carrying out the desires of the body and the mind."* The continuing influence that our remaining sin has on us is a type of warfare against our souls. In Romans 7:21-23 the apostle Paul says that his sin nature is *"waging war"* against his own knowledge of that which is right and true. Likewise, Paul describes a similar conflict in Galatians 5:16-19 where the *"desires of the flesh are against the Spirit."* [LESSON 23: FIGHTING SIN will focus on this battle against the sins of our flesh.]

THE WORLD

When we begin to follow Jesus we will soon find ourselves coming into opposition with people around us. We no longer value or uphold the same beliefs as we used to before we came to faith. Just as an individual can be opposed to God, the values and beliefs of groups and societies of people can be opposed to the truth of Christ. The Bible refers to this collective opposition to Christ as the *world*. *"If the world hates you, know that it has hated me before it hated you. If you were of the world, the world would love you as its own; but because you are not of the world, but I chose you out of the world, therefore the world hates you."* (John 15:18-19) First John 2:15-17 gives a threefold description of the values of the world, *"the desires of the flesh and the desires of the eyes and pride in possessions."* Consider this short list of the differences in how a Christian thinks from a person of the world:

The Christian:	The World:
loves God	loves self
treasures heaven	treasures possessions
denies lusts	gratifies lusts
humbles themselves	exalts themselves
trusts God	relies upon themselves
submits to God	loves autonomy
seeks wisdom	despises truth

As we are transformed into the likeness of Christ, we will find that opposition with the world will be inevitable. *"Indeed, all who desire to live a godly life in Christ Jesus will be persecuted"* (2 Timothy 3:12). The Bible records the consistent theme that the righteous in this age are always persecuted by the ungodly. Whether it is Cain against Abel, Pharaoh against Moses, Saul against David, or the Pharisees against Jesus, sinful people will oppose those who are truly following God. Jesus came into the world to *"not bring peace...but rather division"* (Luke 12:49-53). Opposition comes not just from non-believers but also from people within the visible church who do not truly know Christ. In this spiritual war we boldly proclaim, *"The LORD is my light and my salvation; whom shall I fear?"* (Psalm 27:1)

THE DEVIL

In our sophisticated modern age we tend to downplay the existence and relevance of demonic activity in our lives. Unfortunately, the devil exists and he does seek to destroy believers (1 Peter 5:8). Our lives are more than likely too small-time to meet the actual devil, but we will come across his minions. The devil and demons are fallen angels who rebelled against God's authority. They have power in this age but they are not all-powerful or all-knowing. God has complete control over their actions and He will use what they intend for evil to suit His good purposes. Of course, they do not stand a chance against Jesus; Jesus has authority over demons and will destroy them with His breath at His return.

THE PLAYBOOK OF EVIL

It is necessary that we become aware of the devil's schemes, purposes and power. Paul said we *"are not ignorant of his designs."* (2 Corinthians 2:11) Knowing the devil's *playbook of evil* aids us in resisting his attacks. Read the following passages and identify the schemes of the devil.

* **Questions:** (Genesis 3:1-5; Ephesians 6:16) _____
* **Accuses:** (Zechariah 3:1-6; Revelation 12:10) _____
* **Tempts:** (Luke 4:1-13) _____
* **Divides:** (Ephesians 4:26-27) _____
* **Deceives:** (1Timothy 4:1) _____
* **Challenges:** (Job 1:6-12; 2:1-6) _____
* **Persecutes:** (Revelation 12:17; 13:5-10) _____
* **Intimidates:** (Nehemiah 6:9, 14) _____

TAKE YOUR STAND

We need not be afraid of the devil, for if we resist him in the name of Jesus he will flee from us (James 4:7). Jesus defeated Satan through His ministry and His death, burial and resurrection, so we can boldly affirm that *"he who is in you* [Jesus] *is greater than he who is in the world* [demonic forces]*."* (1 John 4:4) The apostle Paul exhorted us in Ephesians 6:10-18 to take a stand against the devil by wearing *"the whole armor of God."* This armor is a figurative representation of the types of virtues we must be girded with in order to combat attacks. We must be clothed with truth, righteousness, readiness, faith, and hope to stand against the persecution of this world and demonic attacks. To fight back we must wield the sword of the Word of God and pray vigilantly in the Spirit. Our ultimate confidence that we will prevail in this spiritual war is that God, who sits on His throne in heaven, is on our side. *"What then shall we say to these things? If God is for us, who can be against us?"* (Romans 8:31)

HITTING HOME

1. Describe a personal experience of fighting against your own *flesh*?

2. Since your conversion can you describe any breaking or tensions in relationships with friends or family because of your new way of life?

3. What are some ways in which you find yourself against the world in your job or recreations?

4. What ways have you experienced the schemes of the devil in the above *playbook of evil*?

LESSON 23: FIGHTING SIN

KEY DOCTRINE: Christians must put to death the sins of their remaining depravity throughout their lives.
MEMORY VERSE: *"For if you live according to the flesh you will die, but if by the Spirit you put to death the deeds of the body, you will live."* (Romans 8:13)
SCRIPTURE PRE-READING: Psalm 119:9-16; Romans 6:1-14; 7:15-20; 8:1-13; Ephesians 4:17-32; 1 John 1:5-10

The way of salvation is hard because of the battles that we wage. Chief among these battles is the fight against our sin nature. At the moment of our conversion we are justified before God, however sin still remains in our flesh. With the entrance of the Holy Spirit an internal struggle against our flesh begins. This battle against sin will continue throughout our Christian life. It is helpful for our sanctification if we do not underestimate the danger of our remaining depravity. Scripture has commanded us, and the Holy Spirit has empowered us, to put to death the deeds of the flesh and put on the new righteousness of Christ.

SAINTS SIN

It would be wonderful if we could say, "I used to sin, but now I do not anymore," but the saints of God still sin. Conversion does not make us perfect all at once—one day in heaven we will be perfect, but not yet. In this life we face the humbling reality that we have a lot of growing to do. The Bible is not bashful about exposing the flaws of the saints. Abraham's faith was weak at times. Jacob deceived his father. David committed adultery and murder. Peter fell into legalism. Paul and Barnabas quarreled. When we see the warts of such mighty men of faith it reminds us not to think too highly of ourselves.

The letter of 1 John seems to teach contradictory doctrines about the possibility of Christians sinning. First John 1:8 says, *"If we say we have no sin, we deceive ourselves, and the truth is not in us."* Yet, 1 John 3:9 says, *"No one born of God makes a practice of sinning, for God's seed abides in him, and he cannot keep on sinning because he has been born of God."* To sin or not to sin, that is the question? The apostle John is talking about sin in two respects; the *power* of sin and the *presence* of sin. If we are born of God and have Christ in us we are no longer living under the *power* of sin. We cannot keep a lifestyle of regular unrepentant sin to which 1 John 3:9 refers. However, the Bible, in 1 John 1:8, also asserts that sin is still *present* within the character of a born-again believer. This sin needs to be confessed and cleansed by the blood of Christ. Claims of perfectionism do not fit the truths of Scripture, not to mention the obvious experience of our life. The Bible maintains the somber reality that we are going to have to fight against our sin however due to the Holy Spirit we can have hope for victory in this life.

THE POWER OF SIN

When we are born-again Christ becomes the Lord of our life. Christ's lordship replaces the lordship that sin once had over us. *"We know that our old self was crucified with him in order that the body of sin might be brought to nothing, so that we would no longer be enslaved to sin."* (Romans 6:6) Though Christ has greater power than our flesh, our remaining sin is still a formidable enemy. A key strategy in sports and warfare is to never underestimate your opponent. If we think we can just coast by and win easily, our opponent will shock and defeat us. We must not underestimate how powerful the flesh can be in our lives. Our sin was a power that controlled us and it wants to enslave us once again. This is why the Bible instructs us to, *"Let not sin therefore reign in your mortal body, to make you obey its passions."* (Romans 6:12)

It is a healthy mindset to be convinced that you can commit any sin under the sun no matter how wretched. The moment we say, "I could never do that..." we are in trouble. Recognizing our depravity protects us against self-righteousness and helps to guard us against temptations. *"Therefore let anyone who thinks that he stands take heed lest he fall."* (1 Corinthians 10:12) When we think we are standing strong we are actually more vulnerable to a fall. It is dangerous to think that we have completely eradicated a particular sin from our lives, for temptation is always around the corner. God warned Cain, who would become the first murderer, *"sin is crouching at the door. Its desire is for you but you must rule over it."* (Genesis 4:7)

One of the great dangers in the fight against our sin is simply not recognizing it. The Lord Jesus often grew angry and railed against the Pharisees because they could not see their own unrighteousness.

In the parable of the Pharisee and the tax collector (Luke 18:9-14), the account of the sinful woman washing Jesus' feet (Luke 7:36-50), and the list of woes against the scribes and Pharisees (Matthew 23:1-36), the Lord confronted this deception of sin. The Sermon on the Mount, in many respects, is a scathing rebuke against the *"righteousness"* (Matthew 5:20) of the scribes and Pharisees who hid behind the Law. The law of God, when correctly applied, should expose the hidden depths of our sin, not inflate our pride. As we progress in the faith we should alway clothe ourselves with humility, confessing with the apostle Paul, *"For I know that nothing good dwells in me, that is, in my flesh."* (Romans 7:18)

PUTTING SIN TO DEATH

Scripture commands us to not let sin control us; instead, by the Spirit we should put sin to death. *"For if you live according to the flesh you will die, but if by the Spirit you put to death the deeds of the body, you will live."* (Romans 8:13) In our own strength we cannot rid ourselves of any sin, but the Holy Spirit can be the effective agent in cleansing and changing us to be more like Christ. Read Matthew 5:27-30 and Ephesians 4:17-32, and answer these questions concerning our fight against sin.

- Describe the *"former manner of life"* which we are told to *"put off"*? (Ephesians 4:17-32)

- What kind of actions characterize the *"new self"* in Christ? (Ephesians 4:24-32)

- What does Jesus mean when He instructs us to cut off sinful body parts? (Matthew 5:27-30)

- What is the danger of leniency toward our sin? (Matthew 5:27-30)

Now the big question is *how* do we put off the *"old self"* and put on the *"new self"*? The key is to set our minds on things that are pleasing to the Spirit. The desire of the Spirit is for us to focus on the attributes, faithfulness, and glory of Christ. The Spirit builds our faith by teaching us to trust in God's steadfast love and faithfulness and causes us to yearn to experience it evermore. On the other hand, our flesh wants to focus on fleeting pleasures associated with lusts, materialism, and our pride. Whatever our mind is fixating on will be the direction we pursue. At the most practical level we need to be aware of what we are thinking about at all times. Little thoughts become big desires, and then grow into actions. *"Then desire when it has conceived gives birth to sin, and sin when it is fully grown brings forth death."* (James 1:15)

The prime instruction to help us set our mind on the desires of the Spirit is to read God's Word. Psalm 1 teaches us that the faithful man's *"delight is in the law of the LORD, and on his law he meditates day and night."* (Psalm 1:2) When we go for a time without reading and studying the Bible we begin to conform to the world and our sin nature starts taking over again. However, when we come back to the Bible the Spirit uses Scripture to direct our faith to *"things that are above"* (Colossians 3:2) and the power of our flesh diminishes. Let us therefore be diligent to study God's Word, to continue in prayer, to fight against our flesh, and to walk by the Spirit. Finally, be encouraged by this promise, *"God is faithful, and he will not let you be tempted beyond your ability, but with the temptation he will also provide the way of escape, that you may be able to endure it."* (1 Corinthians 10:13)

HITTING HOME

1. How well do you have a grasp on how dangerous and powerful your sin can be in your life?

2. Have you seen victories over the power of sin in your life? Describe how the Spirit used Scripture to lead you out of a temptation to sin.

3. Are there sins in your life that you are allowing to live instead of putting them to death ?

4. What practical steps have you taken in your life, or will now take, to guard yourself against temptation?

LESSON 24: THE TRIALS OF LIFE

KEY DOCTRINE: Christians will have their faith tested and matured by various trials that God brings into their lives.

MEMORY VERSE: *"Count it all joy, my brothers, when you meet trials of various kinds, for you know that the testing of your faith produces steadfastness."* (James 1:2-3)

SCRIPTURE PRE-READING: Ruth 1; Ecclesiastes 3:1-14; Romans 8:18-25; Hebrews 12:1-13; 1 Peter 4:12-19

Many people have a naïve expectation that God should make life easy for us. We need to recognize that God will orchestrate numerous trials in our lives to refine and test our faith. Some of these trials involve simply living in a fallen world. Others will be used to expose and chasten our sin. We will also be persecuted for being associated with Christ. All these trials will serve to test the genuineness of our faith and increase our trust in God's love and care for us.

IT'S A HARD KNOCK LIFE FOR US

For Adam and Eve, life was a paradise in the garden of Eden. Since the sin of Adam, this paradise was lost and we now live in the fall-out of God's judgments on all of creation. These judgments were pronounced by God in Genesis 3:14-19. The whole creation was subjected to corruption; the evil one opposes the children of God; the marriage relationship is marred; childbirth and rearing is painful; work is toilsome and our bodies will get sick and die. The totality of this curse has caused the world to be like a woman in childbirth, groaning until the day when Christ's return creates all things new (Romans 8:20-23).

Though we are born again into Christ we must still remain living in this fallen world and experience the effects of sin in our life and the world around us. We cannot escape the trials that are associated with the fall: suffering violence and crime, sickness, job loss, broken relationships, death of loved ones, want, etc. The book of Ecclesiastes chronicles many of the frustrations of living in this vain world. In Ecclesiastes 3:1-8 we learn that there is a time to experience every type of gain and loss in life. Even as believers we will not be able to steer our lives away from all the hardship in order to only obtain the good things.

As we live in this fallen world, we must live by faith trusting that God is in control and cares for us. Persevering in this trust is a battle, as our carnal flesh and the world desire to be in control and discount the role that God plays in the daily affairs of mankind. Yet we need to trust that God is providentially guiding every purpose and event on the earth. Our faith will be tested to reveal whether or not we trust that God cares for us, His children. When the world and our flesh scream that we have to fend for ourselves, we must believe Jesus when He says that God clothes and feeds His children even more than the flowers and birds (Matthew 6:25-30). During natural calamities and acts of unspeakable evil, skeptics will question God's goodness or existence, but we affirm that God still sits on His throne and will make all things beautiful in His time (Ecclesiastes 3:11).

TAKING UP OUR CROSS

One specific type of trial that Christ has planned for us involves remaining faithful to Him in the face of an unbelieving world. *"If anyone would come after me, let him deny himself and take up his cross daily and follow me...for whoever is ashamed of me and of my words, of him will the Son of Man be ashamed when he comes in his glory"* (Luke 9:23, 26). Taking up our cross does not refer to the basic hardships of life, but to the unique persecutions that come from being identified with Jesus. *"Indeed, all who desire to live a godly life in Christ Jesus will be persecuted"* (2 Timothy 3:12). Keeping Christ's word and publicly being recognized as someone who believes in Jesus may cause people to mock, distance, challenge, or even kill you. [LESSON 25 TAKING UP YOUR CROSS deals with this subject in more depth.]

THE FATHER'S DISCIPLINE

When life is going well and we are taking care of business, we are usually blind to the reality of our sin and our need for more faith. God sends trials into our life to expose our sin and lack of faith. *"Behold, I have refined you, but not as silver; I have tried you in the furnace of affliction."* (Isaiah 48:10) Just as fire burns away impurities within silver, fiery trials burn away sin within us.

In Hebrews 12:10-11 the writer makes the claim that God *"disciplines us for our good, that we may share in his holiness. For the moment all discipline seems painful rather than pleasant, but later it yields the peaceable fruit of righteousness to those who have been trained by it."* God will use painful trials that we do not like in order to train us in holiness. This Fatherly discipline should not be seen as a form of retribution or a natural consequence of our sin. Rather, persecution, trials, and suffering in general are part of God's comprehensive plan to cause us to be more like Christ.

STRENGTH IN WEAKNESS

An important purpose of a trial is to weaken us and take away our self-reliance, which will then compel us to trust in the Lord. When God delivers us He gets the glory. A recurring theme throughout the letter of 2 Corinthians is the principle of weakness. Read the following three passages in 2 Corinthians and explain the weaknesses mentioned and the positive outcomes from the trials.

- 1:8-10 _____

- 4:7-11 _____

- 12:5-10 _____

The book of Judges gives an account of a weak man named Gideon who became a mighty warrior for the Lord (Judges 6:11-7:25). In the face of impossible odds Gideon was commanded by God to lead the Israelites into battle against the Midianites. When the time came for the battle instead of increasing Gideon's army God reduced the army from thirty-two thousand to a meager three hundred men. Was God looking for "a few good men?" No, just a few men, so that He, not Israel, would get all the glory. We should not despise our trials when they weaken us. In times of trouble, when we are too weak to save ourselves, God reveals His saving power and glorifies His holy name.

A GENUINE FAITH

Refined faith is a true faith, and refined faith is a deep faith. One of the purposes of trials is to reveal the genuine nature of our faith. Suffering and persecution will separate true believers from Christians in name only. The second seed in the parable of the sower (Matthew 13:20-21) that fell on the shallow, rocky soil died off because of persecution and tribulation due to Christ's word. Many people can maintain a shallow trust in God when life is going as they wish, but when a life-crisis, suffering, or great temptation confronts them they reveal their true nature. It is through various trials that our faith is tested to show that it is real, *"In this you rejoice, though now for a little while, if necessary, you have been grieved by various trails, so that the tested genuineness of your faith—more precious than gold that perishes though it is tested with fire—may be found to result in praise and glory and honor at the revelation of Jesus Christ."* (1 Peter 1:6-7)

Every test of our faith will challenge the core truth of our faith--God loves us. With every trial we are tempted to think that God has forsaken us, and perhaps we are too sinful for God to bless. We then question His goodness, His ability, and the plan of His providence. As we wrestle with these questions the Holy Spirit will bring to our minds the promises of God's grace from the Scriptures. We may not smell like roses as we go through trials, but in the end we will have the aroma of Christ and our faith will grow deeper. So let us not despise the trials we are going through but patiently submit to our Father's kind and wise purposes to make us more like Jesus.

HITTING HOME

1. What trial are you going through now that is causing pain in your life, and what aspects of your faith and character is this trial exposing?

2. Have you ever suffered any kind of persecution for your faith in Jesus? Explain.

3. Describe a trial where God weakened you in order that He might show His strength.

4. How have you seen your faith grow through the trials you have experienced? In what ways are you now more prepared for the next trial?

LESSON 25: TAKING UP YOUR CROSS

KEY DOCTRINE: In this age Christians who desire to live a godly life in Christ should expect to endure persecution.

MEMORY VERSE: *"Then Jesus told his disciples, 'If anyone would come after me, let him deny himself and take up his cross and follow me.'"* (Matthew 16:24)

SCRIPTURE PRE-READING: Daniel 3:8-25; Psalm 35:11-24; Luke 14:25-33; John 15:18-27; Hebrews 12:1-4

After Peter made his first confession that Jesus is the Christ, Jesus predicted His own sufferings of the cross, and then He charged each of His followers to also bear their own cross. The command to take up our cross does not refer to our daily trials of life but to the expected opposition we will face in this world because of our faithfulness to God. We should expect opposition in many forms, whether it is merely mockery or ultimately death. Persecution will become a blessing to us as we experience fellowship with Christ and a greater measure of His Spirit.

THE DARKNESS HATES THE LIGHT

Since the fall of mankind sinful people have always opposed the righteous followers of the LORD. After the fall of Adam God pronounced a curse on the serpent and foretold that there would be *"enmity between you and the woman, and between your offspring and her offspring"* (Genesis 3:15). Eventually a descendent from Eve would come who would destroy the serpent--*"he shall bruise your head"* (Genesis 3:15)--therefore the devil throughout the history of the Bible attempted to eradicate the people of God. The very first record of this enmity between the offspring of the serpent and believers occurred when Cain murdered his righteous brother Abel (Genesis 4:1-12). The history of the nation of Israel is one of persistent conflict with adversaries of the one true God, whether it was Pharaoh, the Canaanites, or the Babylonians. In the book of Esther, Haman, *"the enemy of the Jews"* (Esther 9:10), sought to wipe out the whole population of Jews throughout the kingdom of Persia. How often King David cried out in the Psalms about the hatred he endured at the hands of the enemies of the LORD, *"I call upon the LORD, who is worthy to be praised, and I am saved from my enemies."* (Psalm 18:3)

This spiritual conflict can be simply summarized in Jesus' teaching that *"people loved the darkness rather than the light because their works were evil."* (John 3:19) At our conversion we change sides from the domain of darkness to the kingdom of Christ (Colossians 1:13). Once we have made a public identification with Christ, the Light of the world, we can expect to receive opposition from the world of darkness which opposes Christ's rule. Jesus taught us that *"the gate is narrow and the way is hard that leads to life, and those who find it are few"* (Matthew 7:14), so as we seek to obey Christ we should not be surprised if the world hates us.

THE APOSTOLIC TESTIMONY OF SUFFERING

Jesus told His disciples in John 14:18 that the world would hate them because it first hated Him. The experiences of the apostles confirmed this word. The first apostles were arrested (Acts 4:3; 16:24), brought before the Jewish religious leaders (Acts 5:27), stoned (Acts 7:58; 14:19), and put to death (Acts 12:2). From their own experience Barnabas and the apostle Paul testified to the elders of the churches that *"through many tribulations we must enter the kingdom of God."* (Acts 14:22) Church history records that, except for John, every one of the apostles died a martyr, and even John was imprisoned on the island of Patmos in his old age. To carry the message of Christ in this world carries a great cost.

The apostles in their letters instructed the church that they should expect suffering for their faith in Jesus. Peter said that we should not *"be surprised at the fiery trial when it comes upon you to test you, as though something strange were happening to you."* (1 Peter 4:12) Expect it; this is your heritage as a Christian! Paul considered his sufferings to be a mark of legitimacy for his ministry (2 Corinthians 11:23-33) and exhorted young Timothy to *"Share in sufferings as a good soldier of Christ Jesus."* (2 Timothy 2:3) We might be tempted to think that suffering is reserved for elite Christians, but the average pew-sitting Christian should expect an easier road. The problem with this thinking is that it negates those all-inclusive words like *all*, *anyone*, and *whoever*. Paul said, *"Indeed, **all** who desire to live a godly life in Christ Jesus will be persecuted."* (2 Timothy 3:12) When Jesus said, *"If **anyone** would come after me"* (Matthew 16:24) and *"**whoever** is ashamed of me"* (Mark 8:38) He was not limiting the application. Why should we exclude ourselves from these challenges?

THE COST OF DISCIPLESHIP

Instead of making church growth the priority, Jesus often seemed intent on reducing His followers. When He saw great crowds following Him, Jesus told them they had to *"count the cost"* (Luke 14:25-33) before they considered being His disciple. Jesus is "up front" with us that fellowship with Him will require renouncing all (Luke 14:33), losing friends and family (Matthew 10:34-37), leaving houses and possessions (Luke 9:58), and never looking back (Luke 9:62).

For those of us who live in societies with freedom of religion we tend to think of persecution as something that happens "over there." However, persecution can take many forms and even the seemingly milder forms are painful. The following list presents a spectrum of persecution that we can expect in this world. Look up the associated verses and see how they might apply in your life.

- **Mockery**: (Psalm 22:6-8; 1 Peter 4:3-4) _____

- **Social Estrangement:** (Jeremiah 15:15-17; Matthew 10:34-39) _____

- **Career and Financial Endangerment**: (Daniel 6:3-5; Revelation 2:9) _____

- **Verbal Assault:** (Nehemiah 2:19; 4:1-5; 1 Peter 3:16) _____

- **Physical Punishment and Death:** (Daniel 3:13-18; Revelation 2:8-11) _____

"BLESSED ARE YOU"

At the end of the Beatitudes (Matthew 5:2-11) Jesus taught that His followers would be blessed when they endured persecution. Jesus listed two forms of persecution that would come to His followers:

- **Suffering for Righteousness Sake:** *"Blessed are those who are persecuted for righteousness' sake, for theirs is the kingdom of heaven."* (v. 10) There will be a type of persecution that comes to us because we take ethical and moral stands in society against the unrighteous standards and practices of the world.

- **Suffering for Jesus' Sake:** *"Blessed are you when others revile you and persecute you and utter all kinds of evil against you falsely on my account. Rejoice and be glad, for your reward is great in heaven, for so they persecuted the prophets who were before you."* (v. 11-12) Our identification with the name of Jesus will elicit hatred and persecution by some, not because of any actions we have done, but because of the world's hostility to Christ.

Since both of these forms of persecution are painful, how can we consider them a blessing? We are blessed because Jesus promised that the Holy Spirit would grant us an extra measure of His grace in the midst of our trials. When we take up our cross we will have a fellowship with Jesus as His sufferings and consolations flow into our life. The apostle Paul said the goal of his life was *"that I may know him and the power of his resurrection, and may share in his sufferings, becoming like him in his death"* (Philippians 3:10). It was in this fellowship of sufferings that Paul knew he would be the closest to Christ and experience more of His righteousness (Philippians 3:8-9). Let us be faithful to our Lord and take up our cross daily, and in so doing become more like Christ in His death and resurrection.

HITTING HOME
1. What forms of persecution have you experienced or are presently experiencing in your life? (See section **THE COST OF DISCIPLESHIP**.)

2. Give an example of how a persecution in your life grew your faith and drew you closer to Christ?

3. In what ways are you not associating with Christ in order to avoid opposition? How can you change this behavior in order to take up your cross and embrace the fellowship of Christ's sufferings?

4. According to Matthew 10:26-32 what should take away our fear of men?

CORESTRENGTH † CORESTRENGTH † CORESTRENGTH † CORESTRENGTH † CORESTRENGTH

LESSON 26: THE WAY OF WISDOM

KEY DOCTRINE: Wisdom is the skillful application of God's truth in life to effect outcomes consistent with God's will.
MEMORY VERSE: *"The fear of the LORD is the beginning of knowledge; fools despise wisdom and instruction."* (Proverbs 1:7)
SCRIPTURE PRE-READING: 1 Kings 3:1-28; Proverbs 3:1-26; Colossians 1:27-2:3; James 3:13-18

The Bible exhorts believers to obtain wisdom because its benefits far exceed that of mere wealth. Wisdom is not just having knowledge, but having a skill in applying truth to a variety of circumstances to achieve good results in life. Wisdom requires knowing how things and people work and anticipating the outcomes of the various choices before us. We must apply faith with our wisdom as we recognize that God is providentially governing the world we live in.

THE WORTH OF WISDOM
The book of Proverbs exhorts us to seek after and obtain wisdom. Wisdom is deemed to be of more value than even silver and gold (Proverbs 3:14). Read the following passages from Proverbs and list a number of the benefits that King Solomon says wisdom will bring us.

- Proverbs 2:5-8 _____
- Proverbs 2:12-15 _____
- Proverbs 3:16-17 _____

THE NATURE OF WISDOM
When we try to define wisdom we generally relate it to *knowledge*. This is a close synonym, but the two are not identical. Wisdom is the skill of applying knowledge and understanding to a variety of circumstances. Just as a worker has skill in using their knowledge to build or fix something, a wise person applies wisdom to achieve a good outcome in their life.

Wisdom is not merely a secular skill but requires faith in the God of creation who has made and governs the world we live in. *"The fear of the LORD is the beginning of wisdom, and the knowledge of the Holy One is insight."* (Proverbs 9:10) As we fear the Lord, we obtain wisdom by learning more about God, ourselves, and the world we live in. Biblical wisdom also has a moral component. The wise man abhors sin and delights in righteousness; he recognizes that his life and soul will be more blessed as he makes choices in accordance with God's commandments (Proverbs 2:9-15). In contrast, *"The fool says in his heart, 'There is no God.'"* (Psalm 14:1) The fool as defined by the Bible is not just an idiot, but a faithless, immoral and unteachable person, *"fools despise wisdom and instruction."* (Proverbs 1:7) The fool has no fear of the Lord and thus his life is characterized by sin, pride and destruction.

God created all things through wisdom, therefore the wise appreciate the order and wisdom of the creation. In Proverbs 8:22-31 wisdom is personified as a *"master workman"* (v. 30) laboring alongside God to establish the world. As Colossians 1:16 says, *"For by him all things were created, in heaven and on earth,"* Christ is this personification of wisdom, skillfully crafting the creation at the beginning of time. The recognition of God's wisdom in the created order aids us in understanding the fundamental order of the world. This knowledge, when applied to our daily lives, will help us live wisely and give God greater glory.

GETTING WISDOM
How do we obtain wisdom? We ask God for it! *"For the LORD gives wisdom; from his mouth come knowledge and understanding"* (Proverbs 2:6). The apostle James says, *"If any of you lacks wisdom, let him ask God, who gives generously to all without reproach, and it will be given him."* (James 1:5) Who lacks wisdom? Everyone. Ironically, the wise in heart are the ones who recognize their lack of wisdom and humbly ask God to grant it to them. God does not rebuke us for asking for more wisdom, but generously supplies it to all who yearn to have greater knowledge of His ways. Such was the case with young King Solomon (1 Kings 3) when he asked God to give him the wisdom to govern Israel. This request pleased God. He not only granted Solomon wisdom but also the blessings of a prosperous rule.

Section C: A Closer Walk with God

WISDOM VERSUS FOLLY

The book of Proverbs contains many comparative proverbs that describe the contrast between wisdom and folly. Read the following proverbs and note the contrast between the wise and the fool.

- **Receiving Instruction:** (Proverbs 9:7-9; 10:8)

  The fool (scoffer) _____

  The wise _____

- **Temper:** (Proverbs 14:29; 18:6)

  The fool _____

  The wise _____

- **Speech:** (Proverbs 12:23; 18:2)

  The fool _____

  The wise _____

- **Humility:** (Proverbs 18:12; 21:24)

  The fool _____

  The wise _____

THE WISDOM OF CHRIST

Solomon is associated with wisdom, but even he had his failings, as the end of his reign revealed (1 Kings 11:1-13). When Jesus debated with the Pharisees, He told them that a *"greater than Solomon"* was in their midst (Matthew 12:42). As Christians we have the blessing of being united to Christ *"in whom are hidden all the treasures of wisdom and knowledge."* (Colossians 2:3) As God remakes us into the image of Christ, He grants us the wisdom we need by the Spirit of Christ. The following list contains ten traits which mark the wise living of a person who is faithfully following Jesus:

1. The wise fear the Lord and seek to glorify Him. (Proverbs 1:7)

2. The wise build their life upon God's Word. (Matthew 7:24-27)

3. The wise have a humble recognition of their own sins and weaknesses. (Proverbs 16:18)

4. The wise are not naïve to the wiles and failings of people. (Matthew 10:16-17; John 2:24-25)

5. The wise learn how things work in this world. (Proverbs 8:12-21)

6. The wise do not compromise morality for the sake of gain. (Proverbs 1:19)

7. The wise have control over their tongue. (James 3:2)

8. The wise trust in the Lord and not merely in human resources. (Psalm 146:3-7)

9. The wise seek the friendship and counsel of the wise. (Proverbs 13:20)

10. The wise prosper in their work. (Psalm 1:3)

HITTING HOME

1. What is your self-assessment concerning your own wisdom?

2. How does your knowledge of God's wisdom in creation affect your daily living and aid you in giving God greater glory?

3. What are important characteristics needed for you to be wiser?

4. In a practical way how can you pursue wisdom for yourself?

LESSON 27: THE LIFE OF LOVE

KEY DOCTRINE: Jesus' commandment for us to love one another is the preeminent sign of our fellowship in the gospel.

MEMORY VERSE: *"A new commandment I give to you, that you love one another: just as I have loved you, you also are to love one another. By this all people will know that you are my disciples, if you have love for one another."* (John 13:34-35)

SCRIPTURE PRE-READING: Leviticus 19:9-18; Matthew 25:31-46; 1 Corinthians 13:1-13; 1 John 4:7-21

Jesus instructs His disciples that they must love one another as He had loved them. Their love for each other would be proof positive to the world that they were disciples of Jesus. The commandment to love is not a mere sentimental notion, but it is the fulfillment of God's moral law. As believers we must demonstrate a practical care and graciousness to other members of the body of Christ. This love, in fact, is the ultimate litmus test to the reality that Christ is truly living within us.

LOVE THY NEIGHBOR

When Jesus was asked about the greatest commandment of the Law, He answered that we must love God and love our neighbor (Matthew 22:34-39). The first four of the Ten Commandments focus on our responsibility to worship God and the last six focus on our moral duty to our fellow man. Commandments five through ten provide for us the essential guidelines of how we should *love our neighbor*, for the summation of the Ten Commandments is love. *"For the commandments, 'You shall not commit adultery, You shall not murder, You shall not steal, You shall not covet,' and any other commandment, are summed up in this word: 'You shall love your neighbor as yourself.' Love does no wrong to a neighbor; therefore love is the fulfilling of the law."* (Romans 13:9-10) Irrespective of who our neighbor is these commandments are the foundation of righteous and loving conduct toward all people. It should be noted that love is not necessarily an affection felt toward people but the character of one's conduct toward them. In other words you can be loving to people you do not particularly like, in fact, you might find them unbearable. However, we are to act lovingly in that we seek their well-being and do not intend them evil or harm.

God has commanded us to live in a righteous and loving manner because He Himself is abundant in mercy and grace. Whether it is God declaring His character to Moses on Mt. Sinai (Exodus 34:6-7), David singing His praises in the Psalms (Psalm 36:5), or Jonah complaining on the hill outside Nineveh (Jonah 4:2), the Bible consistently describes God as being abundant in love and faithfulness. If we are to be a people who walk with God, then we need to be prepared to love like God. *"He has told you, O man, what is good; and what does the LORD require of you but to do justice, and to love kindness [or steadfast love], and to walk humbly with your God"* (Micah 6:8) and as Jesus said, *"Be merciful, even as your Father is merciful."* (Luke 6:36) In Jesus' rebukes of the Pharisees He asserted that mercy was the preeminent characteristic of true religion, not outward observance and ritual, *"Go and learn what this means, 'I desire mercy, and not sacrifice.'"* (Matthew 9:13; see also Matthew 12:7 and 23:23)

THE GREATEST LOVE OF ALL

In Jesus' final discourse He instructed His disciples that they must love one another just as He had loved them. This love for one another will show the world that they truly are His followers (John 13:34-35). Jesus took the commandment to love as established in the Old Testament law and argued its importance within the New Testament church. Two aspects of this commandment in John 13:34 are noteworthy: *"As I have loved you"* and *"one another"* (John 13:34).

As I Have Loved You: The standard by which we are to love one another has been set by Christ's life and death. First John 3:16 says, *"By this we know love, that he laid down his life for us, and we ought to lay down our lives for the brothers."* The kind of love we are to have is a sacrificial love that is based upon grace. Jesus did not die for the righteous, but rather He laid down His life for sinners. Therefore, our love for the "sinful brethren" needs to express a graciousness which is long-suffering, forgiving, and delights in showing mercy. The ability to be gracious to one another is vital, for without it our relationships will break down under the weight of our mutual sin. When we consider how much we have been forgiven by God we should be motivated to forgive others.

One Another: This gracious love is to be shown especially to fellow believers. In those passages that contain commandments to love *"one another"* (Romans 12:10; Ephesians 4:32; 1 Peter 4:8), the *"one another"* references are to the family of believers and not to humanity as a whole. We who have God's Spirit dwelling within us will have a compulsion to be affectionate toward other people who have the same Spirit. As we love one another the world will see the love that the Father has for His children. Two major characteristics of Jesus' love that we need to show to other believers are *care* and *grace*. In what ways are we to demonstrate love to one another as commanded in the following passages?

- **Care:** A focus on the needs of others.

    Acts 4:32-37 _____

    Romans 12:3-13 _____

    Philippians 2:1-5 _____

- **Grace:** A willingness to love people even through their failings.

    Matthew 18:15-35 _____

    1 Corinthians 13:4-7 _____

    Ephesians 4:29-32 _____

THE LITMUS TEST

Our obedience to Jesus' commandment to love is not optional. It is the ultimate litmus test that we are saved. If a person is unwilling or unable to love another believer it is evidence that they are not in Christ. *"We know that we have passed out of death into life, because we love the brothers. Whoever does not love abides in death"* (1 John 3:14) and *"Anyone who does not love does not know God, because God is love."* (1 John 4:8) Our ability to love one another is rooted in our experience of God's saving love upon us; therefore we will demonstrate this love to other believers (1 John 4:19). Jesus taught in the Sermon on the Mount that the person who hates, slanders, or accuses is tantamount to a murderer and *"will be liable to the hell of fire."* (Matthew 5:22)

In the parable of the sheep and the goats (Matthew 25:31-46), Jesus taught that our final destination is determined by whether or not we demonstrate love toward the body of Christ. Whenever we care for believers we are actually caring for Jesus Himself, since believers are all members of the body of Christ. Likewise, if we neglect to love believers we are neglecting to love Jesus. At first glance it might seem that Jesus is teaching that we are justified by our works, but He is not. We are not justified by works of love, rather our works of love demonstrate the genuineness of our salvation. *"What good is it, my brothers, if someone says he has faith but does not have works? Can that faith save him?...So also faith by itself, if it does not have works, is dead."* (James 2:14, 17) Without love we are nothing, *"if I have all faith, so as to remove mountains, but have not love, I am nothing."* (1 Corinthians 13:2) Of the three great virtues, faith, hope, and love, *"the greatest of these is love."* (1 Corinthians 13:13)

HITTING HOME

1. In what ways do you show mercy to people outside the faith which demonstrates the mercy of God?

2. Give an example of a time you experienced love from within the body of Christ?

3. How can you move your relationships in the church from the merely friendly to genuinely loving?

4. What practical efforts will you take to shown a sacrificial care for the interests of other believers?

5. What relationships with believers do you have which are requiring much grace on your part? How can Christ's love commandment be obeyed in this relationship?

LESSON 28: HOLINESS

KEY DOCTRINE: We are called to pursue holiness, without which we will not enter God's presence.
MEMORY VERSE: *"As obedient children, do not be conformed to the passions of your former ignorance, but as he who called you is holy, you also be holy in all your conduct"* (1 Peter 1:14-15)
SCRIPTURE PRE-READING: Exodus 20:1-21; Psalm 51; Mark 7:14-23; Colossians 3:1-17; 2 Peter 1:3-11

When God saves us He calls us to enter into fellowship with Him. As God is holy we are also called to live in a holy manner. We are to put off the practices of our former lifestyle and put on the new practices consistent with Jesus Christ. This commandment to live a godly life assumes that God's grace through the Holy Spirit will grant us the power to fulfill this obligation. However, there is also an expectation that we will deliberately make every effort to act in ways that are pleasing to God. Without some level of sanctification there can be no assurance that we will be in heaven some day.

MAKE EVERY EFFORT

Some of us may initially object to working on our holiness, but the Bible plainly instructs us to put effort into being holy. We might say, "I am a totally depraved sinner saved by grace. I can't make myself holy!" This statement is only partially true--we are sinful. However, our depravity does not negate the clear imperatives of Jesus and the apostles for us to live holy lives. Jesus commands us to *"sin no more."* (John 5:14; 8:11) The apostles exhort us to put off the *"old self"* of sin and put on the *"new self"* in Christ (Ephesians 4:22-24; Colossians 3:9-10). We are commanded to *"work out your own salvation with fear and trembling"* (Philippians 2:12), to *"make every effort to supplement your faith with virtue"* (2 Peter 1:5), and that we should live holy lives because God is holy (1 Peter 1:12-15). We cannot use the doctrine of depravity as an excuse to ignore the Bible's commandments to put effort into living according to the righteous calling of God.

The kind of effort that we are to put into our holiness primarily involves the regular use of the ordinary means of God's grace. Within the fellowship of God's people we hear the Word of God and partake of the Lord's Supper. The people of God encourage us and keep us accountable in our doctrine and practice. The regular exposure to the Word of God reproves, corrects, and trains us in righteousness. As the Lord convicts us of sin we should be quick to confess. *"I acknowledged my sin to you, and I did not cover my iniquity; I said, 'I will confess my transgressions to the LORD,' and you forgave the iniquity of my sin."* (Psalm 32:5) Our prayer protects us from temptation and restores our soul when we falter.

GRACE PRECEDES WORKS

We are able to *work out* our salvation because God is working in us by His Holy Spirit. Grace always precedes and empowers the good works of believers. The *grace precedes works* principle is shown throughout the Bible. The Ten Commandments open with a declaration of God's saving acts to Israel before God calls them to obey Him. The Epistles generally begin with a discussion of the grace we have in Jesus, and then follow with instructions about godly living. The order is paramount in importance; if we were to switch the order to *works precedes grace*, then we would fall into a deadly legalism. Second Peter 1:3-11 helps us understand how the grace of God has preceded and enabled us to participate in His holiness. Read 2 Peter 1:3-11 and answer the following questions.

- In verses 3-4 list the ways in which God has enabled us to be holy.

- How does God's grace and promises motivate us to make efforts at our own righteousness?

- List the types of godly characteristics we are called to add to our lives. (v. 5-7)

- What are the benefits to our life and our faith that come from godly living? (v. 8-11)

THE OLD AND NEW WAYS

Since God has called us to holiness, it is necessary that we put off the ways of our old self and put on the new ways of Christ. The Bible contains several passages which group words that describe both sin and righteousness (see Romans 1:29-31 and Galatians 5:16-25). The following comparison/contrast will help us in our task to replace the sins of our *"old self"* with the righteousness of the *"new self"* (Colossians 3:9-10):

PUT OFF SINFULNESS	PUT ON GODLINESS
Lusts: sexual sins, drunkenness, covetousness, greed, pride, ambition, power	**Self-Control:** purity, self-denial, patience, speech control, temperance, humility
Hurtful Relationships: enmity, strife, dissensions, divisions, jealousy, envy, rivalries, vengeance, false testimony, gossip	**Healthy Relationships**: kindness, generosity, love, hospitality, peaceful, affection, forgiveness, trust, submission, sharing
Deceptiveness: lying**,** false testimony, charm, deception, false promises, unreliability, stealing	**Integrity:** truthfulness, dependability, goodness, faithfulness
Hatefulness: hate, fits of anger, unforgiving, maliciousness, bitterness, cynicism, criticalness	**Gracefulness:** love, joy, peace, gentleness, patience, faithfulness, hope

The challenge with the process of sanctification is in the *how* to put off sins and put on righteousness. The first step requires having a sober-minded humility and honesty regarding our own sins. The Word of God and the Holy Spirit will reveal the areas in our life that need changing. Once we identify our sins, we should examine all that the Scripture says on the subject and have a holy determination to change. We confess and pray for God's grace and then see how, by faith, we can gain victory in this area of sin. Wisdom also dictates that we should seek godly counsel and accountability.

NO HOLINESS, NO HEAVEN

The Bible teaches that only the righteous will go to heaven. If we claim to have faith in Christ yet there has been no transformation of our character, we should not presume on entering Christ's presence when we die. It is not that our works will save us, but that sanctification always accompanies genuine justifying faith. God's purpose in salvation is to prepare a people who are fit for His holy presence and to whom He will say, *"Well done, good and faithful servant...enter into the joy of your master."* (Matthew 25:23) The following warnings should dispel any misconceptions about the necessity for our holiness:

- *"Strive for peace with everyone, and for the holiness without which no one will see the Lord."* (Hebrews 12:14)

- *"Or do you not know that the unrighteous will not inherit the kingdom of God? Do not be deceived: neither the sexually immoral, nor idolaters, nor adulterers, nor men who practice homosexuality, nor thieves, nor the greedy, nor drunkards, nor revilers, nor swindlers will inherit the kingdom of God."* (1 Corinthians 6:9-10)

- The parable of the wise and wicked servants. (Matthew 24:45-51)

Living righteously in Christ grants us the blessing of having a greater assurance of our salvation and hope of heaven. Though the doctrines of election and justification are the final grounds for our assurance of heaven, the experience of sanctification in our life strengthens our confidence that we are truly God's children and heirs of salvation. As we become diligent to make our *"calling and election sure"* (2 Peter 1:10) we are providing for ourselves a rich *"entrance into the eternal kingdom of our Lord and Savior Jesus Christ."* (2 Peter 1:11)

HITTING HOME

1. Discuss the importance of the, *grace precedes works* doctrine.

2. How does growing in holiness help our assurance of salvation?

3. Using the list under **THE OLD AND NEW WAYS** section, which characteristics "jump out at you" as particularly needing work in your personal transformation?

4. Make a game plan! How can you put off your old self with its specific sins, and put on the new self?

LESSON 29: SEXUAL PURITY

KEY DOCTRINE: God has called believers to enjoy sex within the covenant of marriage and resist sexual immorality in its various forms.

MEMORY VERSE: *"Flee from sexual immorality. Every other sin a person commits is outside the body, but the sexual immoral person sins against his own body."* (1 Corinthians 6:18)

SCRIPTURE PRE-READING: Leviticus 18:6-23; Song of Solomon 4:1-16; Matthew 5:27-30; 1 Corinthians 6:12-20; 1 Thessalonians 4:1-8

God created sex to be enjoyed by a husband and wife within the marriage covenant. After the fall mankind perverted this gift through a multitude of sexual sins which God will judge. As Christians we are called to put off all forms of sexual immorality and live self-controlled lives. Sexual sins are dangerous for both our body and our soul, as our eternal destiny is dependent on our living a holy life. We should make every effort to guard against all sexual temptations in our life.

NAKED AND WITHOUT SHAME

Contrary to what the world thinks, God is not against sex. He invented sex. We are the ones who have perverted it. He created men and women, and He created their bodies to enjoy the pleasure of sex. The very first chapters of the Bible give the account of the way sex was meant to be. Before we examine and learn about the sinful perversion of sex it is best to have a healthy understanding of what God originally intended. Read Genesis 2:18-25 and answer the following questions.

- Was the man complete without the women? Was God not enough? (v. 18-20)

- What is the significance of the woman coming from the rib of the man? (v. 21-23)

- In what way can a man and woman become *"one flesh"*?

- Why did they not know shame? How can we experience that today?

God created sex to exist within the marriage covenant between a man and a woman. The pleasure of sex that exists within marriage is based upon the relationship of trust and commitment to one another, wherein the man and the woman emotionally and spiritually know each other intimately. The sexual act is the expression of this love that exists between them. The expectation for a marriage is that sex should only get better with time and should be a continual and frequent experience (1 Corinthians 7:5). As the love and intimacy deepens between the husband and wife, in the sexual act they will experience the blessings of God who says, *"Eat, friends, drink, and be drunk with love!"* (Song of Solomon 5:1) Sex is also the natural means of procreation which fulfills God's commandment to *"Be fruitful and multiply and fill the earth"* (Genesis 1:28). Within this framework of love and procreation God looked down at His creation of the man and the women and said that it was *"very good."* (Genesis 1:31)

THOU SHALT NOT...

The seventh commandment in the Ten Commandments says, *"You shall not commit adultery."* (Exodus 20:14) This simple sentence (in the Hebrew only two words: "No adultery!") is the prohibition in the law against all forms of sexual sin. The law is prohibiting, not just adultery, but all associated sexual sins. In other passages the Bible specifically chronicles the multitude of these sexual perversions:
- **Adultery** (Genesis 39:6-10; 2 Samuel 11:1-5; Hebrews 13:4)
- **Incest** (Genesis 19:30-38; Leviticus 18:6-18)
- **Homosexuality** (Genesis 19:4-11; Leviticus 18:22; Romans 1:26-27; 1 Corinthians 6:9)
- **Bestiality** (Leviticus 18:23)
- **Promiscuity and Orgies** (Romans 13:13; Galatians 5:19; 1 Thessalonians 4:3-6)
- **Prostitution** (Genesis 38:12-26; Leviticus 19:29; 1 Corinthians 6:15-16)
- **Rape** (Genesis 34:2; Deuteronomy 22:25-27; Judges 19:22-26; 2 Samuel 13:7-17)

The Bible is clearly not naïve about mankind's sexual perversions. More than anyone, Jesus understood the heart of man and the intention of God's law. Even if we have not outwardly committed any of the above acts, we have sinned when our hearts lust in any way. Jesus warned us, *"everyone who looks at a woman with lustful intent has already committed adultery with her in his heart."* (Matthew 5:27). For this reason we must guard our hearts against sexual inclinations and lusts. When we indulge in any form of pornography or voyeurism we are allowing sexual sin to grow in our heart. Eventually we will not be satisfied with images alone. *"But each person is tempted when he is lured and enticed by his own desire. Then desire when it has conceived gives birth to sin, and sin when it is fully grown brings forth death."* (James 1:14-15)

A Stern Warning

The world scoffs saying, "What is the big deal about sex? It's only a physical thing." Sexual sin is a sin against the body, and sins against our body also damage our souls and emotions (1 Corinthians 6:18). When people turn away from God they tend to head down the road of sexual sin. In passages where ungodliness is described, sexual immorality is always at the forefront (Romans 1:24-27; 13:13; 1 Corinthians 6:9-10; Galatians 5:19-21; Colossians 3:5-6; 1 Thessalonians 4:3-8; 1 Peter 4:2-4).

Whenever the apostles challenged believers to live a holy life they always challenge them to put away sexual immorality. To live a holy life requires that we exercise bodily self-control of our passions. Though the world rejoices in sexual perversion we must recognize how damaging sexual sin is to our lives. At the human level sexual sins lead to emotional damage, broken families, and violence against men, women and children. At the spiritual level our eternal destinies are at stake. The Bible clearly warns that the call of God requires us to abstain from sexual sins:

"For you know what instructions we gave you through the Lord Jesus. For this is the will of God, your sanctification: that you abstain from sexual immorality; that each one of you know how to control his own body in holiness and honor, not in the passion of lust like the Gentiles who do not know God; that no one transgress and wrong his brother in this matter, because the Lord is an avenger in all these things, as we told you beforehand and solemnly warned you. For God has not called us for impurity, but in holiness." (1 Thessalonians 4:2-7)

Similar Bible passages state that those who engage in sexual sins will incur the wrath of God and be excluded from heaven (Ephesians 5:5-6; Hebrews 12:14-16; Revelation 21:8; 22:15). Do we recognize the danger of our sexual lusts and put them to death, or do we allow them to have a continual home in our life? Jesus challenged His disciples to be willing to even cut off body parts to get rid of sin (Matthew 5:30). This hyperbolic exhortation of Jesus should impress upon us the importance of making every effort to uproot sexual sin and save our souls from hell.

Helpful Advice
* Recognize that indulging in sexual lust never satisfies.
* Sexual sins can never replace true love and intimacy in a marriage.
* Sexual immorality always brings shame and guilt.
* Pride often fuels much of our sexual desire.
* The damages of sexual sins far outweigh the pleasures.
* Smaller sexual sins will escalate to greater perversions.
* Never "dabble" in sexual temptation--you will eventually give in.

Hitting Home

1. Are there areas in your life where you are allowing sexual sin to foster and gain control? For example: the internet, relationships at work, television and movies, bars and night clubs. How can you protect yourself?

2. Do you fear God and the consequences that will come by allowing sexual immorality to exist in your life? How does your fear of God help you to flee sexual immorality?

3. What are the prerequisites to a healthy and fun sex life?

4. Why does sex within a marriage bring glory to God?

LESSON 30: PRAYER

KEY DOCTRINE: Prayer is our communication with God whereby we offer up to God praise, thanksgiving, petitions and confessions according to His will.

MEMORY VERSE: *"do not be anxious about anything, but in everything by prayer and supplication with thanksgiving let your requests be made known to God."* (Philippians 4:6)

SCRIPTURE PRE-READING: Psalm 34 and 116; Matthew 6:5-15; Luke 11:1-13; 18:1-8; James 5:13-18

Prayer is essential for the Christian life. Unfortunately our prayer life often feels inadequate. In prayer we confess our sins, give thanks and praise, and make requests to God for His hand of blessing in our life. God is pleased when we pray because prayer demonstrates our trust in Him and manifests the power of God as He glorifies Himself through His deliverance. The Bible gives us many instructions on how to pray, what to pray for, and the need to stay persistent in our prayers.

TEACH US TO PRAY

Once when Jesus had finished praying His disciples asked Him to teach them how to pray (Luke 11:1). To their credit the disciples recognized the great difference between their own prayer life and that of Jesus. If we are honest we will admit that we are also not very good at praying. Prayer is often our last resort. When we do pray our thoughts wander and daydream, we lose focus and endurance, and we lack confidence that God is going to answer our requests. There is not a magic formula to good prayer--it must be something we do and in which we must grow. The Bible does give us instructions about prayer that should serve as encouragement and guidance for us.

THE LORD'S PRAYER

Jesus taught his disciples a format for praying in Matthew 6:9-13 (see also Luke 11:2-4):
"Our Father in heaven, hallowed be your name.
Your kingdom come, your will be done, on earth as it is in heaven.
Give us this day our daily bread,
and forgive us our debts, as we also have forgiven our debtors.
And lead us not into temptation, but deliver us from evil."

Exercise: Study each of the five lines in the Lord's Prayer and answer the following questions.

- What is the focus of the first line of the Lord's Prayer? What does it mean that God's name should be *"hallowed"*?

- What should be our heart's desire and prayer in respect to God's kingdom on the earth? What does that mean practically?

- What is our expectation and attitude to God's *"daily bread"* in our life? Does this only refer to food?

- What is the significance of forgiveness in our lives as believers? Why should we pray for this?

- Does God tempt us? What are we praying for in respect to evil and temptation?

GOD'S PLEASURE IN OUR PRAYER

How does God regard our prayers? It is tempting to think that God expects self-sufficiency from us and that our continual petitions quickly become annoying to Him. However, the Bible consistently describes God as being pleased when His children cry out to Him. *"The eyes of the LORD are toward the righteous and his ears toward their cry"* and *"The LORD is near to the brokenhearted and saves the crushed in spirit."* (Psalm 34:15, 18) Integral to our relationship with God is an honest line of communication where we can pour out our hearts to our heavenly Father. The Bible goes even further to exhort us, *"casting all your anxieties on him, because he cares for you"* (1 Peter 5:7) and *"do not be anxious about anything, but in everything by prayer and supplication with thanksgiving let your requests be made known to God."* (Philippians 4:6) As God's children we have the privilege to call upon our Father and we can have the confidence that He is compassionate concerning our needs.

When we call upon the Lord it gives Him pleasure because our prayers reveal our trust in His steadfast love. *"His delight is not in the strength of the horse, nor his pleasure in the legs of a man, but the LORD takes pleasure in those who fear him, in those who hope in his steadfast love."* (Psalm 147:10-11) Our own strength does not please God, but our trust and confidence that He is willing and able to deliver us does please Him. Prayer is the expression of our *"hope in his steadfast love."* For this reason the Lord often brings trials into our lives which overwhelm and compel us to cry out to Him. In our times of need God is most pleased with us when we trust in His power and glorify Him for His deliverance.

APPROPRIATE ATTITUDES OF PRAYER

What kinds of attitudes should we adopt as we enter into prayer? The following is a list of biblical characteristics of appropriate attitudes in prayer:

- **Genuine**: Prayer is not for show to impress anyone (Matthew 6:5). It need not be formal, as if high vocabulary will incline God to listen. Our prayer must be honest as God is the searcher of hearts. We should not hold back our confession of sin, praises, fears, frustrations and desires; He already knows them.

- **Faith**: When we pray we must believe that we are truly speaking with God and He is there with us listening. We are not talking into thin air but to our all-powerful God. He can do the impossible if He so pleases. We should expect that if we ask and knock our loving, heavenly Father will give us good gifts and open doors (Luke 11:9-13).

- **Persistent:** We can easily lose heart and give up in our prayers. Jesus taught that we should always persist in prayer (Luke 11:5-8; 18:1-8). Persistent prayer tests if we actually believe that God is in control and that His heart is predisposed to bless us. To *"pray without ceasing"* (1 Thessalonians 5:17) is to maintain our prayer life in the face of all adversity and disappointment.

- **Spirit-Filled:** God has given us His Spirit who intercedes to the Father on our behalf through our prayers. He directs us to pray according to God's will and gives us the fervor of heart to cry out during hard times. At times the Spirit is praying through our heart's groaning (Romans 8:23-27).

Scripture states that if we pray according to God's will we can have the confidence that He hears us and our prayers will be answered (1 John 5:14-15). While we cannot know the often mysterious plans of our sovereign God, we can through knowing the Scriptures understand His prescribed will. As our grasp of the Bible increases we will understand God's will better and pray more often in the Spirit. As we pray we will find that God conforms our hearts to His will so that we ask for things pleasing to Him.

A helpful aid for our prayer life is a prayer journal to write down prayer requests and praises. This will chronicle and build a written history of God's mighty deeds in our life. Written prayer requests can also help guide our thoughts as we pray. Over time we will be able to see how God responded to all our requests and it can be a great encouragement for further prayer.

HITTING HOME

1. Over the course of a typical week, describe your prayer life?

2. Give a testimony of an instance in your life when you knew that God answered your specific prayer request?

3. What attitudes in your prayer life do you need to change?

4. What practical ways can you increase the frequency and vitality of your prayer life? (Making time, praying with others, keeping a prayer journal, etc.)

LESSON 31: MONEY MATTERS

KEY DOCTRINE: God has entrusted us with resources to use for His glory and the good of mankind.
MEMORY VERSE: *"No one can serve two masters, for either he will hate the one and love the other, or he will be devoted to the one and despise the other. You cannot serve God and money."* (Matthew 6:24)
SCRIPTURE PRE-READING: Ecclesiastes 5:10-20; Matthew 6:19-34; Luke 18:18-30; 1 Timothy 6:6-10, 17-19

How we use and work with money is a key part of our discipleship. Many times Jesus taught about the dangers of covetousness and how our life does not consist merely of our possessions. We have been called to seek God's kingdom and not just live to make money and gain security. As recipients of God's generosity we likewise need to use our resources to do good and reveal the generous nature of God to others. As we seek His kingdom God has promised to care for us as part of His covenantal faithfulness.

THE ROOT OF ALL EVILS

As a typical practice men and women go to work, earn a paycheck, and use the income to buy things. We hope to improve our lifestyle with the benefits of our new possessions. However, in the pursuit of more money we often sin by breaking the tenth commandment that forbids covetousness. Covetousness is the never-satisfied greed for more of anything. *"You shall not covet your neighbor's house; you shall not covet your neighbor's wife, or his male servant, or his female servant, or his ox, or his donkey, or anything that is your neighbor's."* (Exodus 20:17)

We might be tempted to think that covetousness is not such a dangerous sin, since it seems like just a normal desire to want more. The Bible, however, considers covetousness to be just as dangerous a sin as murder, sexual immorality, and idolatry. Jesus warned us to *"be on your guard against all covetousness"* (Luke 12:15) and told the parable of the rich fool (Luke 12:13-21) to warn us about its danger. The apostle Paul equates covetousness with idolatry (Ephesians 5:5) and argues that covetous people will not enter the kingdom of heaven.

The love of money is considered *"a root of all kinds of evils"* (1 Timothy 6:10) because covetousness draws our hearts away from the worship of God unto the worship of this world. As created beings we need the things of this world to live, but we are not to live merely for the pursuit of this world's goods. When we direct our desires to the things that we can see instead of to the eternal, invisible God our covetousness has turned into idolatry. Jesus said we cannot love God and love money at the same time--we have to pick a master (Matthew 6:24)!

SEEK YE FIRST THE KINGDOM OF GOD

Jesus commands us to seek God's kingdom and righteousness first (Matthew 6:33) and not to make the pursuit of an income and physical security our primary aim. People without faith only have one purpose on this earth--to run after obtaining as much of the world as possible. The Preacher in the book of Ecclesiastes asked the question, *"What does man gain by all the toil at which he toils under the sun?"* (Ecclesiastes 1:3) He concluded that all of mankind's labor was *"vanity of vanities!"* (Ecclesiastes 1:2) Jesus asked a similar rhetorical question, *"For what does it profit a man to gain the whole world and forfeit his soul?"* (Mark 8:36) Jesus is not teaching us that we need not work, but that our work should be for God's glory.

We all need to discover the purpose for which God created us so that our labors on this earth will further His kingdom and be eternal pursuits. The parable of the talents (Matthew 25:14-30) reveals that God grants to people resources that they are to utilize for the growth of the kingdom of God. Read Matthew 25:14-30 and answer the following questions.

- Who owns the money and talents originally?

- What expected outcome does the master want from the servants?

- What is the excuse of the man with one talent for his lack of productivity?

- What are the rewards and punishments for faithful and faithless service?

ALL THESE THINGS SHALL BE ADDED

After Jesus instructs us in Matthew 6:24 that we cannot serve God and money He goes on tell us that we should not be anxious about our material needs, for God knows our needs. These two teachings go together: not living for money and trusting God to provide for our needs. Much of our desire for more money is driven by our financial anxieties. Jesus knows that we have these anxieties, so He seeks to allay our fears by showing us the magnitude of God's care for us. *"Therefore I tell you, do not be anxious about your life, what you will eat or what you will drink, nor about your body, what you will put on. Is not life more than food, and the body more than clothing? Look at the birds of the air: they neither sow nor reap nor gather into barns, and yet your heavenly Father feeds them. Are you not of more value than they?"* (Matthew 6:25-26)

Jesus' promise of provision from our heavenly Father is not only a New Testament promise. God has faithfully cared for His people throughout the whole Bible. In the Old Testament God entered into a covenant with Israel where He pledged to protect and provide for them if they worshiped Him alone as their God. During Israel's forty-year desert wandering God provided manna from heaven (Exodus 16:35) and water from the rock (Deuteronomy 8:15). When they entered the promised land God gave them cities, houses, vineyards, cisterns--all which they did not build (Deuteronomy 6:10-11). Lest they take credit for their own prosperity, God warned Israel, *"Beware lest you say in your heart, 'My power and the might of my hand have gotten me this wealth.' You shall remember the LORD your God, for it is he who gives you power to get wealth"* (Deuteronomy 8:17). We always need to remember that the LORD is caring for our every need and give Him the credit and thanksgiving He deserves.

WISDOM WITH OUR WEALTH

As stewards of God's resources we are called to use them in a wise and profitable manner. We are not to squander our resources through foolish and covetous living. The Bible states that *"those who desire to be rich fall into temptation, into a snare, into many senseless and harmful desires that plunge people into ruin and destruction."* (1 Timothy 6:9) The desire to "get-rich-quick" often leads people away from hard work into deceptive schemes which bring about financial ruin. This lust for quick riches also leads many people into gambling at casinos and government-run lotteries (Proverbs 13:11). Our boundless covetousness has give birth to vast amounts of consumer debt that enslaves us to our debtors, *"the borrower is the slave of the lender."* (Proverbs 22:7) A wise person is content with and trusts in the Lord's daily provision, and exercises self-control over their spending habits. Wealth creation which is based upon providing goods and services, working skillfully, benefiting society, and trusting in God's providence and provision is the type of prosperity which God blesses.

All the wealth of this world can be destroyed or stolen (Matthew 6:19), so our best investment is to store our treasures in heaven. If we are faithful with the *"very little"* (Luke 16:10) that God has given us on this earth, He will give us *"much"* when we get to heaven. Faithful stewardship of our money occurs when we use our resources to show God's steadfast love in this fallen world. God's Spirit may burden us to help someone we see in need. We become a conduit of God's mercy, thereby glorifying Him with our good deeds. As we give from our means, God in turn generously provides for us. *"You will be enriched in every way to be generous in every way, which through us will produce thanksgiving to God. For the ministry of this service is not only supplying the needs of the saints but is also overflowing in many thanksgivings to God."* (2 Corinthians 9:11-12) When we are faithful stewards we discover that, *"by working hard in this way we must help the weak and remember the words of the Lord Jesus, how he himself said, 'It is more blessed to give than to receive.'"* (Acts 20:35)

HITTING HOME

1. In what ways has covetousness crept into your day-to-day living? What does your heart long for? What possessions or lifestyle activities would be the most difficult for you to give up?

2. Do you recognize that your life, possessions, body, and talents are all "on loan from God?" How does that change your perspective on how you should use all these resources?

3. How do you spend or give your money so that it glorifies God's mercy in the world?

4. How have you experienced God's faithful provision in your life when you were unable to provide for yourself?

SECTION D:

CHURCH LIFE

"There is one body and one Spirit—just as you were called to the one hope that belongs to your call—one Lord, one faith, one baptism, one God and Father of all, who is over all and through all and in all."
(Ephesians 4:4-5)

God saves individuals, but He always includes them into a group. Our Christian lives are not to be lived in isolation, but lived within the context of the church. The Lord has gifted the church with leaders who minister to us so that we can all attain *"to a mature manhood, to the measure of the stature of the fullness of Christ, so that we may no longer be children, tossed to and fro by the waves and carried about by every wind of doctrine, by human cunning, by craftiness in deceitful schemes."* (Ephesians 4:13-14) Within the church we receive the blessings of the sacraments and the continual ministry of the Word of God to build us up in our most holy faith. A benefit of being a member of the body of Christ is that other members of the body will serve us, and we are also able to serve them as God's grace ministers to us all.

Life in the church, just as in human families, can be both a pleasing and a frustrating experience. We will witness the glories of evangelism, missions, merciful benevolence, and sacrificial service. Sadly, we will also endure fighting, abuse, and compromise. Since Jesus loves His church and has promised that it will endure, we can rest secure that, even though it is deeply marred, the church will be gloriously triumphant in the end.

LESSON 32: THE CHURCH

KEY DOCTRINE: God saves people and includes them in the body of believers, the church, so that they may jointly grow into the likeness of Christ.

MEMORY VERSE: *"So then you are no longer strangers and aliens, but you are fellow citizens with the saints and members of the household of God."* (Ephesians 2:19)

SCRIPTURE PRE-READING: Deuteronomy 7:6-13; Matthew 16:13-20; Ephesians 4:1-16; 1 Timothy 3:1-15; 1 Peter 2:1-12

When God saves us He includes us in a spiritual body that stretches across the world and throughout eternity. All genuine believers enter into the body of Christ, the church, with Jesus as the head. The church is a distinct people through whom God glorifies Himself in the world. As Christians we should all be willing to publicly profess our faith in Christ and join a church. Within the context of the church we are built up in our faith, encourage one another, and receive pastoral oversight.

NOT NEGLECTING TO MEET TOGETHER

Is it necessary to be a part of a church? Sometimes we are tempted to go it alone and rely upon our own faith in Christ. The Bible does not give us the option of being a "lone ranger" Christian; we need to join and worship at a local church. *"And let us consider how to stir up one another to love and good works, not neglecting to meet together, as is the habit of some, but encouraging one another, and all the more as you see the Day drawing near."* (Hebrews 10:24-25) The Bible recognizes that it is the tendency of some people to drift away from the church, however this is a dangerous practice that will ultimately be harmful. When we were saved we were spiritually grafted into the body of Christ and together we are to encourage and spur on one another. Neglecting to come together with other believers in the fellowship of the church is foolish because doing so severs us from the vital relationships we need for our Christian growth. As an exercise read Ephesians 4:1-16 and answer the following questions.

- Why is the word *"one"* given such an emphasis? (v. 4-6)

- What is the ultimate goal of all ministry within the church? (v. 12-13)

- Describe the state of people who have not benefited from the fellowship of the church? (v. 14)

THE PEOPLE OF GOD

Not everyone who has been born is a child of God; only those who have trusted in the Lord become God's children. God's relationship with His people is a unique covenantal relationship wherein He sets them apart from the world to demonstrate what it means to know God. *"I will make my dwelling among them and walk among them, and I will be their God, and they shall be my people. Therefore go out from their midst, and be separate from them, says the LORD."* (2 Corinthians 6:16-17) God dwells in the midst of us and becomes our helper in our time of need. We, in turn, serve God by trusting Him and obeying His commandments. Our lives should reflect the holiness of the God we love. *"Keep them and do them, for that will be your wisdom and your understanding in the sight of the peoples, who, when they hear all these statutes, will say, 'Surely this great nation is a wise and understanding people.' For what great nation is there that has a god so near to it as the LORD our God is to us, whenever we call upon him?"* (Deuteronomy 4:6-7)

In the New Testament God's people are defined as those of us who have placed faith in the Son of God. At the point of regeneration the Spirit gives us life and includes us in a spiritual house (Hebrews 3:6) which is called the body of Christ. *"For just as the body is one and has many members, and all the members of the body, though many, are one body, so it is with Christ. For in one Spirit we were all baptized into one body—Jews or Greeks, slaves or free —and all were made to drink of one Spirit...Now you are the body of Christ and individually members of it."* (1 Corinthians 12:12-13, 27) If we have placed our faith in Christ, then we are a part of the body of Christ. *"And he put all things under his feet and gave him as head over all things to the church, which is his body, the fullness of him who fills all in all."* (Ephesians 1:22-23) Christ controls His church by the Holy Spirit so that each member of the body manifests Christ's glorious grace to others in the church and to the outside world (John 13:34).

THE VISIBLE VERSUS THE INVISIBLE CHURCH

Where is the church found? Is it the church buildings, or is it everyone on the membership roles of a church? In defining the church theologians have distinguished between the *visible* and *invisible* church. The *visible* church is the sum of those who have professed faith in Jesus Christ and have joined themselves to the public body of believers throughout various denominations and churches across the world. The *invisible* church is the actual number of regenerate believers joined to Christ spiritually. Though there is significant overlap, these two groups are not the same. There are many church members who do not have genuine saving faith. Likewise, there are people who are in Christ but are not on the membership roles of any church.

The visible church has always been a mixed bag. The biblical record shows that many who belonged to Israel or the New Testament church did not have real faith. *"For not all who are descended from Israel belong to Israel."* (Romans 9:6) Churches may depart from sound doctrine or be diluted with so many nonbelievers that God's blessing and presence is removed. All churches are a combination of genuine and nominal believers. Having a realistic understanding of the mixed nature of the church can protect us from either idealism or cynicism when we are confronted with problems in the visible church.

THE MARKS AND STRUCTURE OF THE CHURCH

What essentials define the visible church? Theologians have singled out three marks of the church: the *Word*, the *sacraments*, and *church discipline*. A true church must correctly preach the Bible and proclaim the gospel message about Christ. Where Christ is not preached, the church ceases to be a church. *"But even if we or an angel from heaven should preach to you a gospel contrary to the one we preach to you, let him be accursed."* (Galatians 1:8) A church must also administer baptism and the Lord's Supper in accordance with the Scriptures. Lastly, all churches must have some form of leadership that exercises pastoral oversight and discipline of the flock of God. Any Christian organization that does not fulfill these marks does not exist as a true church.

God has ordained there to be two types of officers in the church: pastors (elders) and deacons (1 Timothy 3:1-13). The qualities required of these leaders are primarily focused on godly character and faithfulness, not on worldly success or influence. The elders (pastors) provide spiritual leadership through teaching the Word, prayer, and maintaining proper conduct within the church (Acts 20:27-32). The deacons serve to meet the practical needs of the congregation (Acts 6:1-7). Each of these offices carry great honor and responsibility in the church. The church should exercise discernment in the election of officers and not expediently appoint unfit candidates (1 Timothy 3:6, 10).

Churches also vary in their organizational relationships with other churches and hierarchies. Congregational churches are formally independent but may associate voluntarily with other churches. Some churches exist within a hierarchical framework where church leaders, often called bishops, have authority over the ministers in churches at the local level. Another form of church government is the presbyterian model where elders from the local churches collectively provide oversight of the doctrine, the ministers, and the practices of the church.

The church is the bride of Christ, but she is far from ready to see her Savior. No single church on this planet is perfect. The adage goes, "The church is not a museum of saints but a hospital for sinners." The Lord loves, and He died for His church so we too should have an affection for the church and look to serve her. May we have the same heart toward God's people as King David did when he sang, *"As for the saints in the land, they are the excellent ones, in whom is all my delight."* (Psalm 16:3)

HITTING HOME

1. Are you a member of a church? If not, why not?

2. How are you showing Christ's mercies and encouragement to people in your church?

3. Do you see your church and yourself living any differently from the world of non-believers around you?

4. How have you come into contact with false believers or hurtful saints in the church?

5. Pastoral care and discipline has fallen by the wayside in many churches. How valuable or important do you think pastoral care and discipline is for the well-being of the church?

LESSON 33: BAPTISM

KEY DOCTRINE: Baptism is a sign and seal of entry into the visible church and being united to Christ with all of the benefits of His grace.

MEMORY VERSE: *"And Peter said to them, 'Repent and be baptized every one of you in the name of Jesus Christ for the forgiveness of your sins, and you will receive the gift of the Holy Spirit.'"* (Acts 2:38)

SCRIPTURE PRE-READING: Matthew 28:16-20; Acts 2:36-41; 8:26-40; 16:25-34; Colossians 2:8-14

Baptism is one of the two sacraments of the New Testament church. Baptism marks the entry of a believer into the visible church of Jesus Christ. Christ commanded His apostles to make disciples and baptize them in the name of the Father, the Son, and the Holy Spirit. Christian baptism is a sign and seal of the spiritual realities and blessings of forgiveness, purification, rebirth and being united with Christ.

GET BAPTIZED

Oftentimes people who profess faith in Jesus neglect being baptized. They wonder why they need to. After all, we are saved by faith, so of what benefit is this external ritual? It is true that the act of baptism does not, in and of itself, save people, and one can go to heaven without being baptized (Luke 23:40-43 the thief on the cross). However, we should be careful about having a flippant attitude to one of the two mandated sacraments of the New Testament church. If Jesus and the apostles commanded us to believe in Christ *and* be baptized, then there is no option--we must be baptized!

- *"Go therefore and make disciples of all nations, baptizing them in the name of the Father and of the Son and of the Holy Spirit."* (Matthew 28:19)

- *"And Peter said to them, 'Repent and be baptized every one of you in the name of Jesus Christ for the forgiveness of your sins, and you will receive the gift of the Holy Spirit.'"* (Acts 2:38)

We should also observe that in the book of Acts the administration of baptism was never delayed. The believers at Pentecost (Acts 2:41), the Ethiopian eunuch (Acts 8:36-38), the apostle Paul (Acts 9:18), Cornelius the gentile (Acts 10:47), and the Philippian jailer (Acts 16:33) were all baptized immediately upon believing in Jesus. Thus, there is no legitimate excuse for procrastinating being baptized if we have placed faith in Christ.

In order for a baptism to be considered a legitimate Christian baptism three components are necessary. First, a minister needs to perform the baptism (Acts 10:47). Secondly, water must be applied to the person being baptized since it represents the cleansing of sins by Christ (Acts 8:36). How the water is applied varies among denominations; some churches require full immersion and other churches may simply sprinkle or pour the water. Thirdly, with the application of the water the minister needs to baptize the person *"in the name of the Father and of the Son and of the Holy Spirit"* (Matthew 28:19).

THE BENEFITS OF BAPTISM

Baptism is often described as being a *sign* and *seal* of all the benefits of being in Christ. The sacrament of baptism has a meaning built into it through the visible symbols of water being applied to the repentant sinner. The following benefits are communicated to us, the church, and the world when baptism is administrated. All of these blessings are related as they express the grace of the gospel:

- **Forgiveness of Sins**: Peter preached in Acts 2:38 that people should *"be baptized every one of you in the name of Jesus Christ for the forgiveness of your sins."* In the new covenant God promised *"I will forgive their iniquity, and I will remember their sin no more."* (Jeremiah 31:34) With Jesus' death, burial, and resurrection God has provided a perfect atonement and forgiveness of sins for all who by faith trust in the grace of Jesus.

- **Washed by the Spirit:** The key element in baptism is water. Water represents the washing away of sins by the grace of the Holy Spirit, *"he saved us, not because of works done by us in righteousness, but according to his own mercy, by the washing of regeneration and renewal of the Holy Spirit."* (Titus 3:5) The Spirit is the cleansing agent of our souls and consciences (1 Peter 3:21) as the power of Christ's atonement is applied to us when we are born again.

• **New Creation:** When we are born again the Spirit does a *"washing of regeneration"* (Titus 3:5). Regeneration is a synonym for being *"born again"* (John 3:3) or created anew spiritually. *"Therefore, if anyone is in Christ, he is a new creation. The old has passed away; behold, the new has come."* (2 Corinthians 5:17) The Christian life is not reforming ourselves or changing our lifestyle but becoming a completely new person.

• **United with Christ**: In baptism we show our complete identification and unity with Jesus Christ. We are His disciples now and we are displaying our allegiance. Baptism displays that our very lives represent Christ living in us. *"I have been crucified with Christ. It is no longer I who live, but Christ who lives in me. And the life I now live in the flesh I live by faith in the Son of God, who loved me and gave himself for me."* (Galatians 2:20) Paul understood that our baptism was our being united to Christ in His crucifixion and burial so that Christ's resurrection would give us new life (Romans 6:3-6).

WHO SHOULD BE BAPTIZED?

When a person comes to faith in Christ they need to be baptized. Baptism is the outward sign of our reception into the visible church of Jesus Christ, and we are no longer considered to be outside the family of God. As a result, we come under the care and authority of the leadership of the church. What about the children of believers? Should they be baptized also, or should they wait until they are older and profess faith in Jesus themselves? The Christian church, at present, differs on this issue of when baptism should be administered:

• **Believer's Baptism:** Those who hold to a believer's baptism position state that only those who confess faith in Christ should be eligible for baptism. Since babies do not have knowledge and faith they should not be baptized. They believe that the realities and benefits that baptism symbolize, such as forgiveness of sins, regeneration, and unity with Christ have not happened in the child, thus they should not receive a sign indicating such. Believer baptism proponents assert that in the book of Acts there is no record of an infant being baptized. Instead of baptizing babies some churches will have a dedication service where the parents promise to raise their children up in the Lord with the hope that God will bring their children to faith.

• **Infant Baptism:** Those who baptize their children do so, not because they believe that the act of baptism saves the child, or that they are already saved, but because they are following the commandment to include their children into the covenant community of believers. Infant baptizers hold that the Old Testament requirement of circumcision corresponds to New Testament baptism (Colossians 2:11-12). Both symbolized justification by faith and both were applied to the children of believers. The parents of baptized children embrace God's promise that He loves their children--even to a thousand generations (Exodus 20:6). They trust that God will cause all the blessings that baptism represents to be fulfilled in their children's lives by the working of the Holy Spirit and in accordance with the counsel of God.

All believers should seek to be baptized, and to witness a baptism is a joyful occasion when we consider that we too were saved only by the grace of God. How humbling to our souls it is when we contemplate that we were lost and blind, but now God has washed, forgiven, and given us all new lives. *"And such were some of you. But you were washed, you were sanctified, you were justified in the name of the Lord Jesus Christ and by the Spirit of our God."* (1 Corinthians 6:11)

HITTING HOME

1. Have you been baptized? If not, what are you waiting for? Talk to the leadership of your church, give testimony to your faith, and get it done!

2. What was the occasion of your own baptism?

3. What aspects of the benefits of baptism mean the most to you?

4. How can you gain assurance in your faith from your baptism?

LESSON 34: THE LORD'S SUPPER

KEY DOCTRINE: Jesus instituted the Lord's Supper as a continual sacrament to strengthen believers in the grace of God.

MEMORY VERSE: *"So Jesus said to them, 'Truly, truly, I say to you, unless you eat the flesh of the Son of Man and drink his blood, you have no life in you."* (John 6:53)

SCRIPTURE PRE-READING: Exodus 12:43-13:16; Luke 22:7-23; John 6:22-59; 1 Corinthians 5:6-8; 10:14-22; 11:17-34

The Lord Jesus, on the night He was betrayed, instituted the Lord's Supper as a continual remembrance of His death and spiritual nourishment for our souls. The bread and the cup represent the great atoning work of the cross that Jesus achieved for His people. As we partake by faith in what Jesus has done for us in the gospel we receive more grace from the Spirit of Christ.

THE PASSOVER

Israel in the Old Testament had an annual feast of the Unleavened Bread (Exodus 12:43-13:16) which celebrated the great redemptive event of the Passover and the exodus from Egypt. Each year the nation of Israel remembered how God had delivered them from their bondage of slavery in Egypt and brought them forth as a free people to worship Him. The physical deliverance from the slavery of Egypt was a sign pointing to their greater spiritual deliverance from the darkness of sin into the truth of God's law and grace.

On the night on which Jesus was betrayed He instituted the Lord's Supper as a continuation of the redemptive theme of deliverance from the bondage of sin. *"For Christ, our Passover lamb, has been sacrificed."* (1 Corinthians 5:7) At the Passover, God's angel had destroyed the firstborn of all who had not put the blood of the lamb on their doorposts. In the New Testament, God's firstborn Son was slain as a lamb and His blood was placed over believers. Jesus knew that He was going to provide the deliverance from sin, death, and the devil, so He instituted a perpetual sign that remembered His work on the cross.

IN A WORTHY MANNER

The apostle Paul instructed the church of Corinth the importance of partaking of the Lord's Supper in a worthy manner. He taught them what Jesus had said and done on that night of His last Passover meal:

"For I received from the Lord what I also delivered to you, that the Lord Jesus on the night when he was betrayed took bread, and when he had given thanks, he broke it, and said, 'This is my body which is for you. Do this in remembrance of me.' In the same way also he took the cup, after supper, saying 'This cup is the new covenant in my blood. Do this, as often as you drink it, in remembrance of me.' For as often as you eat this bread and drink the cup, you proclaim the Lord's death until he comes." (1 Corinthians 11:23-26)

The two elements of the meal, the bread and the cup, both point to His death on the cross and the life that Jesus gives to a believer. Bread is a life-sustaining food which feeds our bodies. Jesus' body, given for us, is the Spirit-empowered life that gives our spirits new life. *"I am the living bread that came down from heaven. If anyone eats of this bread, he will live forever. And the bread that I will give for the life of the world is my flesh."* (John 6:51) The cup represents the blood of Jesus, shed for the forgiveness of sins for His people. Without the shedding of blood there is no forgiveness, so Jesus' blood was the perfect sacrifice accomplished in heaven that provided atonement for our sin (Hebrews 10:14-18).

Interpretation Exercise: Read 1 Corinthians 11:17-34 and answer the following questions.

- What were the problems occurring during the Corinthian Lord's Supper feasts? (v. 17-22, 33-34)

- What kind of self-examination should we do before we eat? (v. 27-29)

- What are the potential consequences of improper partaking of the Supper? (v. 29-32)

THIS IS MY BODY

A debate that has continued since the days of the Reformation is the question of how present is Jesus at the Lord's Supper. The Roman Catholic Church upholds a view of *transubstantiation*, which purports that the bread and wine turn into the actual body and blood of Jesus. Lutherans hold that Jesus is *with* the elements (*consubstantiation*). Some Protestants hold a view that Jesus is not present in any way at the meal; it is a mere memorial service. Those of the Reformed tradition maintain that Jesus is present spiritually at the meal through the Holy Spirit, and His grace is experienced by those who partake with faith.

At the core of this debate is the question of how God grants grace to the people who partake of the meal. Those who fall into the error of thinking that the sacraments work in and of themselves (*ex opere operato*) will downplay the necessity of faith in the participant. However, faith is the primary element in the effectiveness of the Lord's Supper. The people who understand who Jesus is and what He has done on the cross to achieve atonement for them will receive blessings from the Holy Spirit when they eat of the Supper. The Holy Spirit uses our remembrance of Christ's death to confer the blessings of Christ on us as we eat and drink. Just as our bodies need food and drink to live, our spirits need the body and blood of Christ to persevere in faith throughout our days in this fallen world.

All churches agree that the Lord's Supper is a continuing and repeated sacrament for the edification of Christians. However, they do not agree on how frequent communion should be celebrated. Some churches partake of the meal at every Lord's Day service, others hold communion only once, or four times a year. Those who advocate more frequent observance of the Lord's Supper argue God's people need its edification on a regular basis. Churches which observe communion less frequently do so in order to maintain its special importance and reverence in the life of the church. They fear that a weekly observance would make the meal a routine, and that God's people will simply be "going through the motions" in their participation. The Scriptures do not prescribe how frequent the meal should be observed, so it is an issue which is typically left to the discretion of church leaders.

WHO COMES TO THE TABLE?

At the beginning of the Lord's Supper service the minister will often invite Christians to partake, explain what the Supper means, and "fence the table" from improper participation. The apostle Paul warned the Corinthian church that many were sick and some had died because of coming to the table in an unworthy manner (1 Corinthians 11:27-30). The primary condition for coming to the table is that we have been saved by Christ. The second condition is that we understand what the meal signifies. The elements all point back to what Christ has done on the cross and how He sustains us in our faith. For this reason children should not be allowed to partake of the table unless they have a credible confession of faith and an understanding of the symbolism of the Lord's Supper. Also, those who are under formal church discipline may be barred from the table until repentance occurs. If we feel reluctant to go to the table due to our struggle with sin then we are the perfect participant to receive grace for our time of need. That is what the Lord's Supper is for!

Since the Lord's Supper is a meal for the whole body of believers it should be celebrated as a unifying event in the church. Paul said we should celebrate *"not with the old leaven, the leaven of malice and evil, but with the unleavened bread of sincerity and truth."* (1 Corinthians 5:8) The Supper is sometimes called *Communion,* denoting that we are partaking of this meal as one body of Christ. The relational dynamics of the church are vital, so people who are at odds with other Christians in the church should, before they eat, examine their heart and seek reconciliation. The meal causes us to *look back* at what Jesus has done, but it also makes us *look forward* in hope to that great banquet in heaven when we, with all the saints, will be united in glory as we feast with our Savior and God.

HITTING HOME

1. How often does your church celebrate the Lord's Supper? How frequently do you like to partake?

2. In what way is Christ present at the Lord's Supper?

3. What aspects of the meal mean the most to you?

4. How do you feel spiritually strengthened from partaking of communion?

LESSON 35: WORSHIP

KEY DOCTRINE: The chief end of man is to glorify God and enjoy Him forever.
MEMORY VERSE: *"But the hour is coming, and is now here, when the true worshippers will worship the Father in spirit and truth, for the Father is seeking such people to worship him."* (John 4:23)
SCRIPTURE PRE-READING: Psalm 150; John 4:1-26; Acts 2:42-47; Ephesians 5:18-21; Revelation 4:1-11

God is seeking worshippers who will worship Him in Spirit and in truth. God saves us so that we will proclaim the praises of Him who has shown us grace. Each Lord's Day (Sunday) churches meet to please the Lord in their worship and to build up the saints through the Word. Worship should be done in accordance with His Word and with a spirit of reverence and joy.

THE END GOAL

God saved us for a purpose—to praise Him for His glory. We were not saved merely because of His pity or so we will not go to hell. God's primary agenda is to create worshippers who recognize and delight in His glorious goodness, grace and power. Jesus told the Samaritan woman at the well that *"the hour is coming, and is now here, when the true worshippers will worship the Father in spirit and truth, for the Father is seeking such people to worship him."* (John 4:23) God still desires today to send forth His Spirit to show mercy to sinners who will worship Him passionately and sincerely.

The Bible is full of descriptions of God's people praising Him for His marvelous deeds toward them. For example, after the crossing of the Red Sea, Moses and Miriam sang a song to the Lord. *"I will sing to the LORD, for he has triumphed gloriously; the horse and his rider he has thrown into the sea."* (Exodus 15:1) The Psalms are full of songs used in worship proclaiming, *"Praise the LORD!"* (Psalm 113:1) In the New Testament the early church met together for fellowship, for teaching, and for praising God (Acts 2:42-47). Finally, in heaven all the angels and saints will be before the throne of God worshipping, *"Holy, holy, holy, is the Lord God Almighty, who was and is and is to come!"* (Revelation 4:8) We need to embrace the reality that God does all His works so that He will be glorified by His creation. In worship our hearts and tongues render back to God thanksgiving for His marvelous favor toward us.

THE LORD'S DAY

In the Old Testament law God decreed that the seventh day of the week, the Sabbath, would be a day of rest to honor God (Exodus 20:8-11). Since the resurrection of Christ the fourth commandment to honor the Sabbath had been fulfilled and observed on the first day of the week, our Sunday (Acts 20:7; 1 Corinthians 16:2). This Christian Sabbath is also called *"the Lord's day"* (Revelation 1:10) in the Bible.

The church since its founding has been meeting on Sundays to worship the Lord and edify one another in the faith. In recent times some Christians have become lax about the worship of God on Sundays and have allowed work and recreation to crowd out their focus on the Lord. It is important that we be on guard against the temptations of the world and still set aside Sundays for worship, rest, and doing good deeds to help Christ's kingdom. For some people, their job makes it necessary for them to work on some Sundays. Emergencies sometimes arise which disrupt our normal practice. Nevertheless, we should be careful to not make missing church a regular occurrence.

IN SPIRIT AND TRUTH

How should we worship God? Churches that are hoping to attract visitors and new members have come up with innovative and creative ways to worship and keep people entertained. However, we do not have the liberty to devise worship according to our own ideas. We need to follow God's Word concerning His own worship. When Jesus met with the Samaritan woman at the well He told her, *"You worship what you do not know"* (John 4:22). The Samaritans' worship of God was a concoction of one part biblical worship and many parts idolatry thrown together by the northern king, Jeroboam (1 Kings 12:25-33). The Scriptures say of all that Jeroboam did *"he had devised from his own heart."* (1 Kings 12:33) We too can err in creating our own worship rather than looking to Scripture for what God desires in our worship. When the priests Nadab and Abihu offered up *"unauthorized fire before the LORD, which he had not commanded"* (Leviticus 10:1), the LORD sent out a fire which consumed them. We should never consider that our forms of worship are a small thing and of little consequence in God's eyes.

Churches should seek to conduct worship in such a way that it is pleasing to God, truly reveals who God is, and builds up the people of God in their faith. The Bible clearly prescribes a number of elements that should be a part of regular worship: teaching, reading the Bible, prayer, singing, the sacraments, and giving. Read the following scriptures and identify which element of worship is being prescribed by God.

- **Matthew 28:19** _____
- **1 Corinthians 11:26** _____
- **1 Corinthians 16:1-2** _____
- **Ephesians 5:18-20** _____
- **1 Timothy 2:8** _____
- **1 Timothy 4:13** _____
- **2 Timothy 4:2** _____

REJOICE WITH TREMBLING

What should worship feel like? There are some churches which have a very somber, reverent atmosphere to them. Other worship services feel like a rock concert or a victory party. Churches try to set a tone or atmosphere that they believe is most conducive to worship. Instead of engineering one mood, worship leaders should look to the whole of Scripture to see how God is to be worshipped. In the Bible, particularly in the Psalms, we find that the LORD was worshipped with a variety of emotions, expressions, and instruments.

In 2 Samuel 6 King David sought to bring the ark of God into Jerusalem. The Israelites incorrectly used an ox cart to carry the ark and Uzzah was struck dead by God when he touched the ark. The fear of the LORD filled David and the people when they considered the holy power of God. Later they carried up the ark correctly with great rejoicing and dancing. Even though he was the king, David danced and whirled before the LORD with great exuberance. The two components of fear and joy need to be held simultaneously in our worship. It seems like an oxymoron to *"rejoice with trembling"* (Psalm 2:11), but the best worship will contain a holy joy. If we lack the fear of God we do not understand that God is holy and awesome. If we lack joy we have probably not experienced His amazing grace.

To worship with holy joy requires that we have both knowledge and emotion in our worship. We have to worship God as He truly is, therefore good theology must undergird all our worship. Merely intellectual or disinterested worship is not pleasing to God for then our hearts are far from Him (Isaiah 29:13). Worship that is pleasing to God will combine a humble spirit (Psalm 51:17), an enlightened mind (Psalm 19:7-9), and an expressive heart and voice (Psalm 100:1).

Our worship of God should never be with a half-hearted or begrudging attitude. The LORD rebuked the attitude of people who said of worship, *"What a weariness this is"* (Malachi 1:13) and who in turn offered blind and lame sacrifices to God. Since God is a great King we must give unto God excellent worship. Our affections, singing, teaching, giving, and service should all be our best offerings.

HITTING HOME

1. David sang, *"I was glad when they said to me, "Let us go to the house of the LORD"* (Psalm 122:1). Does that describe your current heart toward worship? If not, why?

2. Do you set aside Sundays for the worship of God? How?

3. What activities often hinder church attendance? Work, sports, TV, kids' activities, sleeping in, shopping, house and yard chores.

4. Describe the typical worship service in your church? Does it contain all of the above worship elements?

5. What kind of tone does your church worship service have? What kind of tone do you prefer?

LESSON 36: IN THE WORD

KEY DOCTRINE: Growing in an understanding and application of God's Word is the key determinant of spiritual growth.

MEMORY VERSE: *"This Book of the Law shall not depart from your mouth, but you shall meditate on it day and night, so that you may be careful to do according to all that is written in it. For then you will make your way prosperous, and then you will have good success."* (Joshua 1:8)

SCRIPTURE PRE-READING: Joshua 1:1-9; Psalm 1; Matthew 13:1-23; 2 Timothy 3:10-4:8; 1 Peter 1:22-2:3

Understanding and obeying God's Word is the primary determinant of whether a believer will grow in the faith. God uses His Word to both encourage our faith and to teach us how to live godly lives in Christ. In order to live a fruitful life that is pleasing to God we should maintain a regular Bible reading and study program, in addition to hearing the preached Word at every Lord's Day service.

THE PRIME FACTOR

To say that knowing God's Word is the essential factor in spiritual growth is a gross understatement. The Bible is ubiquitous with exhortations to know, trust, and obey God's Word. Joshua is commanded to mediate and do all of God's Word in order to take the promised land (Joshua 1:1-9). All of Israel's prosperity in the land, or their expulsion from the land, was contingent on her obedience to the Law of God (Deuteronomy 30:11-20). Jesus' teaching should be the foundation on which our lives are built and the mark of a true disciple of Christ (Matthew 7:24-27; 28:19-20).

Our very faith originates from the hearing and trusting in God's Word. The apostle Paul says that *"faith comes from hearing, and hearing through the word of Christ."* (Romans 10:17) In the same passage Paul states the obvious that in order to believe you have to hear, and nobody can hear unless someone goes and preaches. The preached Word gives life to the spiritually dead. The Bible teaches us that our spiritual rebirth was caused by the Word of God we heard, *"since you have been born again, not of perishable seed but of imperishable, through the living and abiding word of God"* (1 Peter 1:23). The Holy Spirit uses the Word of God preached (or taught) by humans to bring about regeneration and saving faith as He convicts our hearts and moves us to believe, *"because our gospel came to you not only in word, but also in power and in the Holy Spirit and with full conviction."* (1 Thessalonians 1:5)

As our spiritual birth is through the Word of God and the Holy Spirit, our spiritual growth is also through these same means. If we want to grow in the faith we need to keep coming back to the Word of God. *"Like newborn infants, long for the pure spiritual milk, that by it you may grow up into salvation— if indeed you have tasted that the Lord is good."* (1 Peter 2:2-3) There is a spiritual hunger and thirst within us, created by the Holy Spirit, which craves for the knowledge and grace of God.

HOPE IN HIS WORD

The primary purpose of the Scriptures is to create faith and hope in God. The prophet cried out in Isaiah 40:1, *"Comfort, comfort, my people, says your God."* The gospel is the message of God's grace toward us in Jesus Christ. Just as we believed in Jesus to receive grace from God at our conversion, throughout our Christian walk we must still keep trusting in God's grace for us in Christ. Paul said at the end of his days, *"I have fought the good fight, I have finished the race, I have kept the faith."* (2 Timothy 4:7) Throughout our days we will be continually tested in our faith to see if we still trust in God's mercy and help. Without the Scriptures reminding us of His promises of help, deliverance, and faithfulness we will easily give up hope. *"For whatever was written in former days was written for our instruction, that through endurance and through the encouragement of the Scriptures we might have hope."* (Romans 15:4) The world tells us that there is no God; the Bible tells us that God is faithful.

TRAINING IN RIGHTEOUSNESS

The second purpose of the Scriptures is to teach us how to live godly lives in this world. *"All Scripture is breathed out by God and profitable for teaching, for reproof, for correction, and for training in righteousness, that the man of God may be competent, equipped for every good work."* (2 Timothy 3:16-17) Just as Israel had God's laws, commandments, and statutes to instruct them in righteousness, we are to live out our days as a holy people, set apart for God. Whether it is the Old Testament laws, Christ's teachings, proverbs, or the apostles' letters, all of the Bible corrects and exhorts us to live humble, loving, and self-controlled lives in this world. God's Word continually convicts and restrains our sin nature so that by relying on His unceasing mercy our character is changed. *"For the word of God is living and active, sharper than any two-edge sword, piercing to the division of soul and of spirit, of joints and of marrow, and discerning the thoughts and intentions of the heart."* (Hebrews 4:12)

A TELLING RESPONSE

One of the key texts and teachings of Jesus about responding to God's Word is found in the parable of the sower. The four soils where the seeds fall represent four types of responses to the Word of God. Read, Matthew 13:1-23, the text and answer the following questions.

- Who is the sower and what is the seed?

- What keeps the seed on the path from growing?

- Does the shallow-soil seed represent a true believer?

- What hinders the seed in the weeds from bearing fruit?

- What characterizes good soil?

DAY AND NIGHT

In Psalm 1 the blessed man has no fellowship with the ways and thoughts of the ungodly; instead, *"his delight is in the law of the LORD, and on his law he meditates day and night."* (Psalm 1:2) There are many other passages that exhort believers to have a constant remembrance and application of God's Word in their lives (Deuteronomy 6:4-9; 8:2-3; Joshua 1:5-9; Psalm 119; Matthew 7:24-27). God's Word is to be in our hearts and on our minds as we recognize that we do *"not live by bread alone, but by every word that comes from the mouth of God"* (Matthew 5:4).

Just a little bit of God's Word once a week will not cut it! Unfortunately for many Christians the Sunday sermon may be all they hear from the Bible each week. We need to have a practice of daily reading the Bible on our own and in our families. We should also be a part of a weekly Bible study in their church, whether on Sunday or midweek. It is folly to think that we have understood everything in the Bible. Even the great preacher Apollos, who *"taught accurately the things concerning Jesus"* (Acts 18:25), had to be taken aside by Priscilla and Aquila and be explained *"the way of God more accurately."* (Acts 18:26) True Bible scholars know and openly confess how little they know of the depth and breadth of the Scriptures.

The Bible is such an extensive, complex book that it takes a lifetime to comprehend its many contours. Our reading and study of God's Word should cover *"the whole counsel of God"* (Acts 20:27) and not simply a few familiar texts. As we study the breadth of Scripture we hone our skill in interpreting the Bible. We will find that a text in one part of the Bible will shed light on other passages. Some passages in the New Testament refer to, or cite, Old Testament passages. For instance, understanding the book of Hebrews requires that we understand Genesis 14 and Psalm 110. Studying the whole counsel of God also protects us from becoming unbalanced in our understanding of doctrine. A comprehensive reading of the Bible allows the Spirit to use the diversity of the Word to instruct us according to His revelation and not our theological "hobby-horses."

We should also re-visit portions of the Bible we know well since we can find fresh insights and applications as we grow in faith and our circumstances and trials change. The living nature of God's Word meets us in our need and speaks to us directly, and we are often amazed how God knew exactly the word we needed to hear at that time. We must stay in the Word! Never neglect it! Our lives depend on it.

HITTING HOME

1. How would you describe your overall disposition to hearing God's Word?

2. How often do you read the Bible?

3. Have you ever read through the entire Bible? (It is a must, however long it takes!)

4. What kind of group Bible studies are you involved in with your church?

LESSON 37: THE COVENANT COMMUNITY

KEY DOCTRINE: Christians are called to be members of the church where they exercise love, faithfulness and submission to others.

MEMORY VERSE: *"Now you are the body of Christ and individually members of it."* (1 Corinthians 12:27)

SCRIPTURE PRE-READING: Numbers 16:1-11; Matthew 20:20-28; 1 Corinthians 12:12-27; Ephesians 4:1-16, 25-32; 1 Peter 5:1-5

As members of the body of Christ we are called upon to be committed to the spiritual and practical well-being of other believers. No longer should we think only of our own interests, but like Christ we should be willing to lay down our lives for each other. As part of a covenant community we need to fulfill our commitments to each other in the church. Church members are to submit to the leaders of the church who are caring for their spiritual well-being.

ONE BODY

In our self-reliant, individualistic age we tend to think that we are on our own. If we do not take care of ourselves nobody else will, nor should they have to. Hence, we do not really think we are responsible for anybody else. When we come to Christ and then join a church often our thinking has not changed much. We may view the church merely as an association of individuals who all meet together on Sundays to receive encouragement in teaching, singing, and friendships. Our membership in a church is a nice addition to our lives but it is not an essential part of our lifestyle.

This perspective of the church falls short of the purpose and design that God has for His church. When we were saved we were incorporated into the spiritual body of Christ, with Christ as our Head. *"Now you are the body of Christ and individually members of it."* (1 Corinthians 12:27) This body is to serve and build each other up so that together we all grow into the likeness of Jesus Christ. *"Rather, speaking the truth in love, we are to grow up in every way into him who is the head, into Christ, from whom the whole body, joined and held together by every joint with which it is equipped, when each part is working properly, makes the body grow so that it builds itself up in love."* (Ephesians 4:15-16) Each of us is a member of the body of Christ and has a vital role to perform to strengthen other Christians. The Bible is replete with commandments to serve, forgive, sing to, be patient with, and be kind to one another.

LIVING IN THE COVENANT COMMUNITY

In the book of 1 Samuel, David and Jonathan form such a close friendship that they *"made a covenant"* to pledge their loyalty to each other (1 Samuel 18:3; 20:16). Jonathan showed his faithfulness by standing up for David against his wicked father, Saul, and warning David of Saul's intentions. David fulfilled the covenant by not slaughtering the descendants of Jonathan after he became king. King David even invited Jonathan's handicapped son, Mephibosheth, to eat at the king's table for the rest of his life.

A covenant is a serious thing. When covenants were cut in ancient days the parties involved walked between bloody, slain animals to indicate the penalty of death for not fulfilling the agreement. A covenant was a pledge that one would be faithful to seek the well-being of another at any cost to himself. The Old Testament as a whole is a record of the old covenant wherein Israel entered into a covenant with the LORD to keep His commandments to love God and their neighbor.

When we are saved by Christ we enter the new covenant with Jesus where we pledge loyalty to Christ and other believers. Paul instructed believers that, having a unity in the Spirit and the mind of Christ, they should *"look not only to his own interests, but also to the interests of others."* (Philippians 2:4) We have to break free from our self-absorbed thinking and become committed to looking out for the well-being of other believers. This commitment to help others has no limitation to it. We are tempted to say, "I will help my brother as long as it does not hurt my interests." That is not Christ's standard. The apostle John admonishes us, *"By this we know love, that he laid down his love for us, and we ought to lay down our lives for the brothers."* (1 John 3:16) John goes on to say that if our brother is poor and we have the means to help but refuse, then how can God's love (salvation) be in us (1 John 3:17)? The most obvious manifestation to the world that we are following Jesus is how we care for each other. *"By this all people will know that you are my disciples, if you have love for one another."* (John 13:35)

The early church exhibited this covenant community faithfulness to each other in Jerusalem. *"And they were selling their possessions and belongings and distributing the proceeds to all, as any had need."* (Acts 2:45; see also Acts 4:32-37)   The Bible never advocates eradicating the right of private property (communism), but it does admonish us to give of what we have to others in need.   Other ways in which the early church demonstrated this gracious mindset was in the feeding of widows (Acts 6:1-7), the love offering for the Jerusalem believers (1 Corinthians 16:1-4), and the supplying of food and encouragement to Christians in prison (Hebrews 10:33-34; 13:3).

In addition to practical needs, we also must be committed to the spiritual care of each other. When a person joins a church, or is baptized, the congregation vows to support the faith of the new member.   The successes and failures of each member affect the whole group.   We should be ready to encourage, teach and, when necessary, restore a brother when he strays, *"if anyone is caught in any transgression, you who are spiritual should restore him in a spirit of gentleness."* (Galatians 6:1)   The children of believers also need the help and guidance of the whole church in their upbringing.   Within churches with multi-generational membership the older saints should bless the younger with the fruits of their wisdom and experience (Titus 3:1-6).   *"One generation shall commend your works to another, and shall declare your mighty acts."* (Psalm 145:4)

AUTHORITY IN THE CHURCH

In many areas of life there is authority to which we must submit: children obey parents, students obey teachers, and citizens obey laws and governments.   God has also assigned authority within the church to whom we must submit.   Jesus Christ is the head of the church with the apostles and prophets as its foundation (Ephesians 2:20).   After the canon of Scripture was completed the Bible became the abiding rule of faith and practice for the church.   Today God calls men to be pastors and elders who care for the flock as under-shepherds of Christ.   These church leaders have been given the responsibility of guarding the doctrine of the church and overseeing the conduct of its membership.

The authority these pastors wield is solely for the purpose of building up the church and not for self-aggrandizement or selfish gain.   The apostle Paul wrote to the church in Corinth that the Lord had given him *"the authority for building up and not for tearing down."* (2 Corinthians 13:10)   A pastor is to be like a shepherd who loves, teaches, and sets an example for the flock.   The apostle Peter exhorted elders to *"shepherd the flock of God that is among, exercising oversight, not by compulsion, but willingly, as God would have you; not for shameful gain, but eagerly; not domineering over those in your charge, but being examples to the flock."* (1 Peter 5:2-3)   Jesus set the example for all church leaders as He became a servant to the church and laid down His life for her.   *"But whoever would be great among you must be your servant, and whoever would be first among you must be your slave, even as the Son of Man came not to be served but to serve, and to give his life as a ransom to many."* (Matthew 20:26-28)

Within the church today we are called to obey the leaders that God has placed over us.   *"Obey your leaders and submit to them, for they are keeping watch over your souls, as those who will have to give an account."* (Hebrews 13:17)   Some mistakenly think that since a pastor is to be a meek servant who does not "lord it over" his flock, he holds no authority.   The humble, godly character of a leader should not serve as a justification for a church member to be disobedient.   When we clothe ourselves with humility and become subject to our elders (1 Peter 5:5), we discover that the pastoral care of our leaders will be of great benefit to our soul.   *"Let them do this with joy and not with with groaning, for that would be of no advantage to you."* (Hebrews 13:17)   If we ever faced a situation where we could not submit to our church leadership due to their unfaithfulness to the Lord and the Bible, then we would need to leave that church.   The pressures and responsibilities of caring for the church are overwhelming, so we should always be praying for our pastors.   Like Paul, all pastors cry out, *"Pray for us"* (Hebrews 13:18).

HITTING HOME

1. What ways are you serving in your own church?

2. Have you ever shown faithfulness (loyalty or help) to another believer where it came at a cost to you?

3. What kind of deacon funds does your church have to help people?

4. Describe the character of your church leadership.   Are there authority/submission issues in your church?

LESSON 38: MISSIONS AND EVANGELISM

KEY DOCTRINE: God has called His church to spread the gospel to the ends of the earth.

MEMORY VERSE: *"How beautiful upon the mountains are the feet of him who brings good news, who publishes peace, who brings good news of happiness, who publishes salvation, who says to Zion, 'Your God reigns."* (Isaiah 52:7)

SCRIPTURE PRE-READING: Genesis 12:1-3; Isaiah 49:1-7; Acts 16:6-15; Romans 10:1-17; 2 Timothy 1:8-14

God's great redemptive plan calls for the gospel of Jesus Christ to be heard by all the nations and peoples of the world. God has sent missionaries into the world to accomplish the task, but He also calls all believers to be prepared *"to make a defense to anyone who asks you for a reason for the hope that is in you"* (1 Peter 3:15). Each of us has a role to play and great blessings to experience when we are faithful in sharing the message of God's grace with others.

A LIGHT FOR THE NATIONS

When God initially revealed Himself to Abraham, He promised that Abraham would be a blessing to all the nations of the earth (Genesis 12:3). That blessing has come through Abraham's descendant, Jesus of Nazareth, as now all peoples of this earth can be in a saving relationship with God through faith in Christ. Old Testament prophecies about the Messiah often foretold that through Him there would be a universal outreach to all people, such as in Isaiah 49:6, *he* [the LORD] *says: "It is too light a thing that you should be my servant to raise up the tribes of Jacob and to bring back the preserved of Israel; I will make you as a light for the nations, that my salvation may reach to the end of the earth."*

The church has a commission from Jesus to send out missionaries throughout the world to share the gospel so that all will hear. The Lord Jesus spoke to His disciples saying, *"All authority in heaven and on earth has been given to me. Go therefore and make disciples of all nations, baptizing them in the name of the Father and of the Son and of the Holy Spirit, teaching them to observe all that I have commanded you. And behold, I am with you always, to the end of the age."* (Matthew 28:18-20) All of us have a calling, wherever God sends us, to make disciples of others with the confidence that God will grant success to our efforts because Christ has been given authority over the whole world.

Missionaries need to be sent out because people will not experience God's saving grace through the light of nature and their own reason. All people, no matter where they are born, will face the judgment of God and can only be saved through the gospel of Jesus. No other religion grants reconciliation with God and without the gospel there is no hope of forgiveness. For this reason, people must be sent out with the message of the gospel. *"How then will they call on him in whom they have not believed? And how are they to believe in him of whom they have never heard? And how are they to hear without someone preaching? And how are they to preach unless they are sent? As it is written, "How beautiful are the feet of those who preach the good news!"* (Romans 10:14-15)

NOT ASHAMED OF THE GOSPEL

The task of spreading the gospel is not just an elite calling of a few anointed missionaries. This calling of evangelizing is something that all of us in the church have a responsibility to fulfill. Sharing the faith is something that can cause fear within us. We might feel ashamed, or feel like we will offend someone. The temptation to be ashamed of our Christian faith in this fallen world is a real danger. Jesus challenged all of us who would follow Him, *"For whoever is ashamed of me and of my words in this adulterous and sinful generation, of him will the Son of Man also be ashamed when he comes in the glory of his Father with the holy angels."* (Mark 8:38) Likewise, the apostle Paul exhorted young Timothy to *"not be ashamed of the testimony about our Lord"* (2 Timothy 1:8). Paul proclaimed that he was *"not ashamed of the gospel, for it is the power of God for salvation to everyone who believes"* (Romans 1:16).

We should all be willing to share the gospel with others since since we know that this gospel can give people eternal life. The Scriptures say that the feet of those who bring the news of salvation are beautiful. To lead someone to the Lord is the most loving act we can do for our neighbor. The gospel brings spiritual life, a relationship with God, forgiveness of sins, deliverance from the oppression of sin, the promise of God's continual help in life, and an assurance of a blessed eternity. This is our hope, so why would we want to hold that back from someone else?

COMPEL PEOPLE TO COME IN

Read the parable of the great banquet found in Luke 14:12-24, and as an interpretation exercise answer the follow questions which address issues of people coming to faith.

- How extensive is the invitation to attend the great banquet? (v. 16-17)

- Describe the myriad of excuses for not attending the banquet? (v. 18-20)

- How determined is the master to have guests at his feast? (v. 21-24)

- What assertive actions are the servants to perform to fill the banquet hall? (v. 21-24)

- What kind of people filled the banquet hall? (v. 12-14, 21-24)

A PEP-TALK FOR EVANGELISM

Sharing our faith is one of the biggest challenges, but it is also one of the most rewarding aspects of our Christian walk. The following is some practical advice about engaging in Christian outreach:

- **The warfare of evangelism:** *"But no one can enter a strong man's house and plunder his goods, unless he first binds the strong man. Then indeed he may plunder his house."* (Mark 3:27) Jesus says in this verse that He is stronger than the devil and can *"plunder"* people from the devil's control. The realm of darkness will resist our efforts to share the gospel and *"plunder his goods,"* so we must undergird our efforts with prayer and an expectation of difficulty in the work.

- **The blessing of evangelism:** *"and I pray that the sharing of your faith may become effective for the full knowledge of every good thing that is in us for the sake of Christ."* (Philemon 6) We understand more about our faith and experience new blessings when we share it with others.

- **The fear of evangelism:** *"And do not fear those who kill the body but cannot kill the soul. Rather fear him who can destroy both soul and body in hell."* (Matthew 10:28) We need not fear death in our faithfulness to the testimony of Christ, for God will keep our souls. God has commanded us to testify of His Son, so we should fear Him more than the threats of men.

- **The credibility of evangelism:** *"Show yourself in all respects to be a model of good works, and in your teaching show integrity, dignity, and sound speech that cannot be condemned, so that an opponent may be put to shame, having nothing evil to say about us."* (Titus 2:7-8) A life of integrity lends credibility to all that we say, since we know that people are watching us.

- **The weakness of evangelism:** *"One who heard us was a woman named Lydia, from the city of Thyatira, a seller of purple goods, who was a worshiper of God. The Lord opened her heart to pay attention to what was said by Paul."* (Acts 16:14) Paul shared the faith but he did not "close the deal." People believe by the power of the Spirit opening hearts. We do not "save" anyone.

- **The discipleship of evangelism:** *"Go therefore and make disciples of all nations...teaching them to observe all that I have commanded you."* (Matthew 28:19-20) Sharing the gospel necessitates that we thoroughly teach people the whole counsel of God. Our commission is not to make *decisions* for the Lord but make *disciples* of the Lord.

As daunting a task as evangelism may seem, it is truly a rewarding experience to see someone come to Christ and to observe how the Lord transforms their life. The apostle John said to his son in the faith, the beloved Gaius, *"I have no greater joy than to hear that my children are walking in the truth."* (3 John 3:4)

HITTING HOME

1. How is your church involved in the task of local and world missions?

2. Have you ever shared your Christian faith with someone else with the hope of their conversion? How did it go?

3. What excuses are you harboring which are keeping you back from sharing your faith?

4. Practice a basic four point outline of the gospel: God' existence, sin, Christ's death, and faith.

LESSON 39: SPIRITUAL GIFTS

KEY DOCTRINE: Christ has equipped the members of His church with spiritual gifts to express God's grace and to build up other believers in their faith.

MEMORY VERSE: *"As each has received a gift, use it to serve one another, as good stewards of God's varied grace"* (1 Peter 4:10)

SCRIPTURE PRE-READING: Romans 12:3-8; 1 Corinthians 12:1-31; Ephesians 4:1-16; 1 Peter 4:8-11

Spiritual gifts have been given by God to all the members of the body of Christ to build up other believers in the Lord. Just as God gives gifts to people He has also set aside leaders to be gifts to His church. Spiritual gifts can be categorized as either word gifts or deed gifts. The Holy Spirit operates through these gifts to manifest God's grace to the church. When we use our gifts the focus should not be on our spirituality but on glorifying God in His mercy.

STEWARD'S OF GOD'S GRACE

When the Holy Spirit regenerated us He included us into the spiritual body of Christ. As members of Christ's body we were given spiritual gifts which enable us to build up other believers. The church often feels weak and outnumbered as it exists in the midst of this fallen world. Due to the challenges of the world's temptations and persecutions the Holy Spirit must supernaturally strengthen us so that we can endure to the end. Spiritual gifts are a means by which all of God's people can mutually share in the building up of one another in Christ.

The first gifts Christ gave to His church were people. *"And he gave the apostles, the prophets, the evangelists, the shepherds and teachers"* (Ephesians 4:11). The Lord has set apart men to be dedicated to the advancement of the gospel and the building up of the church throughout the world. The two most important groups of men were the apostles and the prophets, who became the foundation of the Christian church (Ephesians 2:20). Once the foundation of the church was laid (and the New Testament Scriptures written) there was no need for the Lord to continue to provide an apostolic and prophetic ministry. However, there is still a continual need for shepherds (pastors), teachers, and evangelists. In every generation Christ is still sending these men to be gifts to His church. They are set aside to love and feed His sheep.

The spiritual gifts are manifestations of God's grace in us which we use to love and serve others. God can directly bless us without using people, but He is pleased to use people as conduits of His mercy. Just as a human body has many parts and organs, the Christian body has a wide variety of gifts and talents. *"Now there are varieties of gifts, but the same Spirit; and there are varieties of service, but the same Lord"* (1 Corinthians 12:4-5). Read 1 Corinthians 12:4-31 and answer the following questions.

- Who determines how spiritual gifts are distributed? (v. 4-11, 18)

- What is the purpose of the gifts? (v. 7, 25-26)

- Why is there such a diversity of gifts? (v. 12-26)

GIFTS OF WORD AND DEED

The list of the spiritual gifts found in the four passages of our Scripture pre-reading is roughly broken into two distinct kinds of gifts: *word* and *deed*. This two-fold division is seen in 1 Peter 4:11, *"whoever speaks, as one who speaks oracles of God; whoever serves, as one who serves by the strength that God supplies."* Word gifts are those spiritual gifts which are associated with communicating God's truth to His people. These are the preeminent gifts in the church and are those which pastors, teachers, and evangelists are equipped with. These word gifts are not exclusively held by ministers, or men, but are dispersed throughout the body of Christ. The word gifts are: **TEACHING, EXHORTING, WISDOM, KNOWLEDGE, DISCERNING SPIRITS, PROPHECY, TONGUES,** and **THE INTERPRETATION OF TONGUES.**

The deed gifts are given to people who will serve the body of Christ through a variety of ways which are not tied to teaching and instruction. God communicates His mercy through us in practical ways, and these blessings fortify, and give credibility to, the spoken word of God's grace. Through these gifts we can meet the physical, financial, and emotional needs of God's people and the community. The deed gifts are **LEADERSHIP, SERVICE, ADMINISTRATION, FAITH, HEALING, MIRACLES, MERCY, GIVING,** and **HELPS.**

THE PRIDE AND THE POWER

One of the great dangers of spiritual gifts is that they can inflate egos and be used to exert power. We may love the thought of being spiritual, and having divine power working through us can fuel our pride and ambition. Acts 8:9-25 recounts a story of how the famed magician Simon, who outwardly professed faith in Christ, tried to buy the power of the Holy Spirit from the apostles. He was severely rebuked and appears to repent, but church historians record that Simon became a virulent opponent of the early church.

The purpose of a gift is not to exalt our spirituality but to serve for God's glory. *"As each has received a gift, use it to serve one another, as good stewards of God's varied grace...in order that in everything God may be glorified through Jesus Christ."* (1 Peter 4:10-11) We actively participate in the use of our spiritual gifts, but we should not take credit for the blessings that result. It is God working through us to bless others, so in the end God should get all the glory.

Sometimes gifts can be misused when we compare and spiritually rank ourselves against other believers. The apostle Paul had to counsel the church of Corinth to not be arrogant in their great esteem for spiritual gifts. To exhort the church to humbly serve, Paul wrote the famous "Love Chapter" of 1 Corinthian 13. A spiritual gift is not an adornment for our beauty, but a tool for the care of others. In all the use of our gifts we should remember that love is the *"more excellent way."* (1 Corinthians 12:31)

THE HOT TOPICS

The use of spiritual gifts is one of the distinctions which often divides denominations and churches. Some people will not go to a church that does not have a visible use of gifts, whereas other Christians flee at the mention of gifts. The differences on this subject revolve around a few key issues:

- **Past or Present?** Are all of the spiritual gifts still in operation today, or have some of them ceased? The most controversial of them are the gifts of MIRACLES, HEALING, and PROPHECY. Those who do not believe that the miraculous gifts continue, hold that these gifts were associated with the apostles (2 Corinthians 12:12) and prophets during the establishment of the church and the New Testament canon. Those who maintain they are still functioning state that there is no biblical instruction that they should cease or were only apostolic, and also point to modern examples of their use. As a mediating position we can boldly say that, even if the gifts of healing and miracles do not exist, God Himself still heals and performs miracles!
- **Does God Still Speak?** Has the gift of prophecy ceased or does it continue through men and women? With the establishment of the New Testament canon the final authoritative Word is the Scriptures of the Old and New Testament. Beware of any person who tries to bring an authoritative "Thus saith the Lord!" without a biblical basis. God still speaks by His Spirit to grant us correction, wisdom, and discernment, by both using the Bible and the "still small voice" inside us. However, God will not give infallible, authoritative revelations that are divorced from, or contrary to, the Scriptures.
- **Tongues and Interpretation?** The issue of speaking in tongues has caused a great division in the church. Some hold that without tongues you do not have the Holy Spirit, and others think you are misguided if you do. Clearly, in Acts 2 the tongues manifested were spoken foreign languages; however, in 1 Corinthians 14 the type of tongues mentioned is not easily discerned. The apostle Paul draws the conclusion that tongues which are only used for self-edification are of minimal value compared with communicating and interpreting truth to someone else. In any event, tongues are listed on the bottom rung of importance for the spiritual gifts in the church (1 Corinthians 12:28), so it is a pity that they have generated such controversy and division.

HITTING HOME

1. Have you ever done a spiritual gift test to discover what gifts you may have? Looking at the gifts mentioned, which can you identify in your own life?

2. Our spiritual gifts often line up with our natural talents. Is that true in your case?

3. In what ways have you observed a misuse of the gifts in the church?

4. How have you seen blessings result from the use of your gifts? How was God glorified?

LESSON 40: THE PEACE AND PURITY

KEY DOCTRINE: The Bible lays forth a process by which the church can address sins committed within the body so that both the peace and the purity of the church is maintained.

MEMORY VERSE: *"Strive for peace with everyone, and for the holiness without which no one will see the Lord."* (Hebrews 12:14)

SCRIPTURE PRE-READING: Deuteronomy 19:15-21; Matthew 18:15-35; Luke 17:1-4; 1 Corinthians 5:1-6:11; Ephesians 4:25-32

Christians should humbly pursue peace with all people. The strength of the church is found in her testimony of peace and love. Inevitably Christians will sin against others in the church, so Jesus laid out a process by which offenses should be handled. The goal of this process is restoration, though in some cases it will lead to the exposure and removal of unrepentant sinners from the church.

STRIVE FOR PEACE AND HOLINESS

"I therefore, a prisoner for the Lord, urge you to walk in a manner worthy of the calling to which you have been called, with all humility and gentleness, with patience, bearing with one another in love, eager to maintain the unity of the Spirit in the bond of peace." (Ephesians 4:1-3) These verses describe the high importance that God places on the unity of peace within the body of Christ. As the Spirit moves us to love one another we should seek to maintain right relationships with other Christians. Satan is always trying to stir up trouble and cause fights and division in the church, so we must be on our guard against his wiles and put on the humble virtues of gentleness, patience and grace.

Jesus said, *"Blessed are the peacemakers, for they shall be called sons of God."* (Matthew 5:9) As God's children we are to live a life of love which seeks peace with all. *"If possible, so far as it depends upon you, live peaceably with all."* (Romans 12:18) This applies to situations with believers as well as with people outside the faith. Anyone can pick a fight, but it takes work to be peaceable and to cool down contentious situations. Being peaceable does not mean everyone will like us, or that we do not take stands. Striving for peace requires that we die to ourselves and not let our pride and anger take control. Unresolved anger can become a foothold for the devil to do great damage (Ephesians 4:26-27).

Along with seeking peace in the church is the commandment to strive for holiness. The goal of *peace and purity* is a vow many ministers and church members take when they join the church and her service. These two goals are not in competition with each other, but are mutually attained when godly living is occurring in the church. We should never sacrifice purity for the sake of peace. When we live according to the Word of God we find that peace reigns in our midst. It is when we sin that both the peace and the purity are broken.

AS WE FORGIVE OUR DEBTORS

The most powerful tool to effect peace is the willingness to forgive others. Throughout our Christian walk we are going to face continual offenses, misunderstandings, insults, and disputes with people in the church. Without a gracious spirit these altercations will escalate and tear apart relationships, divide the church, and destroy her testimony and vitality. The foundation and motivation for forgiving others is based on what Jesus has done for us. Read the parable of the unforgiving servant from Matthew 18:21-34 and answer the following questions.

- What is the limit for how many times we are to forgive someone?

- What was the relative size of the two debts owed?

- What was the king's judgment against the unforgiving servant?

- What will God do to unforgiving Christians?

THE DISCIPLINE PROCESS

Jesus places great importance on relationships and the health of the church, so He instructed us in Matthew 18:15-20 how offenses in the church should be handled. When we follow this process, problems can be addressed in an orderly and peaceable manner. When we fail to follow Christ's guidance, issues and problems tend to linger, grow, and eventually divide a congregation.

When a Christian sins against us we first must decide if it is serious enough to even deal with. There are numerous little offenses that happen in life which we simply need to overlook, forgiving the person for Christ's sake without telling them. Confronting the person would probably just hurt our relationship with them. *"Good sense makes one slow to anger, and it is his glory to overlook an offense."* (Proverbs 19:11) In these cases *"love covers a multitude of sins."* (1 Peter 4:8) If an offense is serious enough to require it to be addressed, Jesus has given us a "how to manual" in Matthew 18:15-20, which is sometimes called the *church discipline process*:

- **STEP 1: Privately Go.** In a spirit of gentleness we privately go to the person and show them their fault. If the offender is teachable, explains their actions and intentions, or is apologetic, then the matter is discreetly resolved and you have *"gained your brother"* (Matthew 18:15; see also Galatians 6:1; James 5:19-20).
- **STEP 2: Take Another.** If the offender justifies himself, or fights back, then we bring another person with us and speak again with the offender. Another person can serve as a witness to the dispute and provide another perspective on the issue at hand (Deuteronomy 19:15-21).
- **STEP 3: Inform the Church.** If the matter is still not resolved we are to take the matter to the leadership of the church. It is then incumbent upon them to make a binding judgment on the matter (Matthew 18:17).
- **STEP 4: Public Judgment.** If the leadership makes a judgment against the offender and he/she is still unrepentant, then that person risks being barred from the Lord's Supper or being removed from membership of the church (1 Corinthians 5:9-13).

Some sins committed in the church are not just private matters between two people, but are more public offenses or sins against the whole church. When a sin is public then the repentance needs to be public. If a person commits a sin against the whole church, such as causing strife or teaching false doctrine, then the matter can immediately go to the church leadership. The goal of church discipline is never to humiliate or excommunicate people. The hope is always that people repent and be restored to the full fellowship of the church (2 Corinthians 2:5-11).

JESUS THE JUDGE OF THE CHURCH

When sin issues come up in our church it is tempting to respond by quoting, *"Judge not, that you be not judged."* (Matthew 7:1) Some say, "After all, we are all sinners. We should not judge." This verse should not serve as an excuse to stop exhortation or discipline within the church. Under the guise of God's grace we cannot allow a tolerance toward sin to creep into our hearts and churches. Jesus is Lord of His church and His ultimate goal for the church is her continual sanctification.

The process of church discipline serves a two-fold purpose: the restoration of erring Christians and the flushing-out of false brethren. In Matthew 7:15 Jesus warned us about wolves in sheep's clothing hiding within our midst, and a wolf in sheep's clothing always starts out looking like a sheep--until we see the fangs! Jesus said that He came to the earth not to bring peace, but rather division (Luke 12:49-53). Part of the sanctification of the visible church is the drawing out of the people who are not actually saved. When confronted with the Word of God a faithful follower will be able to repent of their sin; however, the false brother will not be able to change his way and will reveal the hidden wickedness and hostility of his heart. When the church is faithful in applying godly discipline, she will be strengthened, both by the casting out of the wolves and trouble-makers and by the repentance of the saints.

HITTING HOME

1. How do you seek peace with people instead of causing hostility?

2. Why is repentance necessary for true forgiveness and reconciliation? (See Luke 17:3-4)

3. Can you recount times in which you have forgiven other people? Have you ever had to repent before someone else in order to restore a relationship?

4. Describe a time when you confronted someone in your past for an offense against you? How did it go?

5. How well does your church conduct the process of church discipline?

LESSON 41: GIVING AND MERCY

KEY DOCTRINE: As good stewards of God's resources, Christians need to give to the work of the kingdom and to the needs of the saints.
MEMORY VERSE: *"They are to do good, to be rich in good works, to be generous and ready to share"*
(1 Timothy 6:18)
SCRIPTURE PRE-READING: Deuteronomy 14:22-29; Nehemiah 10:32-39; 2 Corinthians 9:1-15; 1 John 3:10-24

As stewards of God's resources we are called to be generous in our financial giving to the kingdom and to the needs of others. The work of teaching the Word and providing for the worship of God requires that we give some proportion of our resources to the church. Giving to the needs of people also glorifies the grace and mercy of God by those who are recipients.

FAITHFUL STEWARDS

The English preacher Charles Spurgeon remarked that the last part of a man to be converted is his back pocket—a reference to where his wallet is located. Money has a strong hold on us and the Lord has to transform our selfish tendencies into hearts and hands of generosity. Many of Jesus' teachings were on the subject of money, with the overall thrust of His message being that we need to be faithful with our financial resources and to use them in a manner that honors God.

By faith we recognize that behind all our efforts at earning income is God's sovereign provision and control of our lives. In 1 Timothy 6:17 the apostle Paul gives a charge to wealthy believers to have the right attitude toward their riches, *"As for the rich in this present age, charge them not to be haughty, nor to set their hopes on the uncertainty of riches, but on God, who richly provides us with everything to enjoy."* One of the most dangerous attitudes we can harbor is the belief that our income is solely a result of our own efforts (Deuteronomy 8:17). If we recognize that our wealth comes from the Lord then we must use it to glorify Him and display His generosity.

BRING IN THE WHOLE TITHE!

A vital expression of faithful stewardship to God is giving financially to the work of His kingdom. Our primary responsibility of giving occurs each week during the Sunday worship service. This practice of giving to the work and worship of God began in the Old Testament and continues in the church today (Deuteronomy 14:22-29; Malachi 3:6-12). Many people may question, or begrudge, having to give their money to the church, as if it was some kind of religious tax. However, if we recognize that all that we have comes from God's hand, then it is no burden to give back to God. There are a few key reasons why we give to the church:

- **Giving Thanks:** Financial giving is a form of worship in giving thanks to God, as we express our faith and trust in His grace and generosity toward us (Deuteronomy 26:10-11).
- **Kingdom Workers:** God has set aside ministers and other people for the work of the kingdom, *"the laborer deserves his wages"* (Luke 10:7), so these workers need to be paid. Just as the Levitical priests did not have a portion of the land in Israel but lived by the offerings of the people, ministers of the gospel live by the offerings of the church, *"In the same way, the Lord commanded that those who proclaim the gospel should get their living by the gospel."* (1 Corinthians 9:14; see also 1 Corinthians 9:1-13)
- **Mercy Ministry:** Collections are made so that we can share with people who are in financial need. This is often the ministry that the deacons in the church oversee (Acts 6:1-7).

To encourage us to generously give, it helps to understand that God blesses us when we give. God gives to us so that we can give to others. When we give generously the Lord rewards us in a multitude of ways. He will often financially repay us, which is why Christians commonly say, "You can't out-give God!" Relationships may also be built with people to whom we give. God is praised by the recipients of the help, and we experience joy in being used by God. In the end our giving should be a cheerful experience and not a reluctant duty (2 Corinthians 9:7). As Romans 12:8 instructs us in the attitude of giving, *"the one who does acts of mercy, with cheerfulness,"* showing mercy can be a joy as we participate in God's joyful heart of mercy.

LOVING YOUR BROTHER

In the developed countries of the world most people adhere to a philosophy of individualistic self-reliance. We should take care of ourselves and not be a burden to anyone else. That kind of thinking ultimately leads to the mindset behind the question, *"Am I my brother's keeper?"* which, of course, was spoken by a murderer (Genesis 4:9). Our attitude should be the opposite--*"we ought to lay down our lives for the brothers."* (1 John 3:16)

God has given us resources to use faithfully. The challenge before us is to know how we are to use them. The faithful way to glorify God with our time and possessions is to use them in a generous and gracious manner. The apostle Paul instructs rich people that, *"They are to do good, to be rich in good works, to be generous and ready to share, thus storing up treasures for themselves as a good foundation for the future, so that they may take hold of that which is truly life."* (1 Timothy 6:18-19) One of the evidences that we know Christ and have His Spirit in us is that we love our brother in practical ways. The apostle John says that if we know of a brother in the faith who needs financial help and we close our hearts, then how can God's love be in us (1 John 3:17)? This financial giving test is used by Jesus to separate the sheep from the goats at the last judgment (Matthew 25:31-46).

The New Testament records a few instances of the church meeting one another's financial needs. Soon after the establishment of the church at Pentecost, the new believers were already sharing their resources with those in need (Acts 2:42-47; 4:32-5:11). After the Jerusalem church suffered persecution they were in financial straits and were dependent on the resources from the Gentile Christians. Paul was instrumental in raising resources from churches to take to these Jerusalem believers (1 Corinthians 16:1-4). Lastly, when many believers were imprisoned for their faith, other Christians visited them in prison to provide for their needs (Hebrews 10:32-34). The early church knew to *"not love in word or talk but in deed and in truth."* (1 John 3:18)

Interpretation Exercise: In the parable of the good Samaritan Jesus teaches us about the heart of mercy for our neighbor. Read Luke 10:25-37 and answer the following questions.

* What was the goal of the lawyer in his questioning of Jesus? (v. 25-29)

* What excuses probably went through the minds of the priest and the Levite when they bypassed the injured man? (v. 31-32)

* Describe the abundance of costly mercy performed by the Samaritan man? (v. 33-35)

* What was Jesus' final instruction? (v. 28, 37)

MERCY FOR THE WORLD

Most of the commandments in the New Testament about helping others are specifically focused on believers helping other believers. However, we should not limit our *neighbor* to those of the household of faith alone. We are called to be merciful just as God is merciful, and God sends the sun and rain on the wicked as well as the righteous (Matthew 5:45). Because God by His very nature is overflowing in mercy, compassion, and goodness, we His children should likewise demonstrate those characteristics in how we relate to the world at large. As we love our enemies and care for those in need God is glorified in His grace. A portion of our resources should be available for works of mercy in the world which demonstrate and give credibility to the gospel. Throughout history it has often been the compassion of the church in addressing the ills of society which has been its greatest testimony to outside observers. Though many people whom we help may never accept the gospel, our help is never contingent on their conversion. We love mercy because God is merciful (Luke 6:36).

HITTING HOME

1. How generous are you with your financial giving to the church?

2. Have you ever contributed to the needs of another family in the church?

3. Describe how you have been blessed and God was glorified in your giving or mercy?

4. Have you participated in any type of ministry in the world where you helped the lost?

SECTION E:

THINKING DEEPER

"We destroy arguments and every lofty opinion raised against the knowledge of God, and take every thought captive to obey Christ" (2 Corinthians 10:5)

When Jesus was asked about the greatest commandment in the Law, He answered that, *"'You shall love the Lord your God with all your heart and with all your soul and with all your mind. This is the great and first commandment.'"* (Matthew 22:37-38) The third aspect of our expression of love to the Lord is the use of our *minds*. Contrary to the criticisms of skeptics, when we place faith in Christ we are not abandoning our reason. Our minds are fully engaged in our faith, and we will be challenged intellectually far more than we can imagine.

In this section we will focus on a number of doctrines which formulate our wider-encompassing theology and worldview. Topics such as the sovereignty of God, covenants, and biblical interpretation, aid us in our understanding of the whole counsel of God. Since we live within the environment of the fallen world we need to grow in our discernment between the way the world thinks and lives and how God is transforming us to be righteous and holy. As our thinking grows deeper and we learn more of the ways of the Lord, we still need to retain a humility that, along with the psalmist, says, *"O LORD, my heart is not lifted up; my eyes are not raised too high; I do not occupy myself with things too great and too marvelous for me. But I have calmed and quieted my soul, like a weaned child with its mother; like a weaned child is my soul within me."* (Psalm 131:1-2)

LESSON 42: THE SOVEREIGNTY OF GOD

KEY DOCTRINE: Everything that occurs in life is in accordance with God's eternal plan and under His sovereign control.
MEMORY VERSE: *"In him we have obtained an inheritance, having been predestined according to the purpose of him who works all things according to the counsel of his will"* (Ephesians 1:11)
SCRIPTURE PRE-READING: Genesis 50:15-21; Job 38; Psalm 47; Isaiah 46; Acts 2:22-24; Ephesians 1:3-14

All things that happen in life are according to the sovereign plan of God from all eternity. His eternal decrees account for the creation, the fall, the salvation of sinners, and the actions of mankind—whether they are good or bad. The sin of mankind is part of the will of God, but that which man intends for evil God can turn for good. The challenge for us is to trust in the faithfulness of God and His ultimate good purposes when we experience the hardship and injustice of this life.

GOD'S ETERNAL PLAN

The *Westminster Confession of Faith* [Ch. II, 1] states that *"God from eternity...ordained whatsoever comes to pass."* This confession states that everything that happens in this world has been decreed by God before the creation of the world. All things, whether good or evil, are a part of His plan: life and death, peace and war, health and sickness, the belief and unbelief of people, fine weather and natural disasters. We cannot attribute only the good to God and the bad to chance, the devil or mankind.

The key verse that teaches the doctrine of the sovereignty of God is found in Ephesians 1:11, *"In him we have obtained an inheritance, having been predestined according to the purpose of him who works all things according to the counsel of his will."* All things work according to the counsel of His will, which was from all eternity. There are no surprises for God. He knows all that shall come to pass because it is part of His plan. Nothing can hinder or triumph over or against His purposes. In contrast to worthless idols made out of wood that do not do anything, the one true God boasts that He can do all that He purposes, *"for I am God, and there is no other; I am God, and there is none like me, declaring the end from the beginning and from the ancient times things not yet done, saying, 'My counsel shall stand, and I will accomplish all my purpose,'...I have spoken and I will bring it to pass; I have purposed, and I will do it."* (Isaiah 46:9-11) The sovereign power of God becomes a joy to us when we know that in this chaotic world He is in control, as Psalm 115:3 boasts, *"Our God is in the heavens; he does all that he pleases."*

The doctrine of the sovereignty of God applies specifically to God's predestination of some men and women to be saved for all eternity, and for others to be passed over [See LESSON 11: ELECTION for a full treatment on this topic.]. *"Even as he chose us in him before the foundation of the world, that we should be holy and blameless before him. In love he predestined us for adoption as sons through Jesus Christ, according to the purpose of his will."* (Ephesians 1:4-5) This most vital of all issues—the eternal destination of the souls of mankind—is not left up to chance or the will of man.

GOD'S WILL IN REGARD TO SIN

An objection is often raised that God could not make sin a part of His plan because of His goodness. The Bible does not shy away from the truth that even man's sins and tragic events (disasters, death, and accidents) are a part of His ordained will. He permits people to make sinful decisions without forcing them to choose to sin, so God is not the author of sin. When we do a sinful act we are to blame, not God. Yet God does plan for the sin to occur to further some good purpose of His will. The two key texts which demonstrate how man's evil deeds are a part of God's plan are the sufferings of Joseph and the crucifixion of Christ. Read Genesis 50:15-21 and Acts 2:22-24 and answer the following questions.
* Did God plan beforehand for Joseph to be sold into slavery and Jesus to be crucified?
* What were the intentions of the actions of Joseph's brothers and the Pharisees?
* Is there any indication from the Scripture that God was coercing them against their wills to commit murder?
* What was God's ultimate intention (purpose) in allowing these two events to occur?
* Were the people who committed these wicked deeds aware of God's wider plan?

THE FREEDOM OF MAN'S WILL

A second objection to the doctrine of God's sovereignty is that if all things have been decreed by God then we do not have free will. God's eternal decree does not nullify our ability to make free decisions. God knows the choices we will make, and we are responsible before God for our decisions. We cannot shift the blame to God for our sins, and simply claim it was His will. In another sense, mankind never has free will, in that our sin natures prevent us from making purely righteous choices. Outside of Christ the will of man is under the bondage and power of sin. Only in Christ are we set free.

In all of our reasoning and decision-making we need to recognize that our decisions are all part of God's purposes. *"Many are the plans in the mind of a man, but it is the purpose of the LORD that will stand."* (Proverbs 19:21) We are called to understand God's prescribed and revealed will in regard to those types of actions that please Him and reveal His glory. Individually, we should seek God's specific calling in our life that fulfills our purpose in His Kingdom. Some aspects of God's broader plan will be revealed to us in this life, but with humility we confess that the *"secret things belong to the LORD our God"* (Deuteronomy 29:29) and we shall simply trust in His sovereign control over the world.

THE PROVIDENCE OF GOD

On the subject of God's providential control in the world the *Westminster Confession of Faith* says in Chapter V, 1 that *"God...doth uphold, direct, dispose, and govern all creatures, actions, and things from the greatest even to the least, by his most wise and holy providence according to his infallible foreknowledge, and the free and immutable counsel of his own will, to the praise of the glory of his wisdom, power, justice, goodness, and mercy."* God not only has a plan for the world, but He is intimately involved in controlling His world to see that His purposes are fulfilled. God is not a distant landlord who has removed Himself from the governing of His creation. He is in control...

• **Over All Things:** *"The LORD has established his throne in the heavens, and his kingdom rules over all."* (Psalm 103:19)

• **Over Nature:** *"O LORD, how manifold are your works! In wisdom you have made them all; the earth is full of your creatures."* (Psalm 104:24)

• **Over Nations:** *"the Most High rules the kingdom of men and gives it to whom he will"* (Daniel 4:32, 34-35; Job 12:23)

• **Over His People:** *"fear not, for I am with you; be not dismayed, for I am your God; I will strengthen you, I will help you, I will uphold you with my righteous right hand."* (Isaiah 41:10)

• **Over "Chance":** *"The lot is cast into the lap, but its every decision is from the LORD."* (Proverbs 16:33)

• **Over the Devil:** *"And they were all amazed, so that they questioned among themselves, saying, "What is this? A new teaching with authority! He commands even the unclean spirits, and they obey him."* (Mark 1:27; Job 1:12)

The challenge we have throughout our life is to be able to keep our faith in God's love toward us in the midst of hardship. God told the prophet Habakkuk, *"but the righteous shall live by his faith."* (Habakkuk 2:4) This charge to trust in God came to Habakkuk while he awaited the oncoming devastation of Jerusalem. In the end, Habakkuk chose to find joy instead of despair (Habakkuk 3:17-19). Likewise, we live by faith and trust that God is in control of all events. The Lord loves us, and He is working His redemptive purposes out for our good and for His glory. *"And we know that for those who love God all things work together for good, for those who are called according to his purpose."* (Romans 8:28)

Hitting Home

1. How does it affect your faith to know that all things that occur in life are according to the plan of God?

2. Can you testify to how you have seen either your own or somebody else's sin ultimately be used for the good?

3. How does the knowledge that your salvation is a part of God's predestination encourage you?

4. In what areas of your life is your trust in God's sovereignty being tested?

LESSON 43: THE CREATION OF THE WORLD

KEY DOCTRINE: God created all things out of nothing by the power of His spoken word.
MEMORY VERSE: *"In the beginning, God created the heavens and the earth."* (Genesis 1:1)
SCRIPTURE PRE-READING: Genesis 1:1-31; Psalm 19:1-6; Psalm 104; Hebrews 11:1-3; Revelation 4:9-11

The overall Scriptural record, from Genesis to Revelation, declares that God created all things by the power of His word and that He continues to uphold the universe by this same power. Christians accept this truth by faith, and the doctrine of creation is a fundamental presupposition which undergirds our worldview. The creation itself speaks to the wisdom, goodness, glory, and power of God Almighty. The Scriptural testimony of God's creation is irreconcilable with atheistic or theistic theories of evolution.

THE PRIORITY OF THE SCRIPTURES

Before considering the doctrine of the creation, we first need to establish a starting point by which we will make determinations about truth. What relative authority will we give to scientific findings and presuppositions versus the biblical text? The Christian's starting point is always that the Bible is authoritative on those matters to which it speaks. The interpretation of the Bible is based upon its own internal terms and not from outside disciplines (archeology, anthropology, paleontology, biology, psychology, and so forth). Through the study of history, science, and culture our understanding of the Scriptures can improve, but no outside discipline should be used to abrogate clear biblical doctrine.

Many of us fall into the temptation of conforming our biblical interpretation of creation to the dominant world opinions; either we fear repercussions from the world, or from evangelistic motivations we hope to remove stumbling blocks to sharing the gospel. Akin to the masses in the tale of *The Emperor's New Clothes* who feared being considered "too stupid and incompetent to appreciate its quality," if they did not praise the Emperor's "new clothing," we too may fear being considered unintelligent for believing what the Bible teaches about creation. Our interpretation of the Bible, however, should be driven by a desire to be faithful to the text, with the knowledge that both our interpretation of the Bible and our understanding of the creation (i.e. the sciences) can err. Let us seek to understand each discipline accurately with God as the starting and ending point of all truth.

GOD CREATED ALL THINGS

In the first verse of the Bible God settled the issue of origins, *"In the beginning, God created the heavens and the earth."* (Genesis 1:1) If we do not believe this verse, our objection is not due to reason but is simply a matter of faith. This verse lays the most important block in the foundation of a biblical worldview (also referred to as a *presupposition* or *paradigm*). Genesis 1:1 establishes that God exists and that God created all things at the beginning of time. By faith we stand on this as an ultimate presupposition that cannot be proven by any scientific means. We cannot reproduce this event or disprove its veracity; all that is left is either acceptance or rejection.

How did God create the heavens and the earth? By speaking. *"By faith we understand that the universe was created by the word of God, so that what is seen was not made out of things that are visible."* (Hebrews 1:3) Throughout Genesis 1 there is a repetition of the statement, *"And God said, 'Let there be...'"* God simply speaks being into existence. He is not working with already existing matter but causes all matter to exist by His word. This is the doctrine of *creatio ex nihilo*, or creation out of nothing. *"By the word of the LORD the heavens were made, and by the breath of his mouth all their host."* (Psalm 33:6) The Almighty God who speaks things into being answers every question about origins and the existence of matter. The universe owes its creation to God, thus in eternity all living creatures will sing before the throne of God, *"Worthy are you, our Lord and God, to receive glory and honor and power, for you created all things, and by your will they existed and were created."* (Revelation 4:11)

THE IMPLICATIONS OF CREATION

The doctrine of creation carries a number of implications for the way we should view the world and ourselves:

- **The Authority of God:** *"For from him and through him and to him are all things. To him be glory forever. Amen."* (Romans 11:36) Since God created mankind He has authority over us. We owe our existence and our worship to Him and are accountable to Him for our deeds in this life. A merely materialistic view of creation which assumes the eternal existence of matter releases the creation and mankind from any obligation to serve God.

•   **The Character of Creation:** *"And God saw everything that he had made, and behold, it was very good."* (Genesis 1:31) The Scriptures say that, *"the heavens declare the glory of God,"* and *"Day to day pours out speech"* (Psalm 19:1, 2). This means that the handiwork of God's creation reflects the nature of God.   The immensity of the stars, the beauty of nature, and the almost infinite diversity and creativity of the various species of animals and flora manifest the divine attributes of God (Romans 1:19-21). The original creation was all pronounced *good* by God. The Proverbs (Proverbs 8) and the Psalms (Psalms 8, 19, 33, and 104) refer to God as having made everything according to His wisdom and glory. It is right for us to delight in and give glory to God for the blessings of His creation.

•   **The Image of God in Man:** *"Then God said, 'Let us make man in our image, after our likeness. And let them have dominion'"* (Genesis 1:26). The creation of Adam and Eve by God establishes our nature as being linked to the character of God--the *image* and *likeness* of God. In the command to create mankind God also gave us the mandate to rule over the world. We have a God-given role to be good stewards of the earth.   We are not the blight of this earth, but are protectors and nurturers of all that God has made.

•   **The Humility of Our Understanding**: *"Where were you when I laid the foundation of the earth? Tell me, if you have understanding."* (Job 38:4) Our study of nature should cause us to marvel at the intricacies and wisdom of all God's works.   Over time mankind has gained an immense amount of knowledge through the study of the world.   The more we learn, the more humble we should become, for how much more have we yet to discover? When God challenged Job, and us by extension, He exposed our ignorance and impotence over the world around us.

THE FAITH OF EVOLUTION

Is a theory of evolution compatible with the biblical account of creation? The theory of evolution is the dominant belief within secular education, and many in the church seek to reconcile the Bible with it. However, the following beliefs cannot be reconciled with the Scriptures:

•   The universe has always existed. (Genesis 1:1; Hebrews 11:3)
•   Matter came into being by chance. (Revelation 4:11)
•   All living things and species evolved from a single life source. (Genesis 1:11-12, 20-25)
•   Chance and time is the creative agency in the development of all species. (Genesis 1:11-31)
•   Adam and Eve did not exist, or were only a link in a chain of hominoids. (Genesis 1:26-2:14)

In order to reconcile the Bible with the theory of evolutionary we will need to compromise portions of the Scriptures, engaging in advanced exegetical yoga. Ironically, many atheistic evolutionists mock the attempts of theistic evolutionists to make evolution and the Bible compatible. As we engage others in these discussions, we should recognize that it is not necessarily proven facts, but emotionally held assumptions, that move people away from the Biblical account. Once these assumptions are exposed it is revealed that the theory of evolution is more of a dogmatic faith than objective science.

Our primary motivation for the defense of biblical creation is the exaltation of God.   As we meditate on the wonders of creation, we should be filled with the praises of God, *"Praise him, sun and moon, praise him, all you shining stars! Praise him, you highest heavens, and you waters above the heavens! Let them praise the name of the LORD! For he commanded and they were created."* (Psalm 148:3-5)

HITTING HOME

1.   How does God's creative power bolster your trust in Him as you live?

2.   Describe your interpretive approach to the Scriptures, that is, how do outside theories influence your interpretation of the creation account?

3.   What aspects of this created world move you to glorify God?

4.   How does the creation of mankind affect your view of yourself and your role in this world?

LESSON 44: INTERPRETING SCRIPTURE

KEY DOCTRINE: Scripture can be correctly interpreted and applied if one diligently, with the help of the Holy Spirit, follows correct interpretive principles.
MEMORY VERSE: *"Do your best to present yourself to God as one approved, a worker who has no need to be ashamed, rightly handling the word of truth."* (2 Timothy 2:15)
SCRIPTURE PRE-READING: Ezra 7:1-10; John 16:5-15; 2 Timothy 2:14-3:17; 2 Peter 1:19-2:3; 3:14-18

The Bible is a difficult book to interpret, but it can be correctly understood. God has not written a book for us about Himself, and at the same time hidden its meaning from us. We can faithfully interpret and apply the Bible if we are guided in our study by a number of key principles: the infallibility of Scripture, the self-interpreting nature of Scripture, differences in genre, the Holy Spirit's illumination of the Scriptures, and the progression of revelation.

THE INFALLIBILITY OF SCRIPTURE

As we come to interpret Scripture our starting point must be a conviction that the Bible is God's Word. As 2 Timothy 3:16 states, *"All Scripture is breathed out by God and profitable for teaching, for reproof, for correction, and for training in righteousness."* God *"breathed out"* His Word by inspiring men through the Holy Spirit to write what He wanted them to write. These authors were conscious that they were writing God's Word, though they did not always understand the totality of its meaning. Though God is the ultimate Author, because He has utilized a variety of men in different historical circumstances, their differences in writing style and subject matter will be evident. The divine inspiration of the Bible gives us confidence that the Bible is trustworthy in all its content.

THE BIBLE INTERPRETS ITSELF

The golden rule of biblical interpretation is that *Scripture interprets Scripture.* Since God is the author of the Bible there is one consistent message which connects all its themes together. There will not be any internal contradictions where doctrines are confused or cancel each other out. That does not mean that there are not paradoxes, ironies, and some incomprehensible mysteries in the Bible. When we face apparent tensions where two different verses seem to be saying opposite doctrines, we need to study them in light of each other and see if they are speaking about different aspects of an issue. For instance, Romans 4 states that Abraham was justified by faith and not works, yet James 2:24 states that Abraham was *"justified by works and not by faith only."* A quick reading shows an apparent contradiction, but through further study one sees that the two authors are addressing two different aspects of faith. Paul is focusing on how faith in Christ is the only means for justification. James is stating that justifying faith is proven to be genuine by works. In summary, we are justified by faith alone, but sanctification proves justification. Only by reading the two passages together can these distinctions be discerned.

Throughout the ages interpreters have recognized that some passages are harder to interpret than others. In these cases we allow the plain texts to serve as a basis for interpreting the more obscure texts. For instance, our understanding of the second coming of Jesus should be driven by the Gospels and First and Second Thessalonians, not by the book of Revelation alone, due to its symbolic nature. Obscure passages should never be used to establish a doctrine if it has no support from other texts within the Bible. A few examples of obscure texts being used to support erroneous practices are: baptism for the dead (1 Corinthians 15:29), tongues of angels (1 Corinthians 13:1), and snake handling (Mark 16:18). All doctrines should be confirmed by a variety of passages within Scripture which all speak to the same topic. There is an old adage that says, "Every heretic has his verse." So we should be careful of any doctrine based upon a single verse from the Bible.

KNOW YOUR GENRE

The Bible is written with a variety of literary genres. Much of the Old Testament is historical narrative (stories), laws, poetical books, and prophetic writings. The New Testament consists of four genres: Gospels, historical narrative (Acts), letters, and apocalyptic writing (Revelation). We need to interpret each of these types of literature according to their own set of unique principles. The following list can aid us in accurately interpreting each of these genres:

- **Poetry**: Poetic books should not be read literally. Metaphors, analogies, and hyperbole are for emotional intent.
- **Narrative:** A narrative account describes what happened in history. Each story may contain many applications concerning the faithfulness and mystery of God's providence and the conduct of people.
- **The Law:** The Moral Law (Ten Commandments) within the Old Testament Law has a lasting authority over the Christian. The ceremonial laws have been fulfilled in Christ, and the civil laws have ceased in their authority since the end of the theocratic nation of Israel.
- **Proverbs:** A proverb is a general principle of truth, but is not a universally binding law.
- **Prophets:** Old Testament prophetic books often have multiple fulfillments within history: in the history of Israel, in the New Testament church, and/or at Christ's return.
- **Parable:** A parable teaches spiritual truths using concrete imagery from life. Each parable taught by Jesus has a main point or a few sub points as the parable allows.
- **Epistles:** The letters of the apostles contain both descriptive doctrine of God's grace and instructions on how we need to live.

WHERE IS MEANING FOUND?

In our day a debate is raging between three perspectives on how the meaning of a text should be determined. If the correct meaning is determined by *the author* himself, then we need to know what he intended to communicate. Some would contend that we can never know what the author intended, so we should only look at *the text* itself. Others hold that only *the reader* can determine meaning as they interact with the text. The bias that we bring to a text will always affect how we interpret it.

By using biblical interpretive principles we can have confidence that we can determine an accurate meaning of a biblical text. Behind the human authors stands the Holy Spirit of God, who also aids us in interpreting its meaning (1 John 2:27). A skillful handling of the books of the Bible requires that we study the words of the original language, the structure of thought within a passage, and the cultural and historical context of each section. We should humbly recognize that our interpretations of the Bible are influenced by our own culture, personality, and presuppositions. Over time we will invariably discover that our understanding of passages of the Bible improves as we become more knowledgable of the whole counsel of God and as we mature in our knowledge of God.

THE PROGRESS OF REVELATION

What is the main theme of the Bible? Simply put, *redemption to the glory of God.* The whole story of the Bible is how God, in His grace, redeems a fallen creation to bring it all back to a future perfection—all for His glory. The whole Bible slowly progresses in revealing this redemptive plan from the creation and fall in Genesis to its consummation in Revelation.

Since it is all one story, we should not place a wedge between the Old and New Testaments. The Old Testament began the story of redemption and looks to its fulfillment in the New Testament with Christ. God always saves His people by His grace, and He does not change over the course of time. *"Jesus Christ is the same yesterday and today and forever."* (Hebrews 13:8) The revelation we have of the glory of God in Christ is of the same nature that we see of God in the Old Testament. *"No one has ever seen God; the only God, who is at the Father's side, he has made him known."* (John 1:18)

HITTING HOME

1. Taking into account the literary genres, read the following passages and answer the questions.
   a. **Narrative:** Should Elimelech have gone to Moab? What should we think about Naomi's complaint at the end of the chapter? (Ruth 1)
   b. **Law:** What distinctions are made in the types of killings? Which judicial death sentences still are implemented in your country? (Exodus 21:12-14)
   c. **Poetry:** Describe how David feels in his distress? (Psalm 102:3-7)
   d. **Parable:** What is the main point of this parable? (Matthew 13:44)
   e. **Proverb:** Interpret, reconcile, and apply these two proverbs. (Proverbs 26:4-5)
   f. **Prophecy:** When was this fulfilled? About whom is this prophecy speaking? (Isaiah 40:1-11)
   g. **Epistles:** Is this passage descriptive of God's salvation or exhortative for Christian obedience? (Ephesians 2:1-10)

LESSON 45: THE CHRISTIAN THINKER

KEY DOCTRINE: The Christian analyzes the world through a reasoning process which presupposes that the biblical revelation is the authoritative truth affecting all areas of knowledge.

MEMORY VERSE: *"Do not be conformed to this world, but be transformed by the renewal of your mind, that by testing you may discern what is the will of God, what is good and acceptable and perfect."* (Romans 12:2)

SCRIPTURE PRE-READING: Genesis 3:1-13; Proverbs 9:1-18; Romans 1:18-32; Acts 17:16-34; 1 Corinthians 1:18-2:16

When we place our faith in Jesus we enter a relationship with God in which we are to love Him with all our heart, mind, and strength. Loving God with our mind means that we will be thinkers who base our thoughts and values upon God's Word, and not on the thinking of this age. As we change our presuppositions to conform to God's Word, we will be able to engage with the thinking of the world around us.

HOW TO THINK

People outside the faith often accuse Christians of not being intellectual and of living by "blind faith." Critics think that Christians do not use reason or engage in critical thinking because we have accepted the Bible as the truth. Our dogmatically held beliefs are seen to be a hindrance to true "open-minded" thinking. In leveling these criticisms, skeptics are unaware of how they themselves are guilty of the accusations they direct at Christians. When a person reasons and draws conclusions about any matter they do so while working from a particular point of view. We all hold certain foundational values, presuppositions, paradigms, or worldviews through which we process facts and events. Much of the time we are unaware of the basic assumptions which affect our reasoning processes. From different presuppositions people draw divergent conclusions, even though they may have the same facts. From a human standpoint there is no true objectivity. Reason always proceeds logically from a starting point.

The presuppositions that we hold, in general, cannot be proven to be true using human reasoning. All people who are serious thinkers consider that they can justify their beliefs and presuppositions, and so also Christians can justify theirs. Part of the justification of the Christian worldview comes as we develop a self-critical awareness of how our presuppositions affect our thinking. What is the starting point for all knowledge? For the Christian, the starting point is God. The world chooses man.

LOVING OR SUPPRESSING TRUTH

One of the key presuppositions is the question of how does anybody discover knowledge. In philosophy this is called the *epistemological* question--where is truth found? The Christian looks to God and His revelation (the Bible) as the authority on the primary questions of life: the existence of God and the universe (ontology), the nature of mankind (anthropology), how to live (ethics), and the meaning of life (teleology). We accept that God has revealed these essential answers to us through the Bible, and we base our beliefs on the presupposition that the Bible is infallible and authoritative.

The world scoffs at the notion that anyone would base their thinking upon the Bible, and instead argues that mankind needs to decide for himself what to think. This argument is not new; it started in the garden of Eden many years ago, when the serpent asked Eve, *"Did God actually say, 'You shall not eat of any tree in the garden?'"* (Genesis 3:1) Satan questioned the veracity of God's word, installed doubt into Eve, and then tempted her to eat of the tree of the knowledge of good and evil. This was the first case of *epistemological rebellion*, when mankind decided to do what was right in their own eyes (Judges 21:25) instead of trusting in God's revelation. Romans 1:18-32 gives a similar verdict against the thinking of the world which rejects the knowledge of God. Read the passage and answer the following questions.

- Does mankind have a clear revelation and knowledge of God's existence and nature? How is this revelation seen? (v. 18-20)

- What does mankind do with this revelation? (v. 21-22)

- With what does mankind replace the knowledge of God? (v. 23-25)

- What happens to the mind, passions, and conduct of people who suppress the truth of God? (v. 26-32)

WORLDVIEWS IN CONFLICT

With the Enlightenment Age mankind felt that they had thrown off the shackles of superstition and faith and entered an age of certainty and science. It was expected that through reason and empiricism mankind would be able to prove all truth. However, over time the confidence of the modern man crumbled as the limitations of knowledge became apparent. Philosophers began to argue that reason was not objective, but was always influenced by the subjectivity of a person. Thus arose the postmodern age, which pessimistically concluded that man could not know anything for certain. All things were subjective and relative.

We live in a world with uncomfortable tensions between conflicting worldviews. The confident modern man, who believes that objective truth can be found through reason and science, is opposed by the relativistic postmodern man, who questions the whole concept of truth, especially in the areas of ethics and religion. As Christian thinkers we engage those around us, knowing that much of our evangelism is an intellectual battle against worldviews. *"For the weapons of our warfare are not of the flesh but have divine power to destroy strongholds. We destroy arguments and every lofty opinion raised against the knowledge of God, and take every thought captive to obey Christ"* (2 Corinthians 10:4-5). With God and the Scriptures as our starting point we are to gracefully and patiently challenge all presuppositions and beliefs which are contrary to the knowledge of Christ (2 Timothy 2:24-25).

THE TRANSFORMED THINKER

As Christians we must critically engage the world in which we live. The first stage of the battle is the self-examination of our own beliefs. Romans 12:2 exhorts us, *"Do not be conformed to this world, but be transformed by the renewal of your mind, that by testing you may discern what is the will of God, what is good and acceptable and perfect."* We are transformed in our minds by the diligent use of the Scriptures, which pierce the soul and discern *"the thoughts and intents of the heart"* (Hebrews 4:12-13). The Spirit will shine a light on areas where we are still conforming to the world and will transform us according to God's will. Christ's calling is to send us *"into the world"* but not be *"of the world"* (John 17:16, 18) and be used as *"salt"* and *"light"* (Matthew 5:13, 14) to transform the world. The following lists show some of the contrasts between the thinking of the Christian and the world:

The Christian	The World
The Bible is the authoritative Word of God	The Bible is a human book lacking authority
God created the heavens and the earth	The world is self-created by impersonal matter
Mankind was created in God's image	Mankind is the product of nature and evolution
All ethnic races are made in God's image	Ethnic races are a result of natural selection
Man's chief end is to glorify God	Man has no purpose except what he values
Ethics are determined by God	Mankind creates their own ethics
There is eternal existence after death	This life is all we can know
Marriage is instituted by God	Marriage is only a legal institution
God creates life in the womb	Life is a purely biological process
Gender differences are God's design	Gender differences are societal constructions
Governments are accountable to God	Governments are secular and not accountable to God

HITTING HOME

1. How have you witnessed the preaching of the Bible and the gospel to be considered foolishness instead of the wisdom of God?

2. Explain how presuppositions control how we think. Give an example in your life of how your thinking changed once a presupposition changed.

3. In your life how have you faced conflict with the values and thinking of the world?

4. From the above comparison/contrast list of presuppositions, where do you still find yourself conforming to the world's view of thinking?

LESSON 46: JESUS REIGNS

Key Doctrine: After Jesus Christ ascended to the right hand of the Father, He was declared Lord and He now reigns over the heavens and the earth.

Memory Verse: *"The LORD says to my Lord, 'Sit at my right hand, until I make your enemies your footstool."* (Psalm 110:1)

Scripture Pre-Reading: Psalm 2 & 110; Matthew 13:31-33; Ephesians 1:15-23; Hebrews 2:1-8

Christians struggle with being obedient to Christ in all areas of life. We tend to make our faith a private matter which we apply to our Sunday worship. Since Jesus was raised to the right hand of the Father, He reigns over the world until God puts all things under His feet. All of creation is required to submit to Jesus' rule lest they be subject to His judgment. We should now apply our faith by being *salt* and *light* in our families, church, work, and society as a whole.

THE DIVIDED LIFE

We tend to compartmentalize our faith and Christian life. Thinking that our faith covers our devotion, our church life, and our families we fail to see our need for obedience to Christ in other areas of our life. Many of us struggle to understand how to appropriately apply our faith to areas like the arts, media, education, work, and politics. For some time the unbelieving world has dominated these spheres within our society, while the church sits on the sidelines, sulking. There are a multitude of factors which have contributed to this state:

- **Church and Kingdom Confusion:** Christ has been made head of the church (Colossians 1:18) and His rule and righteousness (His kingdom) is to permeate other institutions in society. Not understanding the distinction between the kingdom of God and the church limits the reign of Christ exclusively to His church.
- **Separation of Church and State:** The acceptance of the separation of church and state dichotomy imposed by secularists and the courts has effectively excluded religious influence from the civic realm in many Western countries. Though the Christian church does not have authority over the civil government, the church and Christian individuals can speak to, and influence, the righteousness and wisdom by which political and educational leaders govern.
- **Modern and Postmodern Worldviews:** Western civilization has adopted a two-level modern and postmodern worldview. Since the Enlightenment, secular intellectuals consider knowledge of nature and science to be objective truth, whereas philosophy, religion and the arts are all seen to be subjective and relative. These worldviews exclude the Bible's claim to authoritative truth.
- **Tolerance Teaching:** In order to respect the beliefs of the individual, any religion which makes exclusive truth claims is considered offensive. In our desire to appear sensitive we often do not make a case for God's truth in its varied applications.
- **Dispensationalism:** Many Christians adhere to the eschatological doctrine of Dispensational Pre-Millennialism which awaits the reign of Christ over the world at the Millennium (Revelation 20:1-7). Until that time, Jesus is Savior and head of His church, but the world is not subject to His rule. If Christ's kingdom is only for the Millennium then we will not seek to advance it now.
- **Christian Ghettos:** Our desire to separate ourselves from the world's ungodly influence has led many of us to become uninvolved with many aspects of society. We might only interact with other Christians and refuse to become involved with corporate business, arts, or politics.

SIT AT MY RIGHT HAND

Is Jesus Lord now? Some of us might say that Jesus is the Savior now, but He will be the Lord at the Millennium or in the new heavens and new earth. The message of the Bible is that, since the resurrection and ascension, Jesus is seated at the right hand of God the Father and has been given all authority over the church, spiritual powers, nations, and the world itself (Ephesian 1:20-21). As an interpretive exercise read Psalm 110 and answer the following questions.

- What does it mean for the Lord to sit at the *"right hand"* of the LORD? (v. 1)

- In what way can the Lord be ruling *"in the midst of his enemies"*? (v. 2)

- When is *"the day of his wrath"*? (v. 5)

We could easily be skeptical about Christ's current reign when we see so much wickedness and disobedience to the gospel. The reality of evil in our day does not nullify Christ's present lordship. *"Now in putting everything in subjection to him, he left nothing outside his control. At present, we do not yet see everything in subjection to him."* (Hebrews 2:8) Just because it does not *look* as if Jesus reigns, He is still *"the blessed and only Sovereign, the King of kings and Lord of lords"* (1 Timothy 6:15). After being seated at the right hand of God Christ reigns until He defeats all opposition to Him:

> *"that he worked in Christ when he raised him from the dead and seated him at his right hand in the heavenly places, far above all rule and authority and power and dominion, and above every name that is named, not only in this age but also in the one to come. And he put all things under his feet and gave him as head over all things to the church"* (Ephesians 1:20-23).

The phrase *"all things under his feet"* originally comes from Psalm 8:6 and speaks about the authority that Jesus has been given by God. The Son reigns over the earth until the final great battle against evil when all God's enemies, both spiritual and human, are destroyed. This means that all things are now subject to His rule and are under His judgment, if they are contrary to His righteousness. Not believing in Christ does not free one from accountability to His rule and judgment. The Bible states that all will appear before the judgment seat of Christ (2 Corinthians 5:10), and there *"every knee should bow, in heaven and on earth and under the earth, and every tongue confess that Jesus Christ is Lord, to the glory of God the Father."* (Philippians 2:10-11) Part of our desire to see the kingdom come is our longing for the day when every knee bows. As we seek His kingdom our confidence in our labors is rooted in our trust in His present authority. *"And Jesus came and said to them, 'All authority in heaven and on earth has been given to me.'"* (Matthew 28:18)

THY KINGDOM COME

A noted Dutch theologian and statesmen, Abraham Kuyper, once stated, "In the total expanse of human life there is not a single square inch of which the Christ, who alone is sovereign, does not declare, 'That is mine!'" Abraham Kuyper contended that the lordship of Christ extends to every part of the creation. All spheres of our life are under Christ's rule, not simply the religious realm. As Christians we have been called to display the justice, mercy, and righteousness of Christ in every aspect of our life.

When we pray the Lord's Prayer we are invoking the Lord to reign in our world. *"Our Father in heaven, hallowed be your name. Your kingdom come, your will be done, on earth as it is in heaven."* (Matthew 6:9-10) We are petitioning God to be glorified in this world by manifesting the rule and righteousness of heaven to come down and exist in our world now. Christ's rule starts in our own lives at our conversion. As we live in the world, like yeast in dough, Christ's rule extends to other parts of our character and lifestyle. Our godliness must be manifest throughout all aspects of our life: marriage, family, work, church, community, entertainments, and political life. In so doing we will be fulfilling the commandment of Jesus when He said:

> *"You are the light of the world. A city set on a hill cannot be hidden. Nor do people light a lamp and put it under a basket, but on a stand, and it gives light to all in the house. In the same way, let your light shine before others, so that they may see your good works and give glory to your Father who is in heaven."* (Matthew 5:14-16)

HITTING HOME

1. How might the following areas of your life be transformed by Christ if you consistently obey Christ's teachings?
   a. **Family:** How does your family adhere to the instructions concerning husbands, wives and children? (Colossians 3:18-21; Ephesians 5:22-6:4)
   b. **Government:** What do you think of this statement? "I do not apply my religion to my political responsibilities." What role do we play as Christian citizens?
   c. **Business:** In terms of work ethic and consideration of the needs of others, are you fulfilling your role as a Christian employee or employer?
   d. **Arts and Culture:** Does the literature you read or the movies you watch cause you to think over things that are true, honorable, and praiseworthy? (Philippians 4:8)
   e. **Education:** Is your education, or that of your family, grounded in God as Creator and Lord over all, thus giving glory to Him as the source of all truth? How can you be more theologically discerning with your formal education involvement?

LESSON 47: MARRIAGE

KEY DOCTRINE: God created the institution of marriage to join a man and woman to become one flesh.
MEMORY VERSE: *"Therefore a man shall leave his father and his mother and hold fast to his wife, and they shall become one flesh."* (Genesis 2:24)
SCRIPTURE PRE-READING: Genesis 1:26-28; 2:18-25; Matthew 19:1-12; 1 Corinthians 7:1-24; Ephesians 5:22-6:4

Marriage is an institution ordained by God between a man and a woman. God created Adam and Eve to become *"one flesh"* (Genesis 2:24) in their mutual obedience and worship of God. After the entrance of sin into the world God still joins men and women together for the blessings of love and children. In order to once again achieve the blessings intended by God of *"one flesh"* the husband should lovingly lead his wife and family, and the wife should obediently help her husband.

ONE FLESH

Any questions about marriage require us to go back to the beginning of creation, which is what Jesus did when He was asked about divorce (Matthew 19:1-12). *"Therefore a man shall leave his father and his mother and hold fast to his wife, and the two shall become one flesh?'"* (Matthew 19:5) The main tenet of marriage is that it is an institution that God has created for the well-being of men and women, and for the raising of children. If we leave the biblical revelation and simply follow our preferences with respect to marriage, we forfeit all the blessings intended by God in marriage.

The greatest blessing of the marriage union is that two souls will become *"one flesh."* God looked on the bachelor Adam and seeing his solitude pronounced, *"It is not good that the man should be alone; I will make him a helper fit for him."* (Genesis 2:18) Isolation is not a good thing, so God put Adam to sleep and took a rib from him to create a perfectly compatible helpmate. The blessing of becoming *one flesh* is not a forever-lost garden of Eden experience, but it is also the goal for which every marriage should now strive. Although it is harder due to our sin--*"hardness of heart"* (Matthew 19:7)-- and our shame hindering true intimacy, the blessing that a man and a woman can intimately know each other is still obtainable. For believers in Christ who are joined by God's Holy Spirit, a husband and wife can be transparent, united in purpose, affectionate, and gracious in their love for each other.

A second obvious blessing of marriage is children. *"And God blessed them. And God said to them, 'Be fruitful and multiple and fill the earth'"* (Genesis 1:28). It is within the marriage covenant that children should be born, nurtured, and grow in the knowledge of God. *"Did he not make them one, with a portion of the Spirit in their union? And what was the one God seeking? Godly offspring."* (Malachi 2:15) The marriage covenant was not created solely for the couple to enjoy its benefits (two incomes, sex, companionship, etc.), it was also designed to become a safe haven to raise godly children with faith. *"Behold, children are a heritage from the LORD, the fruit of the womb a reward."* (Psalm 127:3)

Many people in our day are in support of gay marriage. If we take the Scriptures as the final authority on the issue of marriage, same-sex unions cannot have God's favor resting on them. God has declared that marriage is to be between one man and one women (Genesis 2:22-25). He has also judged homosexuality to be a sin (1 Corinthians 6:9), and same-sex unions cannot, on their own, procreate and raise godly children. Governments are with greater frequency legalizing same-sex unions, however the church should never acknowledge the legitimacy of gay marriage before God.

The Bible does not grant license for polygamous marriages. Although the Old Testament records that a number of the Israelites had multiple wives (Abraham, Jacob, David), polygamy was not God's original design and not the design for Christian marriage. Jesus' teaching on marriage brings us back to God's original purpose and ideal plan for the man and the woman to become one flesh. The entrance of any other party destroys the sanctity of this marriage union. The Bible's prohibition of polygamy for church leaders (1 Timothy 3:2, 12) indicates that one man and one wife is the only rule for God's people.

THE LOVING HEAD

In order for a married couple to experience the blessing of *one flesh* they need to fulfill the roles and responsibilities which God has assigned to them. The trend in our culture is to maintain that men and women are "equal partners" with no differences in their roles and responsibilities. Although men and women equally bear God's image, in the family God has assigned them unique and complimentary roles.

The husband's primary role is to be the head of the wife and family. As the head he assumes ultimate responsibility for all people and aspects of his home: wife, children, house, provision, safety, morality, and spiritual health. The father, or husband, is to be the pastor of his home in order to oversee the teaching and the practice of the Word of God for all members of his family. God's specific command for the husband is to love his wife. *"Husbands, love your wives, as Christ loved the church and gave himself up for her"*(Ephesians 5:25). A husband is called to deny his selfishness, arrogance, and irresponsibility and to sacrificially love his wive, in spite of her weaknesses and disrespect. As an exercise read the following passages and answer the questions.

* In what manner should a husband love his wife? (Ephesians 5:25-33)

* How should the *one flesh* doctrine motivate a husband to love his wife? (Ephesians 5:25-33)

* What does it mean to *"live with your wives in an understanding way"*? (1 Peter 3:7)

* In what ways is the wife a *"weaker vessel"*? (1 Peter 3:7)

THE PERFECT HELPMATE

God's original description of Eve was that she was a *"helper fit for him."* (Genesis 2:18) Two blessings can be found here: *compatibility* and *help*. Since women are also created in the image of God and have come from the man's rib, they can become a perfect fit for men intellectually, emotionally, spiritually, and practically. When we discover that perfect fit, it ignites our passions and excites our hearts. The second description of the woman is that she is a *helper*. Though modern feminism may consider the role of a *helper* to be a demeaning or inferior role to the man, it is an honorable position. God Himself is described as the *helper* of mankind (Psalm 46:1; 124:8) throughout the Scriptures. The help that a woman gives is not merely menial labor, but assisting the man to lead and be faithful, as they together seek to glorify God. A godly wife will help her husband to worship God, to obey Scripture, to trust the Lord, and to advance God's kingdom and glory in this world.

Just as the command for husbands to love their wives can be difficult, the command for wives to submit to their husbands can also be difficult for women. *"Wives, submit to your own husbands, as to the Lord. For the husband is the head of the wife even as Christ is head of the church"* (Ephesians 5:22-23). In general we do not like to submit to authority, so it can be difficult for a woman to have to submit to a husband with his flaws. This command will challenges the faith of wives. In order to submit to a fallen husband, a wife needs to trust in her sovereign God to care for her and her family. A women's faith is not in her husband but in the Lord. Such a faith is pleasing to God, refines her character, and makes her attractive to all. *"but let your adorning be the hidden person of the heart with the imperishable beauty of a gentle and quiet spirit, which in God's sight is very precious. For this is how the holy women who hoped in God used to adorn themselves, by submitting to their own husbands"* (1 Peter 3:4).

TRAIN UP A CHILD

The Scriptures call parents to bring up the next generation in the *"discipline and instruction of the Lord."* (Ephesians 6:4) How parents raise their children can be a contentious issue within the church. The Bible does not give great specificity in parental philosophy, but it does lay down a few key principles about how we should *"train up a child"* (Proverbs 22:6):
* Parents must teach their children the fear of the Lord. (Deuteronomy 6:4-9; Ephesians 6:4)
* Parents must love and care for their children. (Titus 2:4; Colossians 3:21)
* Parents must discipline their children. (Proverbs 13:24; 22:15)
* Children must honor and obey their parents. (Exodus 20:12; Colossians 3:20)

HITTING HOME

1. In what ways do you see the Biblical marriage being compromised in your society?

2. How have you seen or experienced the *one flesh* reality in marriage?

3. Husbands, in what ways are you faithful as a loving head? How are you failing?

4. Wives, how do you help your husband in his headship, and are you faithfully submitting to him?

LESSON 48: FLEE IDOLATRY!

KEY DOCTRINE: Idolatry exists whenever people no longer trust and worship God, but begin to hope in, and worship the things of this world.
MEMORY VERSE: *"Therefore, my beloved, flee from idolatry."* (1 Corinthians 10:14)
SCRIPTURE PRE-READING: Exodus 20:1-17; Deuteronomy 4:15-31; Isaiah 44:9-20; 1 Corinthians 10:1-33

The first of God's Ten Commandments charges that we are to have no other god before Him. In the Old Testament the nation of Israel repeatedly fell into the idolatry of the nations around them. In the Christian church God's people must also flee idolatry. Idolatry is not just the worship of statues and images, but may also be the worship of idols that we have created in our own hearts. Greed and covetousness are a manifestation of our hearts' idolatry which will lead to sexual immorality.

THAT OLD-TIME PAGAN RELIGION

Understanding idolatry in the Old Testament seems simple enough, even if we have a problem with grasping the attraction. Instead of worshipping the LORD God of Israel, whom no one could see, the pagan nations worshipped gods that were carved images. There were statues and poles for gods such as Baal, Asherah, or Dagon. These images were worship-aids which helped the worshipper conceptualize the god they believed to be behind the idol. As people prayed to these gods they expected that their everyday life would be blessed in terms of crops, rain, fertility, business prosperity and overall luck. They expected the gods to do something for them in their life. Likewise, they feared that if they failed to worship the gods, dire results would follow.

The LORD's primary commandment to the nation of Israel was to flee from the idolatry of the surrounding nations. Due to this idolatry and the wickedness of these nations God drove them out from before Israel (Deuteronomy 9:4). The LORD repeatedly commanded Israel not to adopt the abominable practices of worshiping images like the pagans did, lest they become wicked like them. Eventually, Israel did fall into the grossest forms of idolatry, even to the point of sacrificing their children to the god Molech. *"And he burned* [Manasseh] *his son as an offering and used fortune-telling and omens and dealt with mediums and with necromancers. He did much evil in the sight of the LORD, provoking him* [God] *to anger."* (2 Kings 21:6) The nation of Israel's destruction and exile from the land of promise was a direct result of her descent into idolatry and wickedness. After experiencing the LORD's chastisement of seventy years exile in the land of Babylon, Israel never again fell into pagan idolatry.

IDOLATRY AS COVETOUSNESS

The worship of statues and images seems primitive and foolish to the modern Western mind. It is only after we understand the essence of idolatry that we can recognize the dangers and prevalence of idolatry in our own culture. Idolatry is equated with covetousness in the Bible. Both Colossians 3:5 and Ephesians 5:5 recognize this correlation. *"Put to death therefore what is earthly in you: sexual immorality, impurity, passion, evil desire, and* **covetousness, which is idolatry**.*"* (Colossians 3:5) The prohibition of covetousness in the tenth commandment is a recapitulation of the first commandment to have no other gods (Exodus 20:3, 17). Just as the LORD rebuked Israel for its idolatry in the Old Testament, the Lord Jesus rebukes us for our love of the things of this world in the Gospels (Mark 8:36).

If we do not love and trust in God we will love and trust in the things of this world. Covetousness is the greed and ambition to accumulate and achieve this world's glory and riches. Even though it is a grave sin, prohibited by the Law, and the covetous person cannot enter heaven (Ephesians 5:5), we tend to feel that greed is an acceptable sin. After all, do we not all want to be better off in life? Our devotion and desire for this world crowds out our love and trust in God, hence the numerous warnings in the Bible concerning riches and the love of money (Matthew 6:24; Luke 12:15).

Idolatry represents the worship of the things of this world. *"Claiming to be wise, they became fools, and exchanged the glory of the immortal God for images resembling mortal man and birds and animals and creeping things...because they exchanged the truth about God for a lie and worshiped and served the creature rather than the Creator, who is blessed forever! Amen."* (Romans 1:22-23, 25) Thus the Bible is accurate in equating idolatry with covetousness. To the extent that we love, delight in, hope in, and strive for things in this world we are engaging in idolatry. When we think about it in these terms it becomes clear how prevalent and dangerous idolatry is in our day.

IDOLATRY AND SEXUAL IMMORALITY

The added danger of idolatry is that it leads to sexual immorality. The pagan religions of Baal and Asherah involved cult prostitution, where worshippers engaged in sexual acts. The pagans believed that by stimulating the God's to copulate the land would become fertile Although God repeatedly warned them the Israelites were easily seduced by this kind of worship--perhaps it met their "felt needs." We see this link between idolatry and sexual immorality in Numbers 25 when the Israelites and the Midianites together sacrificed to idols and engaged in fornication (1 Corinthians 10:8). In Romans 1:23-27 the apostle Paul argues that the idolatry of the pagans led to their sexual perversions. In the Bible passages which list the many sins to be put off in a Christian, idolatry and sexual immorality are usually paired denoting their connection (1 Corinthians 6:9; Colossians 3:5; Ephesians 5:3-5; Galatians 5:19-20; and Revelation 2:14, 20).

When we do not worship and serve the unseen holy LORD we will focus on the pleasures of our senses. The pleasures of materialism, success, and sexual gratification will become our new god. The Bible commands us to flee both idolatry and sexual immorality (1 Corinthians 6:18; 10:14) because, if we do not worship the Creator by His Spirit, we will worship the creation with our flesh (Romans 1:24-27).

TRUSTING IN IDOLS

Idols represent things of the earth, but they are also considered gods in and of themselves. In the Old Testament people actually trusted and prayed to the idols with the expectation of help from the god. *"And the rest of it he makes into a god, an idol, and falls down to it and worships it. He prays to it and says, "Deliver me, for you are my god!"* (Isaiah 44:17) The idolater hopes that the god will help him, but in reality their hope is in demons. When the Scriptures recount the infidelity of Israel it says, *"They served their idols, which became a snare to them. They sacrificed their sons and their daughters to the demons."* (Psalm 106:36-37) The apostle Paul rebuked the church of Corinth's practice of sharing in pagan idol feasts by saying, *"No, I imply that what pagans sacrifice they offer to demons and not to God. I do not want you to be participants with demons."* (1 Corinthians 10:20)

In God's eyes idolatry is completely asinine. *"All who fashion idols are nothing, and the things they delight in do not profit."* (Isaiah 44:9) The idol cannot help us, no matter how much we trust in it. Why not? Because idols are nothing, lifeless, and powerless to save. *"They have mouths, but do not speak; eyes, but do not see. They have ears, but do not hear; noses, but do not smell. They have hands, but do not feel; feet, but do not walk; and they do not make a sound in their throat. Those who make them become like them; so do all who trust in them."* (Psalm 115:5-8) God declared that He made the heavens and the earth and He is mighty to save. *"Our God is in the heavens; he does all that he pleases."* (Psalm 115:3) This contrast between an omnipotent Lord and impotent gods should challenge us when we are tempted to trust in idols.

Theologians have noted that our hearts are idol factories. If we do not trust in the Lord we will create another god. The idols of our age are not necessarily made of wood and stone but they are still made by our hands. Our job, wealth, achievements, church, house, and family can all become idols in our hearts. Anything in this world in which we place our trust, which is not God, is an idol. The greatest and most secretive idol of all is our selves. The Lord, who searches hearts, knows what we actually worship and trust in. God is jealous and He will not allow an idol to remain in our life. He will test our heart and faith until we come to repentance and closer to our goal of loving God with all our heart, soul, mind, and strength. *"Little children, keep yourselves from idols."* (1 John 5:21)

Hitting Home

1. Prior to your conversion, what idolatry were you engaged in?

2. Since idolatry and covetousness are correlated, in what ways are you tempted by covetousness in your life?

3. What are the dangers of sexual sin when you start living only for this world?

4. What thing(s) in this world are you trusting in to deliver you? Can you describe an experience in your life where God exposed and removed an idol from your life?

5. What is God's cure for the idolatry of self? (Mark 8:34-37)

LESSON 49: GOD'S COVENANT

KEY DOCTRINE: In salvation God graciously enters into a covenant relationship with His people whereby He promises to save and bless them, and they in turn worship and obey Him.

MEMORY VERSE: *"But this is the covenant that I will make with the house of Israel after those days, declares the LORD: I will put my law within them, and I will write it on your hearts. And I will be their God, and they shall be my people."* (Jeremiah 31:33)

SCRIPTURE PRE-READING: Genesis 17:1-14; 2 Samuel 7:1-17; Jeremiah 31:31-34; Luke 22:14-23; Hebrews 9:11-28

When God saves us, He enters into a covenant with us. God always initiates the covenant and it is based upon His grace extended to us. In both the Old and New Testaments God shows mercy to us and declares that He will be our God and we will be His people. In the covenant God blesses us with His manifold salvation, and we in return love and keep His commandments.

THE CONCEPT OF COVENANT

What is a covenant? At the simplest level a covenant is a binding relationship between two parties. A marriage is a covenant, as are many legal contracts. Covenants occur throughout the Bible, so the term *covenant* is not a human theological construct imposed upon the biblical text. Jonathan and David made a covenant where they swore loyalty to each other (1 Samuel 20:16-17). Kings in ancient days made covenants with their defeated enemies, obligating loyalty to their rule. These covenants were not just loose agreements but *bonds in blood*. In a covenant ceremony animals were cut in two and both parties would walk between the pieces. The penalty for breaking the covenant was death, as portrayed by the slain animals.

More important than any human covenant is the covenant that God enters into with mankind. A covenant is a formal, mutual relationship of loyalty and faithfulness between both persons. God enters into such a covenant with us by proclaiming, *"I will be their God, and they shall be my people."* This is salvation in a nutshell: The LORD is our God and we are His people. We pledge to love God and obey His commandments, and God pledges to be our refuge and strength for all of eternity.

How do we enter into this covenant with God? We do so through faith and by His grace. Throughout the Bible God always entered into a relationship with people by His grace. God initiated the relationship by showing favor to an individual (Noah, Abraham, etc.), who then responded with faith in God's mercy. God's people were not saved because of their merit. Abraham was an idolater in the Ur of Chaldeans. The nation of Israel was enslaved in Egypt. *"Know, therefore, that the LORD your God is not giving you this good land to possess because of your righteousness, for you are a stubborn people."* (Deuteronomy 9:6) God chooses to be merciful, and we respond with faith and obedience to His grace. *"We love because he first loved us."* (1 John 4:19) This principle of God leading with grace may be the most important truth in the Bible.

GOD'S OLD COVENANT

God entered into a number of covenants with His chosen people throughout the Bible. The first recorded covenant in the Bible occurs in Genesis 9:9 when, after the flood God swore to never flood the whole earth again. Later God entered into a covenant with Abraham, promising to give him descendants who would inherit the land of Canaan (Genesis 15:1-21). At Mt. Sinai the people of Israel entered into a covenant to be God's people and to keep His law (Exodus 34:10-28). God swore to King David that He would maintain his kingly line (2 Samuel 7:1-17), which ultimately led to Jesus Christ.

God initiated all of these covenants and the human parties involved responded in faith to God's promises. God pledged to faithfully bless His people by defeating their enemies, granting productivity to the land, and giving them offspring. In turn, Israel was forbidden to worship other gods, like the nations around them, or break God's laws, as summarized in the Ten Commandments. The old covenant, however, had a planned obsolescence built into it. The sacrificial system did not provide a full atonement for sin, and the sin of God's people prevented them from keeping God's requirement of holiness. Thus, a new covenant was required that would grant forgiveness, enable obedience, and provide fellowship with God. Many of the Old Testament prophetic books, such as Isaiah and Jeremiah, looked forward to when this new covenant would be inaugurated.

Interpretation Exercise: Read Jeremiah 31:31-34 and answer the following questions.
• Did God have an intimate relationship with Israel in the old covenant? (v. 31-32)

• Did God or man break the old covenant? (v. 32)

• In the new covenant how will God's people be able to keep the law? (v. 33)

• List the four main benefits of the new covenant? (v. 33-34)

GOD'S NEW COVENANT

Since the coming of Jesus Christ, God has commanded all people to enter into a covenant relationship with Him by faith in His Son. *"The times of ignorance God overlooked, but now he commands all people everywhere to repent"* (Acts 17:30). Due to the failings of the old covenant God inaugurated a new covenant based upon better promises (Hebrews 8:6). The new covenant is similar to the old in that it brings about a relationship with God, but it far surpasses the old covenant in its effectiveness and fuller revelation of God's glory. In Jesus Christ we see the fullest revelation of the glory of God and the final word in respect to knowing God. With Christ's death and resurrection we have the perfect sacrifice given by the perfect Priest in God's heavenly sanctuary. With the giving of the Holy Spirit believers can experience a more full and effective sanctification and obedience to God. The new covenant gives a greater experience of salvation than that which believers enjoyed under the old covenant.

Understanding the new covenant in Jesus should greatly increase our assurance of faith. In this covenant our heavenly Father has promised to defend, provide, and bless our earthly existence (Matthew 6:26). He has granted us a full forgiveness of sins and has promised that His condemnation will not be upon us. God not only fulfills His side of the covenant, He also fulfills ours. We may justifiably fear our own failings in obedience, but Christ aids us in fulfilling our commitment to faithfulness by granting the Spirit to preserve us throughout our life. Christ has become *"the founder and perfecter of our faith"* (Hebrews 12:2), who completes what He starts (Philippians 1:6).

An additional dimension of the covenant is that God brings not just individuals, but whole communities into covenant with Him. When we are saved God adds us to His church where we find a covenant community of people who have pledged to serve the Lord. The Lord enters covenant with the whole of God's people and His commandments are always addressed to the whole community. As God's people we are all obligated to keep the covenant by being faithful to the Lord and loving one another according to His commandments.

When God saves someone His favor is also extended to that person's family. Noah and Lot's children were also delivered from destruction (Genesis 7:1; 19:12), and Rahab's (Joshua 6:23) family was saved along with her. The apostle Paul promised the Philippian jailer that both he and his whole household would be saved through the gospel of Christ (Acts 16:31). The deepest longing of any Christian parent is the desire for their children to be blessed by the Lord. Thankfully, God has promised His love to a thousand generations of those who love Him (Deuteronomy 5:10). As we train up our children in *"the discipline and instruction of the Lord"* (Ephesians 6:4) our confidence rests in God's promise that He will place His truth in their hearts. *"'And as for me, this is my covenant with them,' says the LORD: 'My Spirit that is upon you, and my words that I have put in your mouth, shall not depart out of your mouth, or out of the mouth of your offspring, or out of the mouth of your children's offspring,' says the LORD, 'from this time forth and forevermore.'"* (Isaiah 59:21)

HITTING HOME

1. How does it help you to understand your faith when you see it as a binding relationship between God and you, with mutual responsibilities?

2. God begins a relationship with us based upon His grace through Jesus. How does that affect any merit-based salvation thinking you possess?

3. How should the idea of a community of people in covenant with God transform your relationships within the church body?

4. How does God's covenant with you affect your children's upbringing and faith?

LESSON 50: THE WORTH OF WORK

KEY DOCTRINE: God has placed all people on the earth to work as stewards of His creation for Him.
MEMORY VERSE: *"Whatever you do, work heartily, as for the Lord and not for men"* (Colossians 3:23)
SCRIPTURE PRE-READING: Genesis 1:26-31; 2:15; 3:17-19; Ecclesiastes 1:12-2:26; Ephesians 6:5-9

Due to the fall of man work has become painful and frustrating. Yet, for the people of God, work can be redeemed if we understand the proper perspective on our labor. Work should not be merely for economic gain but to improve the well-being of this world and to glorify God. Only with this perspective can we find significance instead of futility in our work. When we seek to honor God in how we work we also discover that God blesses us and helps us in all that we do.

A DREAM JOB

At times we might dream of becoming so financially secure that we can retire early and lead a life of leisure. We may hope that by not working we can simply rest, play, and finally enjoy life. It sounds enticing but such a lifestyle cannot fulfill our calling from God. This dream stems from the reality that much of our work is wearisome, but we would be wrong to conclude that work itself is intrinsically bad. The grief and pain associated with work is a result of the fall of man (Genesis 3:17-19). In God's original design work would only have been a blessing.

When God announced that He was going to create mankind He gave them a job to do. *"Let us make man in our image, after our likeness. And let them have dominion over the fish of the sea and over the birds of the heavens and over every living thing that moves on the earth."* (Genesis 1:26) Mankind had dominion over the earth and everything in it. Adam and Eve were responsible for the upkeep and prosperity of all living creatures on the earth. Adam had a job in paradise. *"The LORD God took the man and put him in the garden of Eden to work it and keep it."* (Genesis 2:15) Everything Adam and Eve did was successful; they did not have to eke out a living since God abundantly gave them food from the trees. They rejoiced in the works of God's hand and joyfully tended the garden as they brought forth its bounty. Adam had a perfect relationship with God and did his work to the glory of God. Likewise, we were designed by God to work and find fulfillment and joy in being productive with our hands and minds. When we do not have work to do, we experience a sense of futility and depression because we have neglected to fulfill our purpose in life.

GRIEVOUS TOIL

After the initial sin of Adam, God spoke to Adam and pronounced a judgment upon his life (Genesis 3:17-19). The earth, which he was responsible for, was now under a curse. It would not produce as freely as before. His work would now become painful labor as characterized by *"thorns and thistles"* and *"the sweat of your face."* (Genesis 3:18-19) Lastly, all mankind would die. The originally blessed labor has become a grievous toil until we die. This is what many of our jobs feel like. The state of our modern economy that is marked by high unemployment, low wages, job insecurity, work place jealousy and competition, cruel bosses, and awful workplace conditions, is a result of God's judgment on the first worker.

The Preacher in the book of Ecclesiastes examined all the work of mankind and was critical of what he saw. Ecclesiastes is mainly an empirical analysis of the folly of much of what we do on the earth. Read the following passages in Ecclesiastes and answer the related questions.

- What motivates the work-ethic of people? (4:4)

- What folly does the "workaholic" experience? (4:7-8)

- What vanity befalls the lover of money? (5:10-11)

- Describe the grievous evil that befalls this father. (5:13-16)

- What vanity often characterizes the labors of people? (2:18-21)

WORKING FOR THE LORD

The Preacher's final word on work in Ecclesiastes is not morbid pessimism, but a call to hope for those of us who have a mature view of our labor on this earth. *"I perceived that there is nothing better for them than to be joyful and to do good as long as they live; also that everyone should eat and drink and take pleasure in his toil—this is God's gift to man"* (Ecclesiastes 3:12-13). Even after the curse God in His redemptive grace gives us the ability to live in such a manner that we can find pleasure and contentment in our work.

How do we work in such a manner that it does not feel futile, but instead feels significant and pleasurable? The primary change in our thinking must be that we do not make our work a form of idolatry, rather we work *"as for the Lord"* (Colossians 3:23). Work does not exist solely for our income. We need to make the primary purpose of our life the glory of God, and our work is a sphere and means by which we obey God's commandments and make the world a better place. With this change of thinking we now serve the Lord in our labors, as we continue the job that was given to Adam. There are a number of principles that the Bible teaches to help us fulfill this calling to work *"as for the Lord"*:

- **Greed is Not Good:** We should not be consumed with greed and ambition in our work. (Ecclesiastes 4:7; Luke 12:13-21)
- **Learn to Obey:** We need to be obedient and respectful to those who have authority over us. (1 Peter 2:18-20; Ephesians 6:5-8)
- **Work Hard and Honestly:** We are ultimately accountable to God, not our bosses for our work. Thus, we should work diligently for the Lord. (Colossians 3:22-25)
- **Be a Good Boss:** Employers and those in authority need to pay and treat fairly those in their employment because God has authority over employers and governments. (Ephesians 6:9; James 5:1-6)
- **Discover Your Calling:** Each of us have been given unique gifts and skills which fulfill a specific calling of God. As we conform to God's purposes for us in this world we will find significance and joy in our labors. (Ecclesiastes 5:18-19)

GOD WORKING FOR US

When we engage in our work we should not think that we are working on our own. Wherever we are working we need to trust that God is with us, helping us in our work. He places us in our employments, *"Beware lest you say in your heart, 'My power and the might of my hand have gotten me this wealth.' You shall remember the LORD your God, for it is he who gives you power to get wealth."* (Deuteronomy 8:17-18) As we seek to glorify God in doing things His way He grants us success in our work. The Bible is replete with examples and promises of God prospering His people in their work. The godly man of Psalm 1 who delights in God's law *"is like a tree planted by streams of water that yields its fruit in its season, and its leaf does not wither. In all that he does, he prospers."* (Psalm 1:3) It is said of Joseph that God blessed him and caused everything that he did in Potiphar's house and in the prison to be successful (Genesis 39:1-6; 19-23). The patriarchs' (Abraham, Isaac, and Jacob) wealth increased at the Lord's hand. The nation of Israel was promised prosperity in the Promised Land if they remained faithful to the Lord's covenant (Deuteronomy 28:1-14).

We should not think that God only blesses His people on the pages of the Bible. God is the same throughout time and He has pledged to be a source of blessing to us when we follow His commandments. With faith let us engage in our work knowing that God has a purpose for us in our labors and He will *"establish the work of our hands upon us; yes establish the work of our hands!"* (Psalm 90:17)

HITTING HOME

1. How would you see your work as having *"thorns and thistles"*? (Genesis 3:18)

2. How is your work a calling before God and not merely a way to make money?

3. In what ways do you honor your boss (authority) and also work *"for the Lord and not for men"* (Colossians 3:23)?

4. How have you seen ways in which God has helped you in your labors?

LESSON 51: THE END TIMES

KEY DOCTRINE: Jesus Christ calls believers to faithfully wait for His return and persevere in the face of all tribulation and persecution in this age.

MEMORY VERSE: *"But stay awake at all times, praying that you may have strength to escape all these things that are going to take place, and to stand before the Son of Man."* (Luke 21:36)

SCRIPTURE PRE-READING: Isaiah 66:15-24; Matthew 24:1-44; 1 Thessalonians 4:13-5:6; 2 Thessalonians 2:1-12; Revelation 20:1-21:8

Eschatology is the study of the end times and the final judgments at the return of Jesus Christ. Eschatology has always been much debated, and many believers may find it to be a confusing topic. The teachings about the last days, as presented in the Bible, should encourage us since Christ will return victoriously. As we await His return we are called to endure by live faithful and godly lives in this age.

DOES THIS STUFF MATTER?

Many people do not care for end-times discussions. This is understandable considering how often modern-day "prophets" falsely (and embarrassingly) predict when Christ shall return, or when the world will end. Some Bible teachers seem to focus inordinately on end times prophecy and inadequately teach the rest of the Bible. Many of us do not read the book Revelation, or, if we do, we find it confusing and troubling. Given the difficulties in understanding eschatology should we just ignore the whole matter?

Since it is a part of the Scriptures, we need to have an understanding of what is taught concerning Christ's return, and why it should encourage our faith. One purpose behind end times doctrine is to warn us about the sober reality of ungodly opposition to the church. In the face of this persecution we should be encouraged by the knowledge that the Lord is sovereign and He will defeat all of His and our enemies. We are held by His hand and no power in heaven or on earth can stop His kingdom. He shall return with wrath and blessings in His hand, and we who love him eagerly await Him saying, *"Amen. Come. Lord Jesus!"* (Revelation 22:20)

A SIMPLE PLAN

There are numerous explanations or schools of thought concerning how the end times will unfold. Matters such as the antichrist, the millennium, the great tribulation, Christ's kingdom, the last judgment, and Christ's return all have to be considered. The following is a simple plan based upon the Old Testament prophets, the Gospels, the epistles, and the Revelation which takes into account these key elements of the end times without trying to force the details:

1. **Gospel Expansion:** The preaching of the gospel and the church will expand throughout the earth to reach all peoples and nations. (Isaiah 66:18-21; Matthew 24:14; 28:19)
2. **The Antichrist Brings Persecution:** The antichrist, or the *"man of lawlessness"* (Second Thessalonians 2:3), will spearhead a great persecution against believers, and will set himself up to be worshipped as if he were God. (Matthew 24:21-24; 2 Thessalonians 2:3-12; 1 John 2:18; 4:1-6)
3. **Cosmic Calamities:** The sun, moon, and stars will be shaken and burned up, indicating the end of the first creation. (Luke 21:25-26; 2 Peter 3:10)
4. **Christ Returns:** The Son of Man will return visibly with the angels in great glory and power, destroying all opposition by His Word. Believers will then be given immortal bodies. (First Corinthians 15:50-55; 1 Thessalonians 4:16-17; Revelation 19:11-21)
5. **The Final Judgment:** All the living and the dead will stand before Christ to receive their just judgment in accordance with their deeds. The righteous will dwell with God in His eternal kingdom and the wicked will suffer with Satan and the demons in the lake of fire. (Matthew 13:36-43; 25:31-32; Jude 14-15; Revelation 20:11-15)
6. **A New Heavens and a New Earth:** The righteous will dwell in glory with God in a new heavens and a new earth that has no curse of sin or death. (Isaiah 65:17-20; 2 Peter 3:10; Revelation 21:1)

Hot Topics!

- **The Rapture:** It became a popular belief many years ago that Jesus would secretly return and steal away all believers (Which would be disastrous if the pilot of the airplane was a Christian!). This idea of an initial return of Christ and a rapture of believers does not have strong support in the Scriptures. Christ will return only once, and all will see His glory in the sky (Matthew 24:30).
- **The Antichrist:** Throughout history many antichrists have come (1 John 2:18) who have opposed God and His people. However, in the last days a preeminent antichrist will come, setting himself up as God to replace the worship of Jesus. He has not appeared yet, and we should not worry because he will be destroyed by one breath from the mouth of Jesus (2 Thessalonians 2:8).
- **The Great Tribulation:** Many people fear the time of great tribulation just prior to Christ's coming (Matthew 24:21-22). This dread of persecution, and of a hope of bypassing it, may have fostered theories of the rapture. The reality of the Christian life is that all who follow Christ must suffer persecution in this age (Acts 14:22), but we will be endure and conquer through the power of God protecting us.
- **The Millennium:** Based upon Revelation 20:1-8, some hold that Jesus will return and set up an earthly kingdom in Jerusalem for a literal thousand years. After that time Christ will return to judge the world. Apart from Revelation 20 there is no other support in the Bible for such a doctrine. A better interpretation of the thousand years is that it refers to the entire church age, when believers who die go to be with the Lord in heaven and reign with Him. Satan is bound in the sense that he has been restrained from stopping the spread of the gospel throughout the world until the whole company of the elect have been brought in. After that time Satan will then be *"released"* (Revelation 20:3) to lead a great persecution prior to his destruction at Christ's return.

Character Counts

What are we supposed to take away from any study of the end times? Perhaps we could invest in a bunker construction in the mountains of Montana with our store of genetically modified seeds. Should we try to identify which world leader will be the antichrist? The problem with these approaches is that Jesus instructed us that no one will know when He is to return (Matthew 24:36, 44).

The Scriptures give us plain instructions of what we should do in the face of end times opposition --live godly lives! *"Since all these things are thus to be dissolved, what sort of people ought you to be in lives of holiness and godliness, waiting for and hastening the coming of the day of God."* (2 Peter 3:11-12) The consistent instruction of Scripture is that we overcome evil by keeping faith in Jesus and by living righteously. After Jesus spoke about the signs of the end of the age He told four parables about holy living in the face of the last judgment: the wise servants (Matthew 24:45-51), the ten virgins (Matthew 25:1-13), the talents (Matthew 25:14-30), and the sheep and goats (Matthew 25:31-46). The apostle John says we will overcome both the world and the antichrist because the Holy Spirit that is in us (1 John 4:4) is greater than all demonic opposition. The overall message of the book of Revelation is that Christ is the sovereign Lord who will defeat all opposition to His kingdom, and we will overcome by the blood of the Lamb and the word of our testimony. *"And they have conquered him by the blood of the Lamb and by the word of their testimony, for they loved not their lives even unto death."* (Revelation 12:11).

Eschatology should not be a depressing, complicated subject. We win in the end! Jesus comes back and it's "game over" for this world and the devil. How do we make it to the end? By believing in Jesus, living righteous lives, and by letting Him who rules on high (Psalm 93:1-2) take care of the rest.

Hitting Home

1. What has been your attitude to end times studies and the Book of Revelation?

2. Would you describe your outlook as optimistic or pessimistic when you think about the last days?

3. How well have you been maintaining your faith in the midst of the *tribulation* of our days?

4. How does the knowledge of the ultimate victory of Christ motivate and encourage you today?

LESSON 52: DOCTRINAL DIFFERENCES

KEY DOCTRINE: It is beneficial for a believer to discern the relative importance of all the Christian doctrines.

MEMORY VERSE: *"Woe to you scribes and Pharisees, hypocrites! For you tithe mint and dill and cumin, and have neglected the weightier matters of the law: justice and mercy and faithfulness. These you ought to have done, without neglecting the others."* (Matthew 23:23)

SCRIPTURE PRE-READING: Matthew 22:34-40; Acts 15:22-29; Romans 14:1-23; Hebrews 5:11-6:3

Within the Christian church there exists a diversity of doctrines between the many denominations. A true Christian church will share identical doctrines with all other true churches in respect to essential doctrines about salvation and the nature of God. There are many other doctrines which affect the life of the church but do not define the existence of the church. In areas of debate amongst believers, mature Christians recognize the relative importance of the various doctrines and will act charitably to the brethren when they have disagreements over non-essential matters.

SO MANY DENOMINATIONS!

As we observe Christianity we may be discouraged by the vast array of doctrinal differences from church to church. We see Roman Catholics, Anglican, Orthodox, Baptists, Presbyterians, Methodists, Lutherans, Assembly of God (to name a few), not to mention all the newer non-denominational churches such as, Vineyard, Calvary, Acts 29, Generic Community Churches, and so forth. Many of us do not even know what the doctrinal differences are between these churches, let alone how each denomination came into being. If we Christians are confused by all the diversity, how will an outside observer understand what Christianity truly is? Would it not be easier to simply have one Christian church?

These differences should not be discouraging because there is much more in common among the churches than there are differences. All Christian churches agree on essential matters of the Trinity, the nature of Jesus Christ, and salvation by faith through the gospel. By knowing at which points churches differ we can then understand the reasons for the existence of each denomination, and also why it is good that groups want to believe in a distinctive manner. When churches recognize the true Christian nature of other churches and their members, it allows for believers to live at peace with other Christians without forcing them to conform.

WEIGHING THE DOCTRINES

A key theological maxim is that not all doctrines are equally as important. The issue of whether women should wear head coverings is not given equal weight with the doctrine of the deity of Christ. The problem comes when people give them the same weight of importance. One of the greatest skills we can learn is assessing the relative value of the numerous doctrines of the faith. The diagram below depicts a helpful way to categorize the relative importance of the various doctrines. The center point is THE GOSPEL itself. A Christian church cannot exist unless the gospel is preached. The first ring, ESSENTIAL, contains essential doctrines which define the Christian faith such as the gospel, the person and work of Christ, the Trinity, saving faith, and repentance from unrighteous deeds. The second ring, IMPORTANT, contains very important doctrines which affect the spiritual health of the believer and the church, but are not essential for saving faith. The third ring, DEBATABLE, contains debatable issues which are of lesser value for the Christian, and which the Bible gives freedom in their practice.

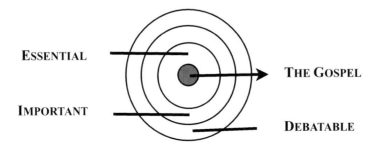

THE GOSPEL

THE GOSPEL is the center point because it is the key to the kingdom. Without having saving faith in Jesus Christ, the Son of God, there is no salvation. The apostle Paul saw the accurate preaching of the gospel as preeminently important. *"But even if we or an angel from heaven should preach to you a gospel contrary to the one we preached to you, let him be accursed."* (Galatians 1:8) Jesus rebuked the religious leaders saying, *"For you shut the kingdom of heaven in people's faces. For you neither enter yourselves nor allow those who would enter to go in."* (Matthew 23:13) Any person or church that errs on the key doctrine of reconciliation with God cannot be considered a true Christian or Christian church.

ESSENTIALS OF THE FAITH

The gospel is firmly fixed within the inner circle of ESSENTIAL Christian doctrine because the gospel itself depends upon these truths. To this group belong such doctrines as the Trinity, the deity and humanity of Jesus, the substitutionary atonement of Christ, the resurrection, justification by faith, repentance from sinful deeds, and eternal judgment. If any of these doctrines are missing within our confession we are standing on very dangerous ground. It is possible that saving faith exists and merely the foundations are faulty; however, without correction great error and damage will result.

IMPORTANT DOCTRINES

A person can be saved and have a solid foundation in the essentials but still be weak in regard to a number of IMPORTANT doctrines. In the area of salvation, a believer may have saving faith and not yet understand the doctrines of election, calling, regeneration, sanctification, and perseverance. To the degree that we grow in these doctrines our faith will be strengthened. Churches maintain differences in some areas of church polity (government) and sacramental practices which effect the spiritual health of the church. However, these differences, such as baptism, the Lord's Supper, the Sabbath, worship style, roles of men and women in office and so forth, do not determine their existence as a Christian church.

DEBATABLE ISSUES

The outside ring contains those doctrines which should not carry substantial weight in our consideration because they are DEBATABLE. The Bible may give latitude in belief and practice in these areas. We should be careful with these debatable issues to not judge our brothers and sisters when they differ from us. Charity should be shown to others even if we ourselves feel strongly about a particular issue. The Bible gives a few examples of these topics: food and drink (1 Corinthians 10:23-33), observing special days (Romans 14:1-12), and the level of financial giving (2 Corinthians 8-9). Other types of doctrines and practices which fall into this area are eschatology (the end times), parenting techniques, women's clothing issues, drinking alcohol, and types of acceptable recreations and entertainment.

HITTING HOME

As an exercise, place the following (non-exhaustive) list of doctrines and practices under the four categories as discussed above: GOSPEL, ESSENTIAL, IMPORTANT, DEBATABLE.

GOSPEL	ESSENTIAL	IMPORTANT	DEBATABLE

The virgin birth of Jesus; The inspiration of Scripture; God's election of believers; Sabbath observance; The use of alcohol; Justification by faith; Infant baptism; The role of women in the church; The sovereignty of God; Spiritual gifts; The extent of the atonement; The millennium; Worship music; The Trinity; The deity of Jesus; Mode of baptism; Frequency of the Lord's Supper; Perseverance of faith; Idol worship; Political views; The practice of homosexuality

MEMORY VERSES

SECTION A: THE CORE BELIEFS

1. GOSPEL: *"For I am not ashamed of the gospel, for it is the power of God for salvation to everyone who believes, to the Jew first and also to the Greek."* (Romans 1:16)

2. GOD: *"Holy, holy, holy, is the Lord God Almighty, who was and is and is to come!"* (Revelation 4:8b)

3. SIN: *"for all have sinned and fall short of the glory of God"* (Romans 3:23)

4. GRACE: *"For by grace you have been saved through faith. And this is not your own doing; it is the gift of God"* (Ephesians 2:8)

5. JESUS CHRIST: *"And the Word became flesh and dwelt among us, and we have seen his glory, glory as of the only Son from the Father, full of grace and truth."* (John 1:14)

6. SALVATION: *"For God so loved the world, that he gave his only Son, that whoever believes in him should not perish but have eternal life."* (John 3:16)

7. THE TRINITY: *"Go therefore and make disciples of all nations, baptizing them in the name of the Father and of the Son and of the Holy Spirit"* (Matthew 28:19)

8. THE CROSS: *"but we preach Christ crucified, a stumbling block to Jews and folly to Gentiles, but to those who are called, both Jews and Greeks, Christ the power of God and the wisdom of God."* (1 Corinthians 1:23-24)

9. THE BIBLE: *"All Scripture is breathed out by God and profitable for teaching, for reproof, for correction, and for training in righteousness, that the man of God may be competent, equipped for every good work."* (2 Timothy 3:16-17)

10. ETERNITY: *"For we must all appear before the judgment seat of Christ, so that each one may receive what is due for what he has done in the body, whether good or evil."* (2 Corinthians 5:10)

SECTION B: SUCH A GREAT SALVATION

11. ELECTION: *"even as he chose us in him before the foundation of the world, that we should be holy and blameless before him. In love he predestined us for adoption as sons through Jesus Christ, according to the purpose of his will."* (Ephesians 1:4-5)

12. CALLING: *"What man of you, having a hundred sheep, if he has lost one of them, does not leave the ninety-nine in the open country, and go after the one that is lost, until he finds it?* (Luke 15:4)

13. REGENERATION: *"he saved us, not because of works done by us in righteousness, but according to his own mercy, by the washing of regeneration and renewal of the Holy Spirit"* (Titus 3:5)

14. JUSTIFICATION: *"Therefore, since we have been justified by faith, we have peace with God through our Lord Jesus Christ."* (Romans 5:1)

15. SANCTIFICATION: *"Therefore, my beloved, as you have always obeyed, so now, not only as in my presence but much more in my absence, work out your own salvation with fear and trembling, for it is God who works in you, both to will and to work for his good pleasure."* (Philippians 2:12-13)

16. PERSEVERANCE: *"And I am sure of this, that he who began a good work in you will bring it to completion at the day of Jesus Christ."* (Philippians 1:6)

17. GLORIFICATION: *"For those whom he foreknew he also predestined to be conformed to the image of his Son...And those whom he predestined he also called, and those whom he called he also justified, and those whom he justified he also glorified."* (Romans 8:29-30)

18. JESUS IS LORD: *"If you love me, you will keep my commandments."* (John 14:15)

19. LIVING BY FAITH: *"Now faith is the assurance of things hoped for, the conviction of things not seen. For by it the people of old received their commendation."* (Hebrews 11:1-2)

20. FEAR GOD: *"Serve the Lord with fear, and rejoice with trembling."* (Psalm 2:11)

21. THE INDWELLING SPIRIT: *"And I will ask the Father, and he will give you another Helper, to be with you forever, even the Spirit of truth, whom the world cannot receive, because it neither sees him nor knows him. You know him, for he dwells with you and will be in you."* (John 14:16-17)

22. THE CHRISTIAN'S WARFARE: *"I have fought the good fight, I have finished the race, I have kept the faith."* (2 Timothy 4:7)

23. FIGHTING SIN: *"For if you live according to the flesh you will die, but if by the Spirit you put to death the deeds of the body you will live."* (Romans 8:13)

24. THE TRIALS OF LIFE: *"Count it all joy, my brothers, when you meet trials of various kinds, for you know that the testing of your faith produces steadfastness."* (James 1:2-3)

25. TAKING UP YOUR CROSS: *"Then Jesus told his disciples, 'If anyone would come after me, let him deny himself and take up his cross and follow me.'"* (Matthew 16:24)

26. THE WAY OF WISDOM: *"The fear of the LORD is the beginning of knowledge; fools despise wisdom and instruction."* (Proverbs 1:7)

27. THE LIFE OF LOVE: *"A new commandment I give to you, that you love one another: just as I have loved you, you also are to love one another. By this all people will know that you are my disciples, if you have love for one another."* (John 13:34-35)

28. HOLINESS: *"As obedient children, do not be conformed to the passions of your former ignorance, but as he who called you is holy, you also be holy in all your conduct."* (1 Peter 1:14-15)

29. SEXUAL PURITY: *"Flee from sexual immorality. Every other sin a person commits is outside the body, but the sexual immoral person sins against his own body."* (1 Corinthians 6:18)

30. PRAYER: *"do not be anxious about anything, but in everything by prayer and supplication with thanksgiving let your requests be made known to God."* (Philippians 4:6)

31. MONEY MATTERS: *"No one can serve two masters, for either he will hate the one and love the other, or he will be devoted to the one and despise the other. You cannot serve God and money."* (Matthew 6:24)

SECTION D: CHURCH LIFE

32. THE CHURCH: *"So then, you are no longer strangers and aliens, but you are fellow citizens with the saints and members of the household of God."* (Ephesians 2:20)

33. BAPTISM: *"And Peter said to them, 'Repent and be baptized everyone of you in the name of Jesus Christ for the forgiveness of sins, and you will receive the gift of the Holy Spirit.'"* (Acts 2:38)

34. THE LORD'S SUPPER: *"So Jesus said to them, 'Truly, truly, I say to you, unless you eat the flesh of the Son of Man and drink his blood, you have no life in you.'"* (John 6:53)

35. WORSHIP: *"But the hour is coming, and is now here, when the true worshippers will worship the Father in spirit and truth, for the Father is seeking such people to worship him."* (John 4:23)

36. IN THE WORD: *"This Book of the Law shall not depart from your mouth, but you shall meditate on it day and night, so that you may be careful to do according to all that is written in it. For then you will make your way prosperous, and then you will have good success."* (Joshua 1:8)

37. THE COVENANT COMMUNITY: *"Now you are the body of Christ and individually members of it."* (1 Corinthians 12:27)

38. MISSIONS AND EVANGELISM: *"How beautiful upon the mountains are the feet of him who brings good news, who publishes peace, who brings good news of happiness, who publishes salvation, who says to Zion, 'Your God reigns.'"* (Isaiah 52:7)

39. SPIRITUAL GIFTS: *"As each has received a gift, use it to serve one another, as good stewards of God's varied grace"* (1 Peter 4:10)

40. PEACE AND PURITY: *"Strive for peace with everyone, and for the holiness without which no one will see the Lord."* (Hebrews 12:14)

41. GIVING AND MERCY: *"They are to do good, to be rich in good works, to be generous and ready to share"* (1 Timothy 6:18)

SECTION E: THINKING DEEPER

42. THE SOVEREIGNTY OF GOD: *"In him we have obtained an inheritance, having been predestined according to the purpose of him who works all things according to the counsel of his will"* (Ephesians 1:11)

43. THE CREATION OF THE WORLD: *"In the beginning God created the heavens and the earth."* (Genesis 1:1)

44. INTERPRETING SCRIPTURE: *"Do your best to present yourself to God as one approved, a worker who has no need to be ashamed, rightly handing the word of truth."* (2 Timothy 2:15)

45. THE CHRISTIAN THINKER: *"Do not be conformed to this world, but be transformed by the renewal of your mind, that by testing you may discern what is the will of God, what is good and acceptable and perfect."* (Romans 12:2)

46. JESUS REIGNS: *"The LORD says to my Lord, 'Sit at my right hand, until I make your enemies your footstool.'"* (Psalm 110:1)

47. MARRIAGE: *"Therefore a man shall leave his father and his mother and hold fast to his wife, and they shall become one flesh."* (Genesis 2:24)

48. FLEE IDOLATRY: *"Therefore, my beloved, flee from idolatry."* (1 Corinthians 10:14)

49. GOD'S COVENANT: *"But this is the covenant that I will make with the house of Israel after those days, declares the LORD: I will put my law within them, and I will write it on your hearts. And I will be their God, and they shall be my people."* (Jeremiah 31:33)

50. THE WORTH OF WORK: *"Whatever you do, work heartily, as for the Lord and not for men"* (Colossians 3:23)

51. THE END TIME: *"But stay awake at all times, praying that you may have strength to escape all these things that are going to take place, and to stand before the Son of Man."* (Luke 21:36)

52. DOCTRINAL DIFFERENCES: *"Woe to you scribes and Pharisees, hypocrites! For you tithe mint and dill and cumin, and have neglected the weightier matters of the law: justice and mercy and faithfulness. These you ought to have done, without neglecting the others."* (Matthew 23:23)

"For as the rain and the snow come down from heaven and do not return there but water the earth, making it bring forth and sprout, giving seed to the sower and bread to the eater, so shall my word be that goes out from my mouth; it shall not return to me empty, but it shall accomplish that which I purpose, and shall succeed in the things for which I sent it." (Isaiah 55:10-11)

Acknowledgments

A work of this nature could not be achieved without the assistance of others. My editors, Helen Ferguson and Paula Burke have shielded me from many an embarrassing mistake. Thanks to William Ntim for his work on the cover. The generous support of Eric and Kelley, and Lynn and Naomi and Abundant Love Christian Center enabled me to focus on the writing of this book and not run after *the things of this world.*

The idea to have a one-year comprehensive discipleship guide was first bounced off and affirmed by Dr. Robert Ferguson who was also helpful with his insights into philosophy and Christian thought.

My wife, Eleanor, and my children, Gaius, Gideon, Esther, and Apollos, were all an intimate part of this task and journey. I thank Eleanor for believing that this labor was not in vain. She has helped and supported me every step of the way.

I must give glory to God. This book has from start to finish been the "brainchild" of the Lord, and out of much affliction and perseverance it was birthed. May the Lord use it as He so pleases.